BRAINWASHED

Diet-Induced Eating Disorders
How You Got Sucked In and
How To Recover

Author: Elisa Oras

Cover design: Elisa Oras

Copyright © 2016 by Elisa Oras

ISBN-13: 978-1532868610 (Paperback)
ISBN-10: 1532868618

All rights reserved. No part of this publication may be reproduced, distributed, or transmitted in any form or by any means, including photocopying, recording, or other electronic or mechanical methods, without the prior written permission of the publisher, except in the case of brief quotations embodied in reviews and certain other non-commercial uses permitted by copyright law.

Disclaimer: The information in this book is based on my own experience. It is not intended as a substitute for the advice of trained medical or mental health professionals. The reader should regularly consult a physician, therapist or counsellor in matters relating to his/her physical or mental health and particularly with respect to any symptoms that may require diagnosis or medical attention. In the event you use any of the information in this book, the author and the publisher assume no responsibility for your actions.

www.followtheintuition.com

elisa@followtheintuition.com

*To Sander who has been there with me
and for me throughout this journey.*

Table of Contents

INTRODUCTION 11

Chapter 1: How diets trigger eating disorders 17

The minnesota starvation experiment 21

Symptoms of starvation 28

The men experienced true eating disorders symptoms 31

Weight gain after starvation (Dieting) 33

How diets lead to an eating disorder 35

But what about "reasonable" calorie restriction for "healthy" weight loss? 44

You can't fight biology 48

Not eating after 6 pm (Aka intermittent fasting) 50

30 Days raw and water fasting 51

Sset point weight 55

BMI (Body mass index) 57

You can't decide your goal weight 58

Different body types and lowering your set-point weight 62
Why are people overweight or obese? 66
Calories in, calories out theory 79
Is starvation mode a myth? 88
Dieting slows metabolism 90
How to get out of diet merry-go-hell 98

Chapter 2: Physical recovery 103

Road to recovery - what to expect 103
Should you recover under supervision? 110
Do we need to count calories to recover? 111
Minniemaud calorie guidelines 115
Refeeding syndrome 118
Should i eat that much if i'm not underweight? 120
What if counting calories triggers me? 122
Why do i need feel hungry? 124
But normal people eat 2000 calories a day? 126
Eating regularly 132
Extreme hunger that feels like bingeing 134
How long will extreme hunger last? 135
Your thoughts can affect extreme hunger 138
Just eat and don't overanalyze! 140

Worshipping purity 141
How to not obsess about eating healthy? 150
Eating fear foods 154
Self-love - eat what your body wants 157
The trap of perfectionism in recovery 159
Exercise as a way to restrict 161
But if i don't exercise, i will gain weight 166
Female athlete triad 167
But can i ever exercise again? 168

Chapter 3: Mental recovery 173
Restriction affects your mental state 173
Triggers 176
Body image 186
Body positive exercises 194
Do not compare 198
Eating disorder thoughts 201
How eating disorder thoughts develop 202
How to change eating disorder thoughts 205
How to separate yourself from the eating disorder 211
Examples of acting on your ed thoughts and how
to change them 215
What if i do not want to recover? 218

It's not working!...220

Emotional eating..221

How to relieve stress/negative emotions in
recovery..229

Right mindset in recovery 238

How to bring recovery to your life 241

Chapter 4: Recovery issues...247

Digestive issues..248

The clean eating digestion disaster 250

Food intolerances...253

Reintroducing foods..255

Tips to relieve stomach problems....................................256

Water retention 260

Drinking water...264

Weight gain..265

Weight redistribution..270

Feeling tired...272

Night sweats..273

Insomnia...274

Amenorrhea(Loss of period)..275

How to get your period back 277

I feel so full and bloated! I can't eat so much food! 278

Bad hair, skin, and nails..280

    Relapse 282

    Eating healthy 288

    Being vegan/vegetarian 290

Chapter 5: Intuitive eating... 293

    Extreme hunger conflicts with intuitive eating............. 299

    What's wrong with the "eat when hungry and stop when full" recommendation in recovery? 302

    Mental hunger 303

    Intuitive eating is awesome!................................ 306

    Science behind intuitive eating 306

    Hunger 312

    Fullness... 316

    How to recover normal hunger cues 317

    It's not black and white!..................................... 327

Free bonus e-book!... 331

Recap of everything we have learned 333

Endnotes 337

Introduction

Do you feel out of control with food? Trapped in your body? Are you constantly overeating, not knowing how to stop or why it happens? Gaining weight and unable to maintain a healthy weight? Are you obsessed with foods 24/7? Eating emotionally? Trying to eat healthy and do the right thing only to fall off the wagon? Do you feel you're not in control of your body, mind, or the food you eat? Maybe you have no idea how you got into this, or how to get out?

If you answered yes to all or any of those questions, then you are exactly where I was several years ago. I developed bulimia and orthorexia without even realizing it. It completely invaded my mind and body. I could not control my eating or my weight. I thought I was doing the best I could to eat healthy, but I just could not stop overeating and throwing up, continuing the cycle of self-hate and bingeing. I was astonished that a mentally stable person could suddenly turn into a nutcase when it came to food. How could I not be in control of what I was eating or feeling? How did this happen?

In this book, I will explain how something as simple as a diet change or wanting to be healthy and lose weight can turn into an eating disorder. I'll show how you get sucked into the never-ending binge-starve-repeat cycle and what you can do to get out and recover.

So what does brainwashing have to do with diets and eating disorders? In my experience – a lot!

These days, we have been made to believe all sorts of lies about our bodies and eating and how to sustain a healthy weight. We've been told that our body doesn't know how to maintain a healthy weight without calorie counting or exercise. We've been told that losing weight is as simple as eating less and burning more. We've been told that we have to restrict certain foods or we will become addicted and eat until we are sick and overweight. We've even been told that we overeat either because we are emotional eaters or because we are trying to fill a "void" in our lives.

Then we are bombarded with messages like "The fat you eat is the fat you wear" or "Carbs make you fat!" or "How to lose 10 pounds in 10 days!" or "Anyone can have a thigh gap if you just work hard and eat clean!" We follow our role models on YouTube, Instagram, and Snapchat, hashtagging #bodygoals, and we read every weight-loss article we can find on the Internet and try to implement those unrealistic strategies. We condition our minds and bodies to not know what is healthy and what is not, what is realistic, and what is downright dangerous.

Introduction

Our mindset has become so brainwashed by believing all this diet nonsense that we do not even know how to listen to our own body and how to eat normally. We stop eating after 6 pm, we binge out on our "cheat day," we go on a three-day water fast to lose weight, and we become frustrated when the scale does not drop – so we adopt even more rigid measures to lose the weight.

I believe if we stopped dieting and restriction, we could literally wipe out most cases of eating disorders. Diet-induced eating disorders have become more prevalent in today's society as we see the rise of unrealistic body standards imposed by the media, by cultural standards, and by today's society in general.

There is so much misunderstanding and confusion about eating disorder recovery and what is normal eating and how to effortlessly maintain a healthy body and healthy weight. Common recovery programs do not focus on the things I am about to tell you. Things that can make your recovery ten times quicker and are scientifically proven to work. In all of my research, I can say that ALL people who have successfully recovered from eating disorders and done so for lifelong results have used these simple yet not so commonly practiced techniques and principles of recovery. They are things that simply work!

But let's come back to where I am now.

I eat when hungry, and I stop when full. I never overeat – I lost the ability to binge. I eat whatever I want, how much I want, and when I want. No willpower is needed. I have no guilt and no obsessive thoughts about food. I have no more bloating or digestion issues. I don't feel sick or cold, I don't have insomnia or messed-up hormones, and I don't have a slow metabolism or experience weight gain. I maintain a healthy weight effortlessly without even having to exercise. I have actually lost some weight naturally without even trying.

I thought I would NEVER be a normal eater again. I had completely forgotten the sensation of hunger and fullness and thought I would always have to "maintain" and "learn how to cope" in recovery, but I never thought I'd be completely free. I thought people who ate when hungry and stopped when full were things of urban legend. It seemed like a nice fairytale but not something that was ever going to happen in real life. But here I am now, one of those lucky people who can eat whatever, whenever and never worry about "consequences."

If you want to experience this, then this book is for you. If you follow the steps outlined in these pages, you can have all that, too!

I managed to recover on my own by reading numerous books, websites, and scientific studies. I learned through my own experiences and those of other people. It took me several years and a lot of trial and error to put together all the puzzle pieces and figure out how recovery actually works. I was totally dumbfounded by what I discovered about eating disorders and recovery – and even more so to discover these things are not even taught in common recovery programs. That was why I was stuck. I did not have the right information from the start!

Many who struggle with disordered eating—people with bulimia, anorexia, orthorexia, or EDNOS and those who binge, overeat, overexercise, or yo-yo diet—have already experienced great success by implementing the tips and tricks found in this helpful how-to book. Through my website, Facebook, YouTube videos, and one-on-one coaching, I have already helped hundreds of people gain back normal eating. You don't have to spend several years searching for an answer because I have put together here everything I know to help you recover successfully and FOR LIFE!

Imagine yourself never thinking or worrying about food or your body. Imagine your eating habits being effortless and balanced. Imagine being free and happy and spending time with your loved ones. Imagine achieving the dreams you never thought possible. Imagine how good it feels to do all these things, and how inspiring you are to everybody around you! And it's all because you took action and did not look back. You became the kind of person other people look at and say, "I don't know how she did it, but I want that, too!"

You can be that person!

CHAPTER 1
How Diets Trigger Eating Disorders

Over the years of having bulimia and orthorexia, I read many helpful books about recovery. Each author had a different experience and unique road to recovery, but although there were differences, I noticed some points that were very similar and repeated in every case of full recovery, things that simply do not work and have to be dealt with or recovery wouldn't be possible. These things are dieting and restriction.

In the following pages, you will learn about the impact dieting and restriction have on our mental and physical health and their role in the development of eating disorders.

> *Even though dieting and weight loss made me feel good about myself, something in my brain told me I was doing something terribly wrong. I started to obsess about food and think about it constantly when, prior to dieting, food simply hadn't been an issue in my life. I felt intense hunger and*

cravings for the type of foods I tried to limit, and I began having cravings to eat abnormally large amounts of food.[1]
–Kathryn Hansen, *Brain Over Binge*

My eating patterns had not been normal for a decade and I no longer trusted my body, and slowly my faith in my mind was starting to falter. I suspected that my ideas and eating plans were not working, and possibly not even correct. I started to associate my insanity, depression, and hopelessness with the unrealistic eating standards that I was imposing. And I started to suspect that the out of control eating was a direct backlash to my self-imposed will, dieting, and restricting.[2]
–Nina V. *Recover from Eating Disorders*

Food restriction and dieting precede the vast majority of eating disorders. Or more clearly: Food restriction is the number one cause of eating disorders.... If you had never restricted your food intake in the first place then the chances are that you would have never felt compelled to binge and purge, meaning you wouldn't now have bulimia. I know for some of you this may come as a bit of a surprise, but it's really that simple.[3] –Richard and Ali Kerr, *Bulimia Help Method*

Dieting is a cultural problem. Today's society obviously puts pressure on us to be a certain weight or size, to look "good" and be "healthy". In order to fully recover, you have to realize that restriction does not work – and it never will! You cannot get better unless you stop restricting. The more you believe diets work, the more you get brainwashed. Trying to recover from an eating disorder while dieting is like trying to recover from a broken leg while still jumping on it. You simply cannot "think" yourself better.

What is the impact of dieting on developing eating disorders?

- Eating Disorders Victoria reports that *"Dieting is the greatest risk factor for the development of an eating disorder. 68% of 15-year-old females are on a diet, of these, 8% are severely dieting. Adolescent girls who diet only moderately, are five times more likely to develop an eating disorder than those who don't diet, and those who diet severely are 18 time more likely to develop an eating disorder."*[4]

- *Journal of Child Psychology and Psychiatry and Allied Disciplines research found that "psychiatric morbidity was the clearest factor associated with extreme dieting and 62% of extreme dieters reported high levels of depression and anxiety. Extreme dieting might reasonably be viewed as lying on a spectrum with clinical eating disorders. Most dieting is unjustified on the grounds of appropriate weight control and appears to reflect a widespread striving of teenage girls towards body shapes at the lower end of age-adjusted norms."*[5]

- National Youth Cultures of Eating Study reports that *"in the 2006 study, disordered eating behaviors for weight control, such as fasting, laxative abuse, smoking, vomiting, chewing food but not swallowing and slimming pills were dangerously present and frequent in girls as young as*

> *12 years old. There appears to be a sharp increase in these dangerous behaviors after pubertal development, which has been suggested by previous authors. Among older girls, these unhealthy behaviors were more common, with as many as one fifth of 16–19-year-old girls regularly fasting for two days or more to try to control their weight."*[6]

- Australian Pediatric Surveillance reported that 25.0% of girls and 13.8% of boys are infrequent dieters. Binge eating was more common among the girls, but in both sexes, it was associated with dieting to control weight. For many adolescents, dieting to control weight is not only ineffective, it may actually promote weight gain.[7]

- European Eating Disorders Review found that *"high frequency of dieting (rather than dieting per se) and earlier dieting onset were associated with poorer physical and mental health (including depression), more disordered eating (bingeing and purging), extreme weight and shape dissatisfaction and more frequent general health problems. The results suggest that there is a need for programs that will enhance self-esteem and weight/shape acceptance and promote more appropriate strategies for maintenance of healthy weight."*[8]

I hope from these statistics you are beginning to understand how critical a role dieting and restriction plays in developing eating disorders. To further convince you, let's look at one of the most important studies of them all.

The Minnesota Starvation Experiment

The first time I read about the Minnesota Starvation Experiment,[9] I was amazed to see the number of similarities regarding eating disorders between the participants. This experiment is one of the best examples of what happens to us when we restrict food and how our body reacts to starvation *(read: dieting)*.

In Minneapolis, Minnesota, Dr. Ancel Keys wanted to help people who suffered from starvation during World War II. He conducted an experiment, hoping to learn the physiology of starvation and the best way to recover from it. Knowledge of the best rehabilitation methods could help to ensure the health of the population and thereby help democracy grow in Europe after the war.

The design of the study was simple: starve the subjects and then refeed them. To achieve this in a controlled, scientific fashion, Keys planned a year-long study which was divided into three parts: an initial three-month control period during which the participants' food intake was standardized, a six-month period of starvation, and three months of rehabilitation.

Keys selected thirty-six physically and mentally strong men from over four hundred volunteers, none of whom had any signs of an eating disorder. They ate when hungry, stopped when full, and did not think about food other than to refuel. It was part of their lives but most definitely not the dominant part. They were normal eaters.

For the next twelve weeks (the control period of the experiment), Keys allowed them 3200 calories a day. He also put them through a battery of tests to gather data on a number of variables such as their heart size, blood volume, hearing, vision, fitness, body fat, and sperm count. He directed the men to maintain an active lifestyle, working jobs in the lab and walking a minimum of twenty-two miles a week.

When the first twelve-week period came to a close, Keys cut the men's calories in half – from 3200 to 1570 calories a day. This reduction began the starvation phase of the experiment, and it lasted for six months.

In today's dieting world, it's very common to suggest somebody to lose weight at 1570 calories a day. Some people may say it's a completely healthy number by which to lose weight. Most people would definitely not consider it "starvation," and some may even think it's too many calories! Let's look what the US National Institute of Health recommends for "healthy" weight loss:

> *A patient may choose a diet of 1,000 to 1,200 kcal/day for women and 1,200 to 1,500 kcal/day for men.... Experience reveals that lost weight usually will be regained unless a weight maintenance program consisting of dietary therapy, physical activity, and behavior therapy is continued indefinitely. After 6 months of weight-loss treatment, efforts to maintain weight loss should be put in place. If more weight loss is needed, another attempt at weight reduction*

can be made. This will require further adjustment of the diet and physical activity prescriptions.[10]

So a "healthy" weight loss is made at 1000-1200 calories a day for women and 1200-1500 calories a day for men? And it can last for six months? And if you can't continue to do it for the rest of your life, you'll regain the weight you lost? Talk about crash-dieting, uncontrollable food binges, and developing a "mental" disease like an eating disorder!

(Note: I put the word mental in quotes intentionally. Dieting is not a mental thing, it's physical, but it can make you go "mental" for sure! I do not believe that eating disorders are mental diseases if they started by dieting.)

I am aware that different sources cite different numbers of calories necessary for healthy weight loss, but some well-intentioned people may set what they think are healthy guidelines without realizing the potential dangers ahead. This is extremely disturbing to me because of the results Keys obtained while keeping men on a low-calorie diet. And keep in mind that his diet was not even full starvation, but only semi-starvation. And the National Institute of Health promotes *semi*-starvation for six months? Nice! Let me explain what Keys' 1570-calorie-day diet did to these men.

As you may have already guessed, this significant reduction of calories had a very rapid effect on the men's health. They experienced a remarkable decline in strength and energy. Keys recorded a 21% reduction in their strength measured with a back lift dynamometer. The men also felt cold and had constant fatigue.

They lost complete interest in subjects that used to interest them like politics and world events. Even sex and romance lost their appeal. Instead, they became suddenly very interested in food.

Some of the men started to read cookbooks and obsessively stare at food pictures. They started to collect recipes (sound familiar?). This is a very common occurrence when people start to diet. All of a sudden food is their number one priority.

When you restrict something, you seem to want it even more. By restricting, you actually give it more attention, more power over you. Eating is a very intuitive part of our lives. People without eating disorders don't think about eating obsessively – they just do it instinctively. But people who diet or restrict foods obsess about it. What to eat, how much, when? If I eat this for breakfast, then what will I have for lunch? How will I prepare it? How many calories does it have? How much fat? Is it healthy, clean, pure? Will I need to burn it off later?

I have definitely been there. Constant thoughts about food are inevitable when you restrict your intake or deprive yourself. It's how we're built. It's natural to want food when you're hungry! The more you try to control your food, the more it starts to control you. And it's very interesting that some men who had no interest in food before the experiment actually became professional chefs afterward!

Meal times became the high point of their day. They grew irritable if they weren't served their food exactly on time, or if they had to wait too long in line. Although the food was quite bland, to the men it tasted delicious. They lingered over the food, savoring every bite. Often they "souped" their meals – mixing everything with water to make it seem as if there was more.[11]

All of the men were very committed when they began the experiment and knew it was all for a good cause – to help the starving people around the world – but cheating became a huge problem in this experiment.

The stress proved too much for one of the men, twenty-four-year-old Franklin Watkins. He began having vivid, disturbing dreams of cannibalism in which he was eating the flesh of an old man. On trips into town (before the buddy system had been implemented), he cheated extravagantly, downing milkshakes and sundaes. Finally, Keys confronted him, and Watkins broke down sobbing. Then he grew angry and threatened to kill Keys and take his own life. Keys immediately dismissed Watkins from the experiment and sent him to the psychiatric ward of the university hospital. There, after a few days on a normal diet, Watkins appeared entirely normal again, so the hospital released him. Watkins' breakdown occurred just a few weeks into the starvation phase of the experiment.[12]

As you can see, this guy definitely went "mental." But was it a mental disease as eating disorders are commonly labeled, or was it a physical side effect of starvation? Are your brain and body being undernourished? This man had nothing wrong with him before he started this semi-starvation experiment – or as it's more commonly known, diet. Think about it before you let a professional tell you that you have a mental disease – is it really your brain working against you, making you a nutcase, or is it a side effect of the dieting and restriction?

Weight loss can have good effects on your health, but when it comes to dieting, our appetite and hunger cues can often get out of control. Our body cannot sustain health when we lower the calories we eat and force our weight down by dieting. It's not at all about having no self-control or willpower. It's a natural instinct to eat more after a period of dieting and restriction, but it's very hard to force ourselves to eat less. No wonder 95% of all diets inevitably fail and 99.5% of dieters gain all the weight back after only five years.[13]

Keys also found that the participants' heart rates fell significantly – from fifty-five beats per minute to thirty-five. This was their metabolism slowing down, and it was a sign that their bodies were trying to conserve calories. They also reported not having regular bowel movements – only one per week. Their blood volume dropped ten percent, and their hearts shrank in size. The men developed edema (water retention). Their ankles, knees, and faces swelled – an odd physical symptom considering their otherwise skeletal appearance.

It is very common to retain water when you have an eating disorder, and if you start to recover, you can have a significant amount of water retention. This is a sign of your body trying to protect you and heal. It's normal to gain ten to fifteen pounds in a matter of days when in recovery. And yes, it's mostly water weight (we will talk more about water retention in Chapter 4).

There was also a decrease in basal metabolic rate (BMR).

(Note: BMR is the amount of energy (calories) that the body requires at rest (with no physical activity) in order to carry out normal physiological processes. It accounts for about two-thirds of the body's total energy needs, with the remainder being used during physical activity.)

At the end of semi-starvation, the men's BMRs had dropped to about forty percent below normal. This drop, as well as other physical changes, reflects the body's extraordinary ability to adapt to low caloric intake by reducing its need for energy. This is scientifically known as *adaptive thermogenesis* aka starvation mode (we will discuss this later in this chapter).

Other effects included dizziness, muscle soreness, reduced coordination, and ringing in the ears. But the creepiest change, which occurred in all of the men, was a whitening of their eyeballs as the blood vessels in their eyes shrank. The skin of some of the men developed a coarse, rough appearance as a result of the hardening of their hair follicles. From the men's point of view, the most uncomfortable change was the lack

27

of body fat. It became difficult for them to sit down for long periods of time because their bones would grind against the seats.

Deprivation and starvation (even *semi*-starvation) have significant effects on our bodies. The following are some typical signs that your body is in starvation mode and you need recovery ASAP (if not sooner!).

Symptoms of Starvation

These are general symptoms that can indicate your body is not getting enough food and you are slowly fading away!

- Easy weight gain when you eat until fullness – gaining weight by eating 2000 calories or less a day

- No menstruation or irregular menstruation

- Unhealthy/damaged/ill-looking skin, hair, and/or nails

- Obsession with food and anxiety around foods

- Depression and nervousness

- Concentration problems, brain fog

- Binge eating and messed-up hunger/fullness signals

- Constant illness due to a weakened immune system

- Mood swings, easily annoyed

- Tired, sleepy, dizzy, and weak

- Sleep problems, insomnia

- Low libido

- Feeling cold all the time, cold hands and feet

- Digestive problems such as constipation or diarrhea, nausea, stomach ache

- Food intolerance, loss of ability to digest certain foods, extreme sensitivity to foods you used to eat

- Bloating, especially after meals

- Water retention (swollen stomach, face, puffy eyes)

- Muscle, joint, or skin pains

Another interesting thing that happened to these men during the semi-starvation period was that even though they were extremely skinny – even skeletal – they didn't see themselves as being too skinny. Rather, they thought everybody else was just fat compared to them! Some participants even avoided eating because they were fearful of weight gain.

This is also a very common mindset in people with eating disorders. Body image and the idea of healthy weight becomes distorted (*body dysmorphia*). You become so used to your extremely fragile look or the way you visualize your "perfect body" that you begin to think it's normal. This is just one example of how dieting brainwashes you. You loose the ability to think rationally or know what is healthy and what is not.

After six months, the rehabilitation period of the experiment started. Keys divided the men into four groups. Each group received either 400, 800, 1200, or 1600 more calories than they had in the semi-starvation period. He did this to observe the effects of the men's ingestion of the optimum amount of calories for them. The men in the lowest calorie groups saw almost no improvement – they still felt hungry all the time and had no signs of recovery. Even after providing them with extra vitamin and protein supplements, there was no improvement. They needed even more calories! He eventually concluded that in order to recover from starvation (1570 calories a day), and rebuild strength a person needs around 4000 calories a day.

During rehabilitation, metabolism speeded up again. Those consuming the greatest number of calories experienced the largest rise in BMR. The group of volunteers who received a relatively small increment in calories during rehabilitation (400 calories more than during semi-starvation) had no rise in BMR for the first three weeks. But consuming larger amounts of food caused a sharp increase in the energy burned through metabolic processes. Their bodies were finally recovering! Yay! The changes in body fat and muscle in relation to overall body weight during semi-starvation and rehabilitation are of considerable interest. Weight declined about 25%, but the percentage of body fat fell almost 70%, and muscle decreased about 40%! Upon refeeding, a greater proportion of the "new weight" was fat – in the eighth month of rehabilitation, the volunteers were at about 100% of their original body weight, but had approximately 140% of their original body fat!

The previous sentence illustrates how dieting, restriction, and deprivation lead to more fat gain in your body than you would normally have. But if you break the cycle and recover, you can healthfully restore your body to its normal weight and fat levels!

(Note: Recovery is not about weight loss or fat loss. I just want you to see how dieting is not making you lose weight or fat effectively as you may think. It's only making it worse!)

The Men Experienced True Eating Disorder Symptoms

Subject No. 20 stuffs himself until he is bursting at the seams, to the point of being sick, and still feels hungry; No. 120 reported that he had to discipline himself to keep from eating so much as to become ill; No. 1 ate until he was uncomfortably full; and subject No. 30 had so little control over the mechanics of "piling it in" that he simply had to stay away from food because he could not find a point of satiation even when he was "full to the gills." "I ate practically all weekend," reported subject No. 26, "and would just as soon have eaten six meals instead of three.[14]

Some of the men even became psychotic. One of them was unable to stick to the diet, started looking through garbage bins for food, and began a cycle of enormous overeating followed by self-induced vomiting. He exhibited a compulsive attraction to refuse and a strong, almost compelling desire to root in garbage cans for food to eat. He became emotionally disturbed enough to seek voluntary admission to the psychiatric ward of the university hospitals.

As you can clearly see, these men – once perfectly healthy physically and mentally – became eating disordered and lost complete control over food and eating. They felt guilt and failure and became self-hateful as a result of restriction and deprivation. It was totally out of their control.

> *The last meal of the study was served on October 20, 1945. The men were subsequently free to depart and eat as they pleased. However, Keys convinced twelve of them to stay on at the lab for another eight weeks so he could monitor them during an "unrestricted rehabilitation" phase. Left to their own devices, Keys observed these men consume over 5000 calories a day, on average. And on occasion, some of them feasted on as many as 11,500 calories in a single day. For many months, the men reported having a sensation of hunger they couldn't satisfy, no matter how much they ate.[15] (In recovery, this is known as "extreme hunger." We will talk about this in Chapter 2).*

This last example is true for eating disorder recovery, and I think it's the most important aspect of it! You need to eat without restriction, and you need to eat as much as you want. Your body knows what it's doing! Experiencing extreme hunger in recovery is normal. It's how our body comes out of starvation (dieting).

Weight Gain After Starvation (Dieting)

The subjects who gained the most weight became concerned about their increased sluggishness, general flabbiness, and the tendency of fat to accumulate in their abdomen and buttocks.

Interestingly, these complaints are similar to those of many patients with eating disorders as they gain weight in recovery. Besides their typical fear of weight gain, they often report "feeling fat" and are worried about acquiring distended stomachs. Although these fears are understandable, it's important to recognize that the body weight and relative body fat of the Minnesota volunteers began to approach pre-experiment levels after only one year in recovery.

During the rehabilitation period, some men did gain more weight back than they'd had before the experiment started, but in time, they lost all the excess weight because they did not restrict again. At the start of recovery, they gained back their original weight plus about ten percent additional, but over the following six months, their weight gradually declined so that by the end of the follow-up period, they were approaching their pre-experiment weight levels.

Keys report highlighted the degree to which the amount we eat can alter both the mind and the body. However, his data also optimistically revealed that starvation didn't appear to have any significant, long-term negative impacts on health. Evolution apparently fashioned the human body to withstand long periods without food.

As you can see, recovery takes time, but it is a sure thing that you can and WILL recover just as those men did, assuming that you do not ever again go back to restriction!

The University of North Carolina at Chapel Hill's Department of Psychiatry conducted a study where they compared previously anorexic women two years out of recovery with normal women. The conclusion was that there was no difference in the BMR of women who'd had anorexia and had recovered and the BMR of normal women. So your metabolism is not broken and doomed to be slow forever – it only needs time to heal. You can restore it 100% if you choose recovery!

Almost sixty years later, in 2003, nineteen of the original thirty-six volunteers of the experiment remained alive. Of these survivors, eighteen were interviewed as part of an oral history project about the experiment. They admitted that there had been some lingering aftereffects of the experiment. For instance, for many years, they were haunted by a fear that food might be taken away from them again. But overall, they uniformly praised the experience as one of the most important events in their lives. And they insisted that if they had the opportunity as young men to do it again, they would do so.

The effects of restriction and deprivation on the body are both significant and dangerous. Our body starts to slowly shut down even with a "moderate" calorie allowance of 1570 calories a day. Shockingly, that's the number of calories many diet "experts" recommend as a healthy daily caloric intake for weight loss (The US Department of Health and Human Services clearly does not see it as a problem!).

Food restriction and diets can turn into uncontrollable food obsessions, binges, and messed-up hunger signals. True, starvation may not have long-term negative effects on our body (thank god!) – our bodies have a built-in pro-life mechanism and are always trying to keep us healthy no matter what – but that is true only when we stop depriving ourselves and begin to eat in adequate amounts after having an eating disorder or dieting in excess.

How Diets Lead to an Eating Disorder

Some people think that "healthy" restriction is okay – that you have to restrict to remain healthy and not become overweight – and this may sound logical to most people, but it could not be further from the truth!

Diets are an ineffective tool to lose weight or get healthy, and science has proven dieting actually triggers binge eating, overeating, eating more food than you need, and eating more junk food than you would normally want. It can result in the loss of normal hunger cues and can even initiate eating disorders. Actually, the most common trigger for a full-blown eating disorder is – you guessed it! – DIETS!

But let's focus on why dieting is a bad idea and why it's not healthy.

Yo-yo dieting increases your risk of heart attack, stroke, diabetes, high blood pressure, cancer, immune system failure, impaired cognitive function, chronic fatigue, depression, and again…eating disorders.[17]

In The University of Pennsylvania study, rats' weight was decreased and increased by weight cycling (yo-yo dieting). The second time the rats tried to lose weight by eating less, they lost weight one hundred percent more slowly and regained the weight three hundred percent faster than the first time they ate less. The rats who yo-yoed the second time stored food as body fat *four hundred* percent more efficiently than rats who maintained a fattening diet! This study shows that doing nothing in regards to eating is four hundred percent better (!) for weight than dieting.[18]

Arthur Frank, medical director of the George Washington University Weight Management Program, reports that out of every two hundred people who start a diet, only ten of them will successfully meet their weight-loss goals. And the odds get significantly worse when you look at the long-term outcomes. Out of those ten people, only one of them will keep the weight off over time. That's a failure rate of 99.5%![19]

A team of experts at UCLA (The University of California, Los Angeles) analyzed every study that followed dieters over a two- to five-year period. *Every* published, long-term dieting study was included. The results were published in the APA (American Psychological Association) journal, *American Psychologist*. When interviewed about the findings, UCLA researcher, Tracy Mann, said that the results of their data were conclusive: *"Diets do not lead to sustained weight loss, or health benefits, for the majority of people."*

She added that most people would be *"better off not going on a diet at all. Their weight would be pretty much the same, and their bodies would not suffer the wear and tear from losing weight and gaining it all back."* Initially, she explained, many people lose five to ten percent of their body weight. But the majority of people regain any weight they lose. So the exhaustive review of every published, long-term dieting study found that diets are ineffective for weight loss.

The UCLA team concluded that *"one of the best predictors of weight gain over the four years was having lost weight on a diet at some point during the years before the study started."* Not only do diets fail at producing (or maintaining) weight loss – they actually make you gain weight![20]

While dieters can consciously override the basic drive to eat for short periods of time, most cannot continue to do so. Hormones such as leptin and ghrelin that stimulate appetite after weight loss do not adapt quickly to reduced body weight. They continue to send out "eat more" signals for as much as a year after weight loss. Eventually, biology wins out.[21]

Not only are diets ineffective for long-term weight loss (and they make you heavier!), studies also show that dieting leads to food obsession, emotional distress, and binge eating as already shown in the Minnesota Starvation Experiment. That's right – dieting has been scientifically proven to lead to binge eating! In reality, restricting what you eat does nothing to restrain you from eating. Instead, it only exaggerates the urge by intensifying your cravings and your focus on food.

When you are forbidden from having something, it dramatically fuels your desire for it. You begin to think about food more and more. When you watch TV, you become fixated on what people are eating. You mentally devour every mouthwatering recipe in magazines. You watch what other people eat and secretly judge them. If someone eats something other than what you allow yourself to eat, it somehow matters to you what they eat and why. The more you restrict particular foods, the more you crave them.

None of this is a sign of weakness on your part. It's simply the natural result of scarcity making something more desirable. Scarcity itself causes us to want something more.

If you are told NOT to look at every red color in the room, you start to seek it out more and focus on it. The more you try to avoid something and not focus on it, the more it starts to pop up everywhere. The same thing happens when you try to restrict food. Restriction makes food a forbidden thing, and therefore, you begin to think about it much more frequently and obsessively. Restricting what you eat doesn't affect only your mental processes – it also changes your actual physiological response to food. Dieting makes you physically crave it more! And it's very important to note that dieting and eating disorders are not only about the restriction of calories but also about the restriction of types of foods – something we see in the rise of orthorexia, an eating disorder where certain foods are obsessively restricted.

Think about the food you last went overboard with. The food that sends you spinning out of control. It's probably something you routinely forbid yourself from having, right? It's not your weakness or a food addiction that creates this intense response. It's the mere fact that the food is forbidden.

Scarcity creates desire. Think about human behavior in stores where the "Last and Only Final Summer Sale" is announced. Everything 50% off for one day only. Or, in your case, *"Binge out on everything for one day only! Tomorrow you will start a new diet, so don't miss out on your last favorite meal!"*

Remember how Adam and Eve were told not to eat the red apple from The Garden of Paradise? Despite all of the available fruit in abundance in the garden, that apple was the only thing they ended up eating. Why? Because it was *forbidden*.

This is something at the core of our human nature. Forbidden fruit is always the sweetest. Do not give unnecessary power and desire to foods by restricting them.

Catherine Liberty from Bulimiahelp.org writes:

> *Researchers have proven time and time again that a restrictive diet has the ability to induce every single physical and psychological symptom we associate with bulimia. What may come as even more of a shock is the fact that this isn't new information. The scientific community has been aware of the link between restrictive eating and the onset of bulimia for nearly 70 years!*[22]

I hope by now you have had many light-bulb moments... Yeah, I know, it's a pretty crazy world we live in!

Here's an example of how dieting leads to eating disorders:

First, you have a goal to lose weight or get "trim, toned, and sexy." Or maybe you just want to eat "healthy" and give up a lot of the "unhealthy" foods you love.

You start to diet – you restrict foods and/or calories. You hashtag #finallygettinghealthy on your protein shake Instagram picture.

Initially, you lose weight, and you think...*Amazzzing!! Finally! #thingsarehappening...*

But then you start to have cravings. At first, you resist the urge and use your willpower to avoid eating and stick to your diet.

But sooner or later, you give in. You binge. You overeat. You let go of the restriction and say *the hell with it!* You eat everything you have been restricting.

After the binge, when you begin to think clearly again and come out of your food coma, you realize what you have done. You have "ruined" your diet. Your life is basically over. You get upset, feel panicky and out of control, and can FEEL how you are getting fatter by the minute. You feel fear and disgust. You feel like you've become this dangerous, insatiable, eat-everything-on-this-planet kind of Foodzilla who has to be stopped.

After this, you promise yourself to be a "good girl/boy" tomorrow and start over. But today? Well, you've already blown it, so you might as well eat for the rest of the day…

(Note: Keep in mind that this binge after dieting is a VERY normal response from your body – you just don't realize it yet! Remember what happened to the Minnesota men who were starved on 1570 calories a day? Yes, they binged hardcore! Why would you think you are any different?)

The next day you start to restrict and diet again, but this time with even more fear and obsession. You want to be sure that yesterday's binge never happens again…and the monster is stopped from doing any further damage to the world's food storage…

But eventually, the same thing happens – you feel the urge to eat more than allowed and the kind of foods that are forbidden on your diet. And eventually, you binge again. You have now entered dieting merry-go-hell.

Of course, thanks to dieting, your metabolism is much slower now, and you've also lost quite an amount of muscle and water weight thanks to restriction. You've lost some digestive enzymes and might find it very hard to digest some of the foods you formerly ate, causing you to get easily bloated and constipated.

So now when you start to eat more – or even normal amounts of foods – you gain weight very quickly. You can gain all the weight back, often times weighing even more than you did originally. You may find it very hard to eat normal amounts and feel totally bloated after a meal.

Welcome, ladies and gents! You are now trapped in a vicious cycle of yo-yo dieting! You have been brainwashed to believe you just need more willpower to continue dieting and it's all your fault it didn't work.

Some stop here and give up dieting (or become chronic yo-yo dieters)…

But some continue with extreme measures to get rid of the weight "once and for all" – welcome, eating disorder!

Some people begin to overeat uncontrollably (binge eating), some binge and purge (bulimia), some starve themselves (anorexia), some obsessively avoid particular foods (orthorexia), some overexercise (bulimia or anorexia athletica), and some may have all of these together (EDNOS – eating disorder not otherwise specified).

> *"Getting rid of dieting could wipe out at least 70% of eating disorders. Get rid of dieting!"*[23]

> *"Dieting is a primary trigger of the downward spiral into an eating disorder."*[24]

> *"Girls who severely dieted were eighteen times more likely to develop an eating disorder within 6 months than those who did not diet. And 2/3 of new cases of an eating disorder came from those who dieted moderately."*[25]

Now you may think, *But my eating disorder is different! I didn't "diet." My problem was more emotional and psychological – eating disorders are mental disorders!*

Yes, some people do develop eating disorders for other reasons and not because of going on a diet. But ultimately, it doesn't matter! No matter the reason behind your eating disorder, as long as you continue to restrict, you cannot recover. When your brain is malnourished, it can't think or function properly. When you start to diet and forbid enough food and calories, your brain is much more likely respond in an eating-disordered way.

> *We know that starvation and weight loss have powerful effects on the body and the brain. Malnutrition impacts on the brain's capacity to think, manage emotions and*

> *process information from its environment. Starvation often exaggerates an individual's personality traits and ways of thinking. Malnutrition may lead to changes in brain development even after they have restored normal eating and weight. We also know that the brain responds to, and has an effect on hormones and other body systems that are undernourished. Food certainly plays a major role; the most urgent task of early recovery and maintenance is restoring the patient's normal weight with adequate daily nutrition. An undernourished individual's brain cannot recover.*[26]

To recover, you need to eat enough calories for your brain to start functioning properly. This is why you cannot recover only "mentally" – you need to recover physically as well so that your body can emerge from the eating disorder. If we recover physically, the mental aspect is much easier to correct. It cannot happen the other way around.

But what about "reasonable" calorie restriction for "healthy" weight loss?

First of all, I want to say that there isn't a single peer-reviewed controlled clinical study of any weight-loss diet that shows success in significant weight loss over the long term. Not one. Remember what we said before? Diets have 99.5% failure rate! Most weight-loss diet studies are done a year or several years after the *initial* weight loss. Yes, calorie restriction may help you lose weight, BUT it's only *temporary*. You will gain the lost weight back in the following years, and that's if you're lucky – often you gain even more weight than you started with.

Don't you agree that if calorie restriction and dieting were so effective, we would all be slim and trim by now? It's not that we lack willpower. In fact, I think constant dieters are the ones with the most willpower of them all! Other people couldn't even be bothered because dieting is Really. Hard. Work. Considering that the weight-loss industry is such a huge business and we spend billions of dollars on weight-loss products and programs every year,[27] shouldn't we be getting results by now? Instead, we have increasing obesity and growing cases of eating disorders each year.

It has been found that restricting calories for "healthy weight loss" does not improve health.

> *Psychologist Traci Mann investigated whether intentional weight loss - regardless of whether people kept the weight off or regained it - improves health. They reviewed studies of dieting interventions, looking for those with common health biomarkers, and chose five measures to compare: total cholesterol, triglycerides, blood pressure (systolic and diastolic), and fasting blood glucose. The results stunned them. "We found basically no relationship between any health outcome and the amount of weight lost or gained," says Tomiyama, adding dryly, "we had some trouble getting it published." Their finding is deeply disturbing, given the fact that virtually everyone in this culture uses weight as a proxy for health.[28]*

The weight-loss industry is designed for us to be stuck there. Stuck for life. Spending even more money when we come back after another disastrous diet that has failed. Why can't we just see it's not working!? Dieting does not work long term, it's not sustainable, and it's not healthy. And the most likely answer to why there are no long-term studies done on weight-loss diets is because nobody can keep restricting forever. It isn't happening because our bodies do not work that way. A healthy and sustainable way of eating should be something you can do for the rest of your life! It shouldn't be just one week or a few months. It won't work and will turn you into the food smashing Zilla again.

So what about "reasonable" calorie restriction programs such as Weight Watchers, you may ask? They don't endorse crash-dieting, just eating healthy, exercising more, and cutting unnecessary calories, right?

NOT.

I remember hearing somewhere that the Weight Watchers program is "the most successful" way to lose weight as it's said to be a "reasonable way to lose weight." But is it truly successful or reasonable? Let's see...

(Note: You can read the full article at https://fatfu.wordpress.com/2008/01/24/weight-watchers/)

> *Thirty-eight thousand people per year who reached goal weight sounds like a lot. But actually, it turns out to be a*

really small number. I found a business article from back then that stated that Weight Watchers had 600,000 attendees in the US in 1993. When I divide 38,000 lifetime members per year into 600,000, my calculator says that each year, only about six percent of Weight Watchers members (give or take) reached their goal weight (presumably 94% failed).

Now before you get all impressed with Weight Watcher's six percent success rate, let's take a step back. For one thing, the successful six percent weren't so fat in the first place. The 2001 study says that most were between a BMI of 25-30 ("overweight" but not "obese" – definitions I find silly). The 2007 abstract says the average starting BMI for that study was 27 –well below the average Weight Watchers participant. So in order to achieve goal weight, the average lifetime member probably had to lose less than ten pounds and would have to include a lot of people who had even less to lose....

And what about the number we're really looking for – how many people actually maintain "normal" weight long term using Weight Watchers? It turns out only 3.9% of the golden six percent were still at or below goal weight after five years. By my calculations, that means 3.9%*6.3% = 0.24% or about two out of a thousand Weight Watchers participants who reached goal weight stayed there for more than five years.[29]

And here it's important to remember that weight regain does not necessarily end when researchers stop following study participants. So we don't know what happens after five years – or ten years.

I found an interesting paper on the research of how "effective" calorie-restrictive diets are for weight loss. The authors reviewed studies of the long-term outcomes of calorie-restricting diets to assess whether dieting is an effective treatment for obesity.

> *These studies show that one-third to two-thirds of dieters regain more weight than they lost on their diets, and these studies likely underestimate the extent to which dieting is counterproductive because of several methodological problems, all of which bias the studies toward showing successful weight-loss maintenance. In addition, the studies do not provide consistent evidence that dieting results in significant health improvements, regardless of weight change. In sum, there is little support for the notion that diets lead to lasting weight loss or health benefits.*[30]

You Can't Fight Biology

The message of the following is to show you how your body always returns to your natural set-point weight no matter whether you try to lose weight or if you gain weight from dieting. This post is meant to be a motivation for you to not diet. *Ever*!

I have been around X pounds all my life (my set-point weight), at least as long as I can remember. It has fluctuated a little bit, but it always seems to be about the same no matter whether I dieted, did a "cleanse," or whatever. Even if I lost weight or gained weight thanks to dieting, I have always come back to this same weight. This is my set-point weight, and this is where my body seems to feel most comfortable.

(Note: Set-point weight is a specific weight that is your body's natural healthy weight where it feels most comfortable, no matter if you eat less or more on some days. It is not a specific number, but more like a small range of weight that is most optimal for you. Set-point weight is different for everybody. We will talk about it more!)

I don't consider myself a skinny-minnie, but I'm definitely not fat or overweight. Overall, I love my body and feel good in it!

I do have some days when I don't like my body and compare it to others, but I have come to realize that it's all normal, and it's "me." Now when I look at myself, I see the beauty in me and, most importantly, the beauty in my "flaws" and my uniqueness. I feel they make me more real, and real people are not perfect (what is perfect anyway?).

But I didn't always think that way, and I was very unhappy with my body. I had some insecurities and, like many people, I tried different things to change them. Some things we do can be beneficial and healthy (like quitting smoking), but some things get out of hand. "Healthy" things can become obsessive and have the opposite effect.

Not Eating After 6 pm
(aka Intermittent Fasting)

When I was younger, about fifteen or so, I tried my first diet. I ate everything I wanted and as much I wanted during the day, but I stopped eating after 6 pm. Unknowingly, I had tried the famous "intermittent fasting" as they call it these days. Back then, I obviously had no clue what I was getting myself into.

Teenage girls go through hormonal changes in their body and often gain more weight at that period of time. They start to develop boobs and a butt, and they start to have more curves. It freaks out most girls because they don't understand that it's natural, and that their bodies will even out in time. Young girls metamorphose into women.

I think this was the reason I started to diet at that age. I felt bigger and uncomfortable, plus I developed much earlier than many other girls in my class. I felt different. I didn't know what to expect.

As this was my first diet, the weight came off very easily. I ate in this way for about half a year, and it worked for me in terms of weight loss. I lost weight until I was about X pounds. I wasn't anorexic, and I didn't feel I needed to lose more weight. But what I was doing was definitely not healthy – some days I forgot to eat before 6 pm, but I didn't allow myself to have dinner after that time, either. Therefore I basically starved on those days. On other days, I had eaten right before 6 pm but got home very late – at about 2 am. I didn't allow myself anything before going to bed, and I went to bed with a growling stomach. As you can see, I was quite strict with this. But as long as it was before 6 pm, I still ate everything and as much as I wanted, so for that reason, I felt what I was doing was healthy and okay.

But then one day my hunger was finally stronger than my willpower. I got home very late one night and felt very hungry, and I decided to eat something. It turned into a binge. Of course, I felt extremely guilty after that and promised myself to start again the next day by not eating after 6 pm – no matter what!

After that binge, though, my body just couldn't do it anymore (thank god!). I couldn't resist eating after 6 pm. And I slowly gained all the weight back and was soon back at my set-point weight.

That was one of my weight-loss stories. But now I'll tell you one of my weight gain stories.

30 Days Raw and Water Fasting

Starting in 2008, I started to change my diet to more plant-based, raw, and healthy foods – mainly to cure the acne I had at that time. I didn't want to take drugs and wanted to heal naturally. As you can see, I had good intentions. I didn't know it could get out of hand.

BrainwashED

In 2011, I went to Australia on a work and holiday visa. I started to eat more raw foods, and a few times, I went thirty days completely raw. I saw improvements in my skin, my energy, and my weight. I noticed it had become more difficult to digest foods I had previously eaten, and I became very sensitive to a lot of stuff. I thought it was because the cooked food was toxic to my body and I had to limit or avoid it, so I wanted to continue being raw as much as possible. My goal was to be 100% raw for optimal health.

But it became more difficult for me. I always had cravings for cooked foods despite eating enough calories. Even so, I still believed that if I only stayed raw long enough, my cravings would disappear and my taste buds would change. I believed I'd lose the cravings for those unhealthy and addictive foods. At least, that's how I was conditioned by the raw food community.

I decided to do my third period of thirty days eating only raw foods. The "proper" way of eating raw healthfully was to only eat low fat, no salt, and only fruits and veggies. I still had cravings this time, but my willpower was stronger and I was able to stick with it somehow.

I did, however, have a never-ending craving for a vegan burrito that sometimes kept me up every night. After that thirty days was over, I still had the burrito craving and decided to have one – just to get it out of my mind and get over it. But that first bite turned into a two-month junk food binge and purge episode. Hello, diet-induced bingeing and eating disorder!

I don't remember gaining weight because of the bingeing episodes (I think I didn't gain because I hadn't been calorie restricting at that time, so my metabolism was still good), but I did feel miserable, stuck, and definitely bloated. I didn't know how to get over it. I didn't understand why it was so difficult to eat the most nutritious foods on the planet, foods we are supposedly biologically designed for.

Every time I binged, I promised myself that I would be back to 100% raw the next day. *This is the last time*, I would tell myself. But it never was because the harder I tried to restrict the foods I craved, the more I ended up bingeing.

To fight this, I decided to do a three-day water fast. I thought that maybe I just needed to clean my system and my taste buds, and then my body would naturally start to crave healthy foods. I could start fresh with a blank sheet.

Before the first day of my water fast, I planned one "final" binge, promising myself to never go back to eating junk again. I bought all of my usual binge foods, ate them all, felt disgusting and bloated, and then vomited. Now I was truly motivated to "start over" with my new sparkly-glittery-hopeful three-day fast.

I fasted those three days and felt great afterward. I felt clean and pure, and I lost weight (water weight). When I decided to eat again, I started with a watermelon and progressed to some other fruit. Then I thought, *Why not have some low-fat, high-carb vegan cooked foods? It's still healthy, right?* After that, I started wanting more fat, so I added some fatty sauce. *Still not so bad, right?* I told myself.

But I felt the hunger get bigger and bigger, and I had a familiar thought. *I'll binge for the last time, and then I promise it will be over.* So I again went out and bought those binge foods and binged, promising to start eating healthy tomorrow. It didn't happen of course. My eating disorder was worse than ever. The cycle had continued. I purged till the blood vessels in both of my eyes broke, and I walked around with completely red, bloody eyes for about a month.

After that, I gained weight. I usually NEVER gained too much weight, so it was scary. I gained about thirteen pounds in a matter of one month after the water fast. I was at my heaviest at that point, and I felt so uncomfortable.

After I realized that I simply could not be #fullyrawforlife, I started to eat cooked foods again. I was still trying to eat clean, and I still felt guilty about certain foods, but since I wasn't doing any calorie restriction or fasting, I slowly lost the extra weight. It took me a whole year to lose that weight by not restricting calories. I also stopped purging for a good while that year, so that helped with normalizing my weight. But my mentality was still eating disordered, I still wanted to eat as clean as possible – I was not recovered. The bulimia came back later on because I still did not understand that by restricting the foods I craved, I couldn't recover. But yeah, my weight eventually went back to my normal set-point weight – the X pounds I had always been no matter what I did.

So the moral of my story is that your body has its own healthy set-point weight, and you cannot *force* it down. If you diet, you can maybe lose some weight for a short period of time, but you will gain it back afterward because your hunger cues are much stronger than willpower, and your body is designed to respond to restriction with increased hunger and cravings. Even when you temporarily gain or lose some weight as a result of dieting or fasting, you will eventually get back to your set-point weight as this is the weight your body feels the best and most healthful at.

Set Point Weight

Set-point weight is the body's natural, healthy weight. It doesn't matter if you eat more on some days and less on others – you still end up in the same weight range. It's important to know that your body has a weight *range,* and it's normal for your weight to fluctuate a little bit. It doesn't stay at the exact number all day every day, so take a deep breath…it's normal. Set-point weight is different for every individual.

A healthy body maintains its healthy set-point weight by prompting you to eat according to hunger and fullness cues without any compensatory behaviors (counting calories, exercising, dieting, etc.). Very few people are naturally BMI 18; most average between 20-25. Your body will do everything to keep you at your set-point weight, no matter if you are naturally BMI 20 and try to gain to BMI 22, or you start at BMI 25 and try to diet down to BMI 20.

"This natural weight is where your body functions best and is the weight your body is meant to be according to your genetic makeup. Just as you have a predetermined height or shoe size, you also have a predetermined biological weight or set-point that your body tries to defend."[31]

Stephan Guyenet from Whole Health Resource explains,

One pound of human fat contains about 3,500 calories. That represents roughly forty slices of toast. So if you were to eat one extra slice of toast every day, you would gain just under a pound of fat per month. Conversely, if you were to eat one fewer slice per day, you'd lose a pound a month. Right? Not quite.

How is it that most peoples' body fat mass stays relatively stable over long periods of time when an imbalance of as little as 5% of calories should lead to rapid changes in weight? Is it because we do complicated calculations in our heads every day, factoring in basal metabolic rate and exercise, to make sure our energy intake precisely matches expenditure? Of course not. We're gifted with a sophisticated system of hormones and brain regions that do the "calculations" for us unconsciously.

When it's working properly, this system precisely matches energy intake to expenditure, ensuring a stable and healthy fat mass. It does this by controlling food seeking behaviors, feelings of fullness and even energy expenditure by heat production and physical movements. If you eat a little bit more than usual at a meal, a properly functioning system will say "let's eat a little bit less next time, and perhaps also burn some of it off." This is one reason why animals in their natural habitat are nearly always at an appropriate weight, barring starvation. The only time wild animals are overweight enough to significantly compromise physical performance is when it serves an important purpose, such as preparing for hibernation.[32]

BMI (Body Mass Index)

BMI shows the balance between height and weight and indicates whether a person is overweight, underweight, or normal weight. It's calculated with numbers – 18.5 to 25 is normal, over 25 is overweight, and 18.5 or less is underweight. The formula isn't completely accurate because it doesn't differentiate between fat, bones, and muscle. Belgian mathematician Adolphe Quetelet came up with BMI in the 1830s to measure weight trends in whole populations – not in individuals as it's used today.

A BMI of 25-30 means overweight in the medical world, but it doesn't indicate health. It only indicates body mass comparison. That's it. The chronic conditions often associated with obesity exist at all weights and are more likely to cause death in those of average or below average weight than those of above average weight. In fact, a *Journal of the American Medical Association* study found that *"Overweight was not associated with excess mortality."*[33] You may be surprised that an article entitled "Excess Deaths Associated with Underweight, Overweight, and Obesity" in one of the world's leading medical journals found that overweight people lived the longest.

Being overweight is associated with numerous diseases, but we have to understand that *correlation does not mean causation.* Just because one thing is correlated with another, it doesn't necessarily mean the one actually caused the other. Similarly, if a dog goes outside, and it starts raining, it's correlated, yes, but does it mean the dog caused the rain? Today we don't actually even know if diabetes comes after a person has gained weight or if the person's weight gain is a symptom of diabetes, as surgeon and nutrition researcher Peter Attia has suggested. There is a big difference. No one truly knows which comes first, the illness or the weight gain. As Robert Lusting wrote in a 2008 editorial in *The Journal of Pediatrics,* "*Behavior can alter biochemistry, but biochemistry can also alter behavior.*" Or maybe there is even a third factor that caused both the illness and, therefore, the weight gain.[34]

You Can't Decide Your Goal Weight

Some people think they can actually decide their goal weight. They may be unhappy with their bodies and want to lose weight, so they decide how much they want to weigh. This mindset can be very dangerous and can cause more anxiety and stress when they find it hard to reach their goal. Many people believe that losing weight is as simple as eating less and burning more. This kind of thinking can lead to an eating disorder. Only *your* body can decide what its healthy weight is, not you and not anyone else. We say we want to lose "just ten more pounds" to be happy with our body. But is it actually necessary and healthy from our body's perspective? These things we do not ask.

Most often, we compare our bodies to other people's. We take somebody as our "bodspiration" and decide that's the way we should look. We find it so hard to accept that we all have different body types and individual healthy set-point weights. Some have wider hips, some bigger boobs, some skinny legs, some thicker thighs, and so on. Some are BMI 21, some BMI 25. Some even have BMI 29 and are perfectly healthy without any dieting background or medical illness. Even when you diet down to a lower number, it doesn't mean it will stay that way when you start to eat after your hunger cues kick in again or you return to a normal way of eating. Even when you diet down to a lower weight, it won't make you healthy – it will just make you sick because your body cannot be healthy and function at its best at that low weight - it's not your healthy set-point weight. If what you are doing is not sustainable for the rest of your life, then it will NOT work! Overexercising, restricting calories, restricting foods you crave, bingeing, and eating-disordered behaviors are not healthy and sustainable ways to have a normal healthy weight for life!

According to BMI, healthy weights range from a BMI of 18.5 to 25. Very, *very* few people are naturally BMI 18.5-20. Most fall between 21-25. And keep in mind that a BMI higher than 25 does not automatically equal unhealthy. Some people are BMI 27 and still healthy – they naturally have more muscle and a dense bone structure. BMI identifies averages and is not an optimum nor a norm, so please keep that in mind!

It's very understandable that people who have gone through years of eating disorders might not even know what their healthy weight (set-point weight) is. But the thing is that you don't have to know your set-point weight in order to recover and maintain your healthy weight! Your body will reach its optimal weight by itself! As you recover, your body will naturally find its best weight. It's the weight that is very easy for you to maintain. You can maintain it without calorie counting or restricting or planned exercise.

If you maintain a certain weight through restriction and/or an intense exercise regimen that's hard for you to keep up with healthfully, then that is not your natural, healthy weight! That's why in recovery it's so important to quit exercising and start eating enough – you must allow your body to find its healthy set-point weight. If you keep restricting or exercising, you might not recover at all but rather stay in a semi-recovered state or even overshoot your set-point because your body is still running slowly and saving up for the next restriction period.

It is actually true that people who "recover" on lower amounts of calories will have more fat on their body after recovery than people who go into full recovery on proper amounts of foods. Remember that in the Minnesota Experiment, men who had the largest calorie increase in the rehabilitation period recovered the quickest! And on average, they gained 140%

more fat than they had before the experiment but over time it went back to normal. It balances out if you give it time!

If you continue to restrict in your recovery – even just a little bit – and try to recover on lower amounts, your body can't relax and come out of its starvation mode. It's still storing extra fat because it thinks the famine isn't over and food is not abundant. You have to eat without restriction and eat as much as you are hungry for. Never deny yourself food when you want it.

> *Furthermore, researchers have shown there is a significant increase in trunk adiposity (fat deposits around the midsection of the body) in recovery ... and this fat mass is evenly redistributed in the optimization period after weight restoration only if the patient continues to eat in an unrestricted fashion.*
>
> *In other words, the initial trunk adiposity and disproportionate fat mass ratio in the early period of refeeding may not resolve unless and until a patient successfully supports the period of hyperphagia [extreme hunger] that is part and parcel of the process of reaching a healthy remission. We also know that trunk adiposity, in particular, is correlated with cardiovascular disease in older men and women...which is all the more reason to encourage those in recovery to allow their bodies to complete the refeeding process fully to allow for a return to optimal fat mass to fat-free mass ratios.*[35]

Also, if you are not underweight and have a BMI in normal range, it still does not mean you are at a healthy weight for *you*. Everybody has a different set-point weight and BMI. For example, for Sandy, it might be BMI 24. If she restricted or exercised down to BMI 21, does it mean that's her new healthy set-point? No! She will have to continue restricting to maintain that new lower set-point. Her body will suffer and run on a deficit. It will slow down and become ill the longer she continues to restrict. She is not clinically underweight – she is still within a healthy BMI range – but it is *not* healthy for *her* body. This weight was not reached healthfully and sustainably. For her body, BMI 24 is easiest to maintain without any form of restriction or compensation.

I want to stress that if you are in a healthy BMI range of 18.5 to 25, it does not yet mean you are recovered or at your optimal set-point weight. Being at "normal weight range" does not automatically mean recovery. If you still gain weight very easily by eating enough or you have to "maintain" that weight in any restrictive way, it's not your set-point weight.

Different Body Types and Lowering Your Set-Point Weight

As we mentioned previously, our bodies have a set-point weight where we feel healthiest and happiest. Some bodies are skinnier, some are curvier, and some are right in the middle.

The media wants us to believe that we should *all* be BMI X, and if we aren't, we are automatically unhealthy, fat, or anorexic. We CAN'T all be the same body weight and size! And if you try to force your body, you can end up with an eating disorder – bingeing, starving, and obsessing.

There are many body types. Some are naturally skinnier, some are average, some are curvy – everything in between and beyond. Look around in real life, and you'll see so many different bodies – and not only the slim and skinny kind.

For example, my boyfriend is a normal eater. He eats whatever he wants in whatever amount he wants. He eats when he's hungry and stops when he's full. He has no obsession with his body or his weight or food. He wants to eat healthy to feel good and nourish his body, but he's not trying to eat perfectly and won't hesitate eating chocolate, chips, pizza, or whatever food he wants.

He is naturally skinny and has been like that all his life. But if he would want to gain weight, he'd have to force-feed himself. It would feel unnatural and unhealthy, and I bet he would be miserable – just the same as someone on any restrictive diet. Even if he gained weight thanks to over-feeding, when he eventually went back to listening to his normal hunger cues, he would lose all the weight without even trying and go right back to his original set-point.

I'm quite average in build. I have some definition but also curves. I've been like this all my life, the same body type no matter if I eat less on some days and more on others. My weight and body build stays the same. If I wanted to be more like my boyfriend's body type – skinny and very slim – I'd have to do something drastic. I would have to either start restricting calories or following some restrictive eating style. I've done it plenty of times in my life, and that's why I developed an eating disorder –I forced my body to be something it isn't!

I ride my bike or go hiking, and I occasionally do some yoga or stretching or take a walk. I am in no way an athlete, and I don't strive to be one, either. I developed exercise bulimia (aka bulimia athletica) in the past, and now I simply want to find my happy medium with exercise or body movement. I want to move my body because it feels natural and good, but I will not force myself to exercise for weight loss, "weight maintenance," or any of that.

I eat plenty of whole foods and home-cooked meals, but I do not have a mindset of #eatcleanordie. I like to eat out sometimes or have ice cream, chocolate, or cookies as a snack – or maybe even as a full meal if I want! I eat when hungry and stop when full. I do not binge or overeat or obsess about foods or calories. In my past, I tried to eat more "clean" and 100% healthy foods, and what did it get me? Orthorexia – food obsessions, food fear, going crazy in my head, bingeing and purging because of my restrictive, clean eating diet (despite eating enough calories!!!). I don't aim for perfection anymore but want to be in a place where my body feels happy and balanced in terms of food – not restricting, not obsessing, and having plenty of nutrition and fuel. My point is that I had to accept that I can't force my body to a lower set-point or to a different body type because I developed a serious eating disorder by doing so.

Lowering your weight affects you mentally as well as physically. It's very stressful and depressing. I don't want to do that anymore. So now I accept my weight and the way my body is naturally built. I accept that I represent women who are quite average and not a skinny body type.

Yes, I – just like everyone else – have plenty of things about my body (according to body "standards") that I could beat myself up about every day. I'm not "perfect" (who the hell is?), and I definitely have some things I feel insecure about, but I have learned to love those things and see them as a part of me. I've learned to love my body that went through bulimia, restriction, and dieting hell! The body I hated and did not love!

I am very lucky to have a body with legs and arms, I'm lucky to be able to run and cycle, I'm lucky to have a healthy body that's able to transport me from place to place. This is the body I will have for the rest of my life, the body that has been with me in good times and bad times, the body that never left me no matter how badly I treated it. The body that *recovered!* The body that is able to heal itself so miraculously if given the chance! My body is truly amazing! And so is yours!

Why Are People Overweight or Obese?

Many people ask me this question when they begin recovery and realize they have to eat more than they previously allowed themselves, more than what is considered a normal amount by society. They think food and eating actually *equal* being overweight, fat, and obese. They're afraid that by eating enough calories to recover, they'll become obese and die! What I have found is that there are many more reasons for gaining weight than just eating and calories.

Fat does not automatically mean there's something wrong. It isn't automatically a sign of disease or bad behavior. Many "overweight" (according to BMI numbers) people can actually be metabolically healthy and live long and healthy lives. So it's not always a sign that something is terribly wrong. However, if a person had a normal weight previously and – suddenly or over time – gained weight way above their previous set-point, then there is a reason behind it. I will discuss some of those reasons below. Note that I am no way an expert on why people are overweight/obese, but this is what I have found in my research.

1. **Dieting**

Dieting promotes weight gain rather than loss. No calorie-restrictive diet is sustainable long term. In fact, 99% of the people regain all the lost weight back after five years. If that's not an incredible failure rate, I don't know what is! But despite that fact, people keep believing that maybe, just maybe, they are the odd one percent…or more like 0.01%…

By dieting and restricting, you teach your body to store more fat. Your healthy metabolic fat burning functions cannot work properly if you starve yourself! Your body thinks, *Oh no! Food is no longer abundant! Better slow down because we don't want to waste energy (calories) when we might need it to get through this famine!*

Every time you diet, your metabolism slows down. Up to seventy percent of lost weight can be muscle loss, and you also lose water weight. But when you start eating again, you will gain even more weight back than you had previously because now your metabolism simply doesn't burn the same amount of calories it did before your diet. In one study of Finnish twins, the more diets the participants went on, the higher their risk of becoming overweight and the faster they gained weight later in life.[36]

Dieting also makes you binge-prone, which means your appetite, cravings, and need for calories skyrockets. You cannot control the binges, and willpower does not help you out here. This is your body's biology in action! Your set-point weight will climb higher and higher. You can only end this by not dieting or restricting ever again and restoring your normal hunger cues.

The following image illustrates how every time you diet and restrict calories, you will lose weight, but along with that, your metabolism slows down. You lose metabolically active muscle tissue, and you also become binge-prone. So when you finally quit dieting (which you will!), it will be so easy for your body to gain weight rapidly because it is running slower and will store more fat and weight in case of future famine. If you don't stop dieting, this cycle can continue until you are obese!

[Illustration: silhouettes showing a stair-step pattern with labels — "set point", "dieting", "binge-prone", "reduced metabolism", "higher set point", "dieting", "reduced metabolism", "binge-prone", "higher set point"]

What can you do?

First off, do not even think about weight loss in recovery. When you have an eating disorder, the last thing you want to think about is losing weight. But because knowing how normal, healthy weight happens may help to calm you down and assure you that you won't become obese just by eating what is enough for your particular body, let's say your weight is truly unhealthy and you need to lose weight. What then is the healthy way to do so?

The only thing you can do is to eat enough as you go through recovery so that any damage you've done with your past of bad eating habits can be fully reversed. Do not – ever – restrict again. Eat whatever foods you want and as much as you want, and do it regularly! This will eliminate all of your urges to binge, eliminate cravings, and restore normal hunger cues. Eat whole foods and home-cooked meals. Take a big, long break from strenuous exercise and instead move your body *mindfully* – take walks, play with your kids, take the stairs instead of an elevator, do some gardening, and so on. Do not overexercise because this can have a negative effect (we will talk about this in Chapter 2). Slow and steady body movement through everyday activities is much more effective for a healthy weight maintenance than any obsessive exercise regimen.

Work on your stress levels and make sure you get enough sleep, sunlight, play, creativity, happiness, and fulfilling relationships in your life! Don't underestimate the things I just mentioned – these are crucial!

All of the above will give your body a full chance to recover and reach a healthier weight if it needs to. If your body decides to let go of any weight, then this is the only healthy way I know to make it happen. But I have to stress again that you should not even think about this kind of stuff while in recovery. Most commonly, a healthy weight is achieved by itself while going through recovery and just giving your body time. You do not have to force it to happen.

I have personally seen my body change thanks only to restoring my normal hunger cues and getting rid of my eating disorder. I include activity in my daily habits – not exercise in and of itself – and that is enough.

2. **Reaction to Medication**

> *Some medications can increase appetite, cause fluid retention, or slowly lead to weight gain over a period of time due to fatigue and lower activity. Drugs that trigger increases in appetite may work in the brain and affect the satiety (fullness) center.*[37]

Just look at the list of drugs that can promote weight gain and increased appetite, and you will see what I'm talking about…

http://www.drugs.com/article/weight-gain.html

http://sideeffects.embl.de/se/C0232461/pt

> *The use of second-generation antipsychotics (SGAs) is associated with metabolic side effects including weight gain, diabetes mellitus and an atherogenic lipid profile. These adverse effects are not only the risk factors for cardiovascular disease, insulin resistance and diabetes mellitus leading to increased morbidity and mortality but may also impair the patient's adherence to treatment. SGAs, in particular, are associated with significant weight gain…*[38]

> *Hyperlipidaemia is often an early metabolic response to some antipsychotics and is thought to be up to five times higher in those who have received antipsychotics than in the*

general population. The most common abnormality is a low level of high-density lipoprotein cholesterol in up to 58% of patients. Raised triglycerides have been found in up to 53% of people with psychosis.[39]

Harriet Brown, the author of Body of Truth, writes about her own experience with taking a medication for anxiety: *"The first time I went on an SSRI [an anxiety drug] for anxiety, I gained forty pounds over three years. When I went off the medication, I dropped twenty-five pounds within a month, and the rest soon after."*[40]

Another commonly used drug is the contraceptive pill. The following are quotes from different people who use/have used this drug.

(Note: Not all people have this side effect from the pill or after quitting the pill, but as you can see, it does happen.)

"It made me bloated, very moody, depressed, and [I] gained 17 pounds and kept on gaining until switched to a different pill. It did its job, prevents pregnancy but definitely makes you gain a lot of weight. Got off the pill [and] lost the 15 pounds within 2 weeks…"

"I haven't gotten pregnant on this pill. Hence, I gave it a 10 for effectiveness. I have been on it for 6 months. I have gained 27 pounds on my 5-foot frame."

"I've been taking this pill for about 6 months now and have gained 20 pounds. I haven't made any change to my diet or exercise routine…I'm just worried about the amount of weight gained in such a short time."[41]

3. **Being Called "Fat"**

Being called "fat" at a young age can increase the risk of becoming overweight later on. Co-author Jeffrey Hunger, a graduate student at UC Santa Barbara, said that simply being called fat may lead to behaviors that later result in obesity. "Being labeled as too fat may lead people to worry about personally experiencing the stigma and discrimination faced by overweight individuals, and recent research suggests that experiencing or anticipating weight stigma increases stress and can lead to overeating.[42]

We are definitely vulnerable to these kinds of comments and do not even realize the effect it has on us. Being called "fat," "ugly," "weirdo," and so on does not necessarily make us obese in and of itself, but it certainly triggers us to diet and have unrealistic goals for our body, and it increases the urge to do something to change ourselves – which often leads to weight and body image problems in the long run.

It can be beneficial to identify the causes of your eating problems when you were younger. It's likely that your parents/friends/environment interrupted your normal eating somehow. Were you called "fat" or any other insulting label? Was there any deprivation or restriction of foods in your family? Any body shaming? Were your parents dieters? All of these can interrupt a child's normal eating habits, even causing eating disorders later on.

If you think this may be the case, you can see that you have the ability to change your eating habits. Your current eating patterns exist not because normal eating habits were not a part of you but because something interrupted them. You can change things by going through recovery.

Being called "fat" or other upsetting names is one of the things that causes young people (and people in general) to go on diets. And because diets do not work, they gain even more weight back. No wonder those people can become overweight or even obese later on in their lives.

There is a great chapter on this issue in the book Intuitive Eating by Evelyn Tribole and Elyse Resch. They talk about how a child can easily turn away from normal hunger and fullness cues through restriction and deprivation. It can start with simple comments like *You can't have dessert when you don't eat your dinner first!* or *You can have only one candy today because it's too much sugar! Sugar makes you fat.* These remarks may sound innocent, but they actually create problems with food.

Often parents are too concerned that their child will be overweight, and this increases the need to control the child's eating – but in reality, it only makes things worse. The child doesn't learn to listen to his normal hunger cues, instead listening to his parents' rules – just like in any other diet! Restriction of any kind can lead to bingeing and overeating.

Parents have to trust their children and their ability to eat normally without passing judgment on them. Even a parent's rolling eyes or looks of disapproval can lead to the child feeling guilty and having food phobias. This never results in a healthy relationship with food!

4. Metabolic Issues

You can develop a metabolic disorder if certain organs (for instance, the pancreas, thyroid gland, liver, etc.) stop functioning properly. These kinds of disorders can be the result of genetics, a nutritional deficiency in a certain hormone or enzyme, consuming certain foods, lifestyle choices, or a number of other factors.

Also, keep in mind as we mentioned before that dieting can be a major factor in the development of metabolic disorders and for the improper functioning of hormones.

The most common types of nutritional and metabolic disorders include the following:

Gaucher's disease – *This condition causes an inability to break down a particular kind of fat, which then accumulates in the liver, spleen, and bone marrow. This inability can result in pain, bone damage, and even death…*

Glucose-galactose malabsorption – *This is a defect in the transport of glucose and galactose across the stomach lining which leads to severe diarrhea and dehydration…*

Hereditary hemochromatosis – *In this condition, excess iron is deposited in several organs and can cause liver cirrhosis, liver cancer, diabetes, and heart disease…*

Maple syrup urine disease – *This condition disrupts the metabolism of certain amino acids, causing rapid degeneration of the neurons. If not treated, it causes death within the first few months after birth...*

Phenylketonuria (PKU) – *PKU causes an inability to produce the enzyme phenylalanine hydroxylase, resulting in organ damage, mental retardation, and unusual posture...*[43]

Since I am not an expert in medical conditions, always seek more information from a professional.

5. **Depression and Stress**

Depression and stress are very destructive to the body. People react to it differently – some lose weight, and some gain weight. At first, stress can decrease your appetite, and you may not eat enough for few days. This, in turn, can lead to bingeing over the following days because your body is simply hungry.

When the body is under stress, it definitely performs differently on a cellular level, affecting organs, hormones, and even fat production.

Depression is very common among people with eating disorders. Sometimes we don't realize that the root cause of the weight gain is not depression itself but the restricting that caused the altered brain function, the feeling of loss of control with foods, and the inability to trust hunger signals.

So first ask yourself – have you been on diets, have you been trying to lose weight, have you done restriction of any kind? If the answer to any of these questions is yes, then the increased appetite and weight gain may be the result of dieting and not depression. The same thing is with stress. Having an eating disorder, bingeing, and dealing with food obsession is very stressful! Heck, dieting is stressful! When you recover your normal eating habits, the stress of eating will be gone!

But what happens first: do we gain weight because we are depressed, or do we become depressed because we gained weight? Nobody knows exactly.

> *It's a chicken and the egg phenomenon," says psychologist Leslie Heinberg, Ph.D., who directs the Bariatric and Metabolic Institute at the Cleveland Clinic. "But we do know that depression has lots of symptoms that can worsen obesity - appetite disturbances, lack of energy, lack of motivation to do things.*[44]

And as I said before, so many drugs (such as antidepressants) for mental issues (depression/stress) actually cause weight gain as a side effect. So it could also be that the drug you're taking to manage depression and stress is causing the weight gain, not the depression or stress itself.

6. **Junk Food – Not Enough Nutrition**

Further on in this book, I will mention many times how important it can be to eat junk food and processed foods when you're in recovery. It's essential that you get over your food fears to achieve full recovery. I do not believe recovery is possible when you still have a fear of foods and a "good" and "bad" food mindset. I'm not saying that your body needs junk food for health or nutrition, but eating those foods is more for your mental health. First and foremost, you must get rid of the food-shame and feelings of guilt when eating particular foods. (We will talk about it more!)

It's okay to eat junk food in moderate amounts, but humans cannot sustain health if junk food is the basis of our meals every day for long periods of time. I'm sure you know that just by common sense. I'm not going to get into details about junk food since this is simply not the right place, given my own experience with eliminating junk food completely and then developing uncontrollable cravings for it. Instead, let's focus on recovery and developing a healthy relationship with food.

I think the solution is to not completely eliminate these foods or deem them "fattening," "unhealthy," "sickening," or "addictive" – this is negative and can further promote an obsession with foods and cravings, especially when you already have an eating disorder. Instead, learn to have a healthy relationship with these foods so they do not become a dominant part of your life or meals. And one step toward that healthy relationship is to not restrict.

I like what Portia de Rossi said in her interview with Oprah about how she recovered from her eating disorder by not restricting food:

> *But really the only way I recovered from my eating disorder and chronic dieting was to never ever restrict. Never restrict ANY kinds of foods, not even the portion sizes. And that really is the only way food loses its power over you. If you can have something every day as much as you want, you tend not to want it as much anymore. And after a period of time, you actually eat what your body needs, you eat what makes you happy, and you will not think about food ever again! And that is how I healed myself.*[45]

Intuitive eating does not mean that you follow your cravings and eat whatever you can get your hands on. Yes, intuitive eating is about listening to your body, but it's also about listening to your brain and emotions as well. The brain and the emotions are not separated from our body. You have to listen to all three to find balance. There is nothing wrong with including nutritious foods in your diet because they make you feel good and healthy and energetic. But eating other things as well is good for you emotionally and mentally. It prevents you from feeling restricted and, therefore, promotes stress-free eating and normal hunger cues.

By learning to eat intuitively, you will want whole foods without feeling restricted! By listening to your body, you will quickly learn that if you eat only junk food, your body will tell you it needs nutritious foods, too! That's where we want to be after eating disorder recovery – healthy, feeling free around food, not restricting, and following our body's signals to be in balance! Eat plenty of whole foods to nourish your body but eat every other food you crave to nourish your soul!

These are just some of the reasons why people may be overweight or obese. There are other factors as well, but my main point is that when you recover, it is very, very unlikely that you will become overweight just by eating when you're hungry and stopping when you're full – it's just not gonna happen! In the last chapter, you will find numerous studies done on intuitive eating and why it's actually a very effective way to get back to your normal healthy weight and stay there for life!

Calories In, Calories Out Theory

Many people think weight loss is as simple as eating fewer calories and burning more. Yes, in terms of thermodynamics, that's absolutely true, but don't forget to take into account other important factors. For example, metabolic rate can vary big time from person to person. You can't "out-calculate" your metabolism because it's too complicated, too dynamic.

Our body is biological, not mathematical. Those kinds of math equations are not accurate when it comes to the body. It's just not that cut and dried. Just as the body knows how to breathe unconsciously, it knows how to keep our weight within a normal range. We just have to follow our hunger cues and not mess with the system by dieting, restricting calories or foods, or trying to "burn off calories." If your body is healthy and not riddled with a history of disordered eating habits, it easily stays at its set-point weight without you having to think about it…or calculate if you can or cannot eat that cookie today and how many steps you have to take to burn it off.

In June 2011, Barry Popkin and Kiyan Duffey, doctors at the University of North Carolina at Chapel Hill, made a startling discovery. They discovered that the number of calories consumed per person per day increased by 570 calories between 1977 and 2006. So if the calories in = calories out theory were true, it would mean if an average person consumes 570 more calories per day, then the average person should have gained 476 pounds since 2006, right? But we know that can't be true.[46]

We should think about our weight in terms of biology, not math. If we drink more, we urinate more. If we inhale more, we exhale more. When we eat more, our body burns more. It is proven that people who eat more have a higher metabolic rate. And this advantage is not solely theirs because *you* can also improve your metabolism or "heal" it after chronic dieting or an eating disorder when you start to eat enough calories. Your metabolism is suppressed by dieting and restriction, and that's why you may gain weight initially when you start to eat more, but you will drop the excess weight when the damage from your past bad eating habits is repaired and your bodily functions – hormones, hunger cues, and metabolism – are back to normal.

> *This "burn more when we eat more" behavior explains how we've gained dramatically less than what would be predicted by calorie math. The "burn less when we eat less" behavior explains why studies show traditional calorie-counting approaches failing 95.4 percent of the time – and often provoking even greater rebound weight gain. When we put*

these two biologic behaviors together, we can see why every weight-loss study ever conducted shows that when people are given a surplus or shortage of calories, they never gain or lose the mathematically anticipated amount of fat. The body just doesn't work that way.[47]

According to the calories in calories out theory, we should lose weight if we just eat a little bit less, right?

Here's another study conducted at Harvard involving 67,272 people.[48] The researchers divided this large sample into five groups according to the quantity of calories they ate and found that the *less* people ate, the *more* body fat they had. People who weighed more ate far fewer calories than people who weighed less naturally – these people simply burned more calories. So this study clearly shows that lowering your calories does not matter in terms of your weight. If you slow down your metabolism by dieting and lose muscle tissue, it's a sure way to eat less and weigh even more in the long run.

Jonathan Bailor, the author of *A Calorie Myth: How to Eat More and Exercise Less with The Smarter Science of Slim*, writes:

> *Let's look at a real-life study: the Women's Health Initiative, a study that tracked nearly 49,000 women for eight years. Just as in our experiment, the women in one group ate an average of 120 fewer calories a day than the other group. Remember, that adds up to 350,400 fewer calories. How much lighter was the average woman who ate 350,400 fewer calories? The answer: 0.88 pounds.*

> *That is not a typo. Eating 350,400 FEWER calories had less than 1 percent of the impact predicted by calorie math. Eating less of a traditional Western diet does not cause a long-term fat loss because this approach incorrectly assumes that taking in fewer calories forces our body to burn fat. That has been clinically proved to be false. Eating less does not force us to burn body fat. It forces us to burn fewer calories. That is why dieters walk around tired and crabby all day. Their bodies and brains have slowed down. When our body needs calories and none are around, it is forced to make a decision: go through all the hassle of converting calories from body fat or just slow down on burning calories. Given the choice, slowing down wins.*
>
> *Even worse, if we still don't have enough energy, our body burns muscle, not fat. Studies show that up to 70 percent of the non-water weight lost when people are eating less comes from burning muscle – not body fat. Only after it's cannibalized this muscle will our body burn fat.*[49]

That's the beauty of set-point weight. Our genes, brain, and hormones work together to maintain balance. A healthy body automatically knows how much food it needs, and it regulates it with hunger cues. It automatically maintains our body's fat levels – not too high, not too low, but just perfect for every individual. When we don't mess with this system, our body has no problem maintaining a healthy set-point weight.

> *Our set-point is determined by a series of hormonal signals released from our gut, pancreas, and fat cells, which travel to*

the hypothalamus in the brain. The brain then regulates how much we eat, how many calories we burn, and how much body fat we store long term through various hormones and neurotransmitters, such as serotonin, leptin, and ghrelin. Our "set-point weight" refers to the level of stored fat our body automatically works to maintain regardless of a number of calories we take in or burn off. Our set-point explains why it's so hard to keep fat off through traditional diet and exercise techniques.[50]

If you eat more, you will burn more. A renowned metabolism expert, Matt Stone, writes in his book *Diet Recovery: Restoring Hormonal Health, Metabolism, Mood, and Your Relationship with Food*,[51] that the more you eat above your appetite and the more sedentary you are to minimize the calories you burn, the more the body fights back against this surplus by:

- Raising the metabolism
- Decreasing hunger
- Increasing physical energy
- Increasing the pulse rate
- Increasing body temperature
- Increasing the rate of lipolysis (burning fat for energy)
- And the list goes on…

In other words, for a normal healthy person, if you do eat "more than your daily calorie allowance," let's say, your body performs all of the above tasks to keep you at your natural, healthy set-point weight. I have experienced this myself. If I eat more some days, I feel I have more energy just to move around. I'm feeling much warmer, my pulse gets higher, and, after that, my hunger decreases for the next meal or the next day. It makes perfect sense!

We do not have to track how many calories we ate today or measure how active we were to know how much we must eat to stay at our healthy weight – our bodies regulate themselves!

Scott Abel, the author of *Understanding Metabolism: The Truth About Counting Calories, Sustainable Weight Loss, and Metabolic Damage* says, *"The calories you eat today will likewise affect the hormonal and metabolic environment of your body tomorrow."*[52] For example, if today you eat "too much," your body will regulate itself to make sure things get balanced again. You don't need to calculate anything! It's when you mess with this artificially, however, that you get into problems because you interfere with this natural, built-in system.

The solution here is to first allow your body to recover and reset its normal hunger cues. Eat when hungry, and stop when full – again, intuitive eating wins! Dieting loses! Pow!

Scott Abel further explains that, when looking at the bigger picture, a calorie is not a calorie. *"Instead, what really matters is the metabolic and hormonal environment of the body within which calories enter."*[53]

Researchers at the Mayo Clinic fed people 1,000 extra calories per day for eight weeks.[54] A thousand extra calories per day for eight weeks totals 56,000 extra calories. Nobody gained sixteen pounds – 56,000 calories worth of body fat if the calories in, calories out theory were true. The most anyone gained was a little over half that. The least anyone gained was basically nothing – less than a pound.

How could that be true? People ate an additional 56,000 calories and gained basically zero body fat? How can 56,000 extra calories add up to nothing? That's because extra calories don't have to turn into body fat. They can be burned off automatically. The medical journal QJM reports, *"Food in excess of immediate requirements...can easily be disposed of, being burned up and dissipated as heat. Did this capacity not exist, obesity would be almost universal."*[55] Eating more and gaining less is possible because when we're hormonally healthy, we have all sorts of underappreciated ways to deal with calories other than storing them as body fat.

Our body does whatever it needs to stay at your healthy set-point weight. You do not need to count calories or exercise to burn more if you eat more. When our body is healthy, and our weight starts rising above our set point, for whatever reasons, hormonal signals cause our metabolic rate to go up, our appetite to go down, and our body fat to get burned. This prevents excess fat from sticking around for too long. We stay at a healthy set point without even trying.

Jeffrey M. Friedman, MD, Ph.D., head of the Laboratory of Molecular Genetics at Rockefeller University in New York, says that our weight stays relatively stable because our body's energy balance is regulated with a precision of greater than 99.5%, which far exceeds what can be consciously monitored.[56] No calorie counting can be better than our body's natural calorie counting system that happens without us even thinking and is regulated by hunger cues. The set point is a precise and powerful biological system that maintains body weight within a relatively narrow range.

Trying to eat less to lose weight is like trying to sleep less to do more work. You may get away with it for a short time, but it has consequences and is not sustainable. You may think that by depriving yourself of sleep you can get more work done, but when the sleep deprivation hits, you will suffer physically and mentally. It's the same with diet-induced weight loss. You cannot go against your body's biology and just decide on your own how much you want to sleep or how much you want to weigh. If you do it that way, there will be negative after-effects.

So can you lose weight by simply eating less and burning more? Sure, if you want to ignore all I've written above and dismiss the facts about how the body will react to this kind of behavior in the long run. But I hope you will see by now that the body is much more complex than a simple mathematic equation.

If you are not metabolically healthy, and your metabolism does not function optimally, then of course even looking at a chocolate cake can make you gain weight! But this does not have to be infinite. You can restore your metabolic and hormonal health by going through recovery!

Your body is designed to balance out automatically. The body never works against us. It doesn't want to be overweight as much as it doesn't want to sleep more than needed. But when you constantly under-sleep, you are about to get so tired that your body forces you to sleep more. You can sleep 24 hours straight when you are seriously sleep-deprived. Same goes with weight. If you restrict food, your body forces you to binge and eat more than you normally would. When you mess with the system, it will become unbalanced, and that's why you need recovery time after eating disorders or dieting.

When we consistently eat enough calories, never restrict foods, and never try to compensate, our weight set point will get back to normal, and our body's hormonal levels will balance out. Then our body will automatically start to regulate how much to eat, when to eat, and what to eat. We simply follow our hunger cues, allow our bodies to do what they have been biologically designed to do. No calorie counting or maniacal exercise regimen to burn calories is required to stay at that healthy weight.

Is Starvation Mode a Myth?

Many people think that the starvation mode is a myth. They think it's not real. They say there's no such thing as being in starvation mode because you *will* lose weight when you keep on eating less and less, so therefore, starvation mode does not exist.

But they fail to understand what starvation mode actually *is*.

They claim that starvation mode is when people continue to eat fewer calories and can't lose weight anymore. Everybody knows if you don't eat, you can die of starvation. That's completely true!

Starvation mode is not the point where body completely stops losing weight the fewer calories you eat, but it's *"a set of adaptive and physiological changes that reduce metabolism in response to a lack of food."*[57]

This means that the body changes its responses to a lack of food. It lowers your metabolism, burns your metabolically active muscle tissue, or even cannibalizes your organs to keep you alive. This system also wants to shut down any metabolically "expensive" bodily functions like your reproductive system. This is why many women lose their period when they diet. Their bodies are not healthy and strong enough to give life.

Starvation mode is not the point where weight loss stops when you continue to eat less and less (because when you eat less and less, you absolutely can die of starvation), it means your body simply runs slower to protect you from dying.

Operating on a deficit of calories slows down your metabolic rate over time. This is known as adaptive thermogenesis (aka starvation mode), and it happens as a result of a prolonged deficit. The more excessive the deficit is, the more significant the drop will be. Remember the Minnesota Starvation Experiment – the BMRs of those men slowed down by forty percent when they consumed 1570 calories a day! That is adaptive thermogenesis in action!

> *Although weight reduction is difficult in and of itself, anyone who has ever lost weight will confirm that it is much harder to keep the weight off once it has been lost. The over 80% recidivism rate to pre-weight-loss levels of body fatness after otherwise successful weight loss is due to the coordinate actions of metabolic, behavioral, neuroendocrine and autonomic responses designed to maintain body energy stores (fat) at a central nervous system-defined "ideal." This "adaptive thermogenesis" creates the ideal situation for weight regain and is operant in both lean and obese individuals attempting to sustain reduced body weights. Much of this opposition to sustained weight loss is mediated by the adipocyte-derived hormone 'leptin'. The multiple systems regulating energy stores and opposing the maintenance of a reduced body weight illustrate that body energy stores in general and obesity, in particular, are actively 'defended' by interlocking bioenergetic and neurobiological physiologies.*[58]

This means that your body will defend your weight loss by slowing down *"metabolic, behavioral, neuroendocrine, and autonomic responses"* so it's much harder for you to lose weight. That's the baseline of adaptive thermogenesis (starvation mode).

My point is that starvation mode does not mean your body stops losing weight (because this is not true – if you continue to eat less and less, you can starve to death), but scientifically, it means that your body slows down its normal processes to help you survive, to protect you from starvation, because that's what your body thinks you're going through when you diet.

So is starvation mode real? If we take it by definition – what starvation mode actually means – it is 100% real!

Dieting Slows Metabolism

Eating less does not cause sustainable and healthy fat loss. You might lose some weight initially, yes, (your metabolism is still high at the beginning, and you lose water weight very quickly…), but the weight will just come back afterward when you eventually binge out. The body does not become an efficient fat-burning machine when we cut back on fuel. If you put fewer logs on the fire, the less fire you get!

Want to know a recipe for weight gain and bingeing? Go on diets! As soon as you get tired of being hungry and irritable all the time, your body will force you to go back to eating as many calories it needs. But now, when you come from dieting, your metabolism is much slower, and you've lost a lot of muscle tissue. Your body thinks you have been starving, and it creates an extra layer of body fat in case of the next famine. It's the body's protection mechanism. Your body doesn't know you just want to lose a few pounds for your next vacation. It slows down your system for protection, making sure have plenty of fat stores because it senses that food is scarce in your life at the moment.

In the absence of adequate energy, our body also uses catabolism (destruction of cells throughout your body) to survive. *In the Journal of the American Medical Association*, George L. Thorpe, MD, a physician within the American Association itself, wrote that eating less makes us lose weight, not *"by selective reduction of adiposis [body fat], but wasting of all body tissues...therefore, any success obtained must be maintained by chronic undernourishment."*[59]

When you under-eat, starve yourself, or diet, your body will literally start to eat itself to get energy. It will catabolize your organs, bones, and other body tissues to survive. It will not only take energy from your fat stores, like dieters think, but from your entire body. That's why diets never work and will never result in health. Even if you're overweight, your body needs enough food to lose weight, to get back to your healthy set-point weight. I know that might sound crazy to you if you're used to dieting, but that's how it works. You cannot eat less and expect your body to do more – and that includes weight loss.

A while back, I got an interesting comment from a viewer who said she'd talked to a woman who had to gain thirty pounds to lose seventy pounds. Her metabolism was at rock bottom thanks to dieting. She went to a sports medicine physician who revamped her nutrition to get her metabolism working. This is exactly what I'm talking about here. If your metabolism is too slow thanks to dieting, you might need to increase your calories and gain some weight to get all the systems working properly, and then you will achieve your healthy sustainable weight loss, if overweight.

The more you diet, the harder it is to maintain a normal healthy weight because your body thinks it's starving. When you do not provide enough calories to your body, it goes into starvation mode as we talked about previously. What does your body want to have more of if it thinks it's starving? Stored energy…aka body fat. What does your body want less of when it thinks it's starving? Metabolically active tissue that burns a lot of calories…aka muscle tissue. So when your body thinks food is scarce and you're starving, it wants to get rid of muscle tissue and store more fat. You will still lose fat when starving but not in the way a healthy, nourished body burns fat. The temporary weight loss is not worth the long-term side effects – bingeing, food obsession, overeating, weight gain, eating disorders.

One of the experiments on starvation dieting took place at the University of Geneva and involved three groups of rats, all eating the same quality of food.[60]

1. Normal Group: Adult rats eating normally.

2. Eat Less Group: Adult rats temporarily losing weight by eating less.

3. Naturally Skinny Group: Young rats who naturally weighed about as much as the adult Eat Less Group immediately after the adult rats were starved.

I want to give you a comparison to humans and dieting so it will be clearer to understand:

1. Normal Group: People who eat normally without counting calories, listen to their hunger cues, and have a normal and healthy set-point weight.

2. Eat Less Group: People who diet and cut calories to lose weight. They were at their normal set-point weight to begin with but wanted to be even skinnier to fit within today's societal norm of the perfect body type.

3. Naturally Skinny Group: People whose set-point weight is naturally lower, but they also eat based on hunger cues and don't count calories.

For the first ten days of the study, the Eat Less Group ate fifty percent less than usual while the Normal Group ate normally. On the tenth day:

1. The Normal Group kept eating normally.

2. The Eat Less Group stopped starving themselves and started eating normally.

3. The Naturally Skinny Group ate normally.

This continued for twenty-five days. The study ended on day thirty-five.

At the end of the thirty-five-day study, the Normal Group had eaten normally for thirty-five days. The Eat Less Group had eaten less for ten days and then normally for twenty-five days. And the Naturally Skinny Group had eaten normally for twenty-five days.

Which group do you think weighed the most and had the highest body fat percentage at the end? The Naturally Skinny Group seems like an easy "no" since these rats were naturally thinner than the other rats to begin with. Traditional fat-loss theory (calories in, calories out) would say the Eat Less Group is an easy "no" as well since these rats ate fifty percent less for ten days. So the Normal Group weighed the most and had the highest body fat percentage at the end of the study, right? Surprisingly, no.

The Eat Less Group weighed the most and had the highest percent of body fat. Even though they ate less for ten days, they were significantly heavier than those who ate normally all the way through. Eating less caused metabolic adjustments that led the rats to gain – not lose – body fat after returning to normal eating.

So this is the side-effect of typical crash-dieting: more fat gain. Eating less is actually WORSE for our body than doing nothing at all.

Researchers at Nagoya University took five healthy, nonsmoking, "normal"-weight women in their twenties and thirties and put them through two major periods of weight loss and regain within 180 days. Studies of weight and health typically use self-reported measures of weight, height, food intake, and exercise routines, which are notoriously inaccurate because most of us under-report what we've eaten and our weights, and overestimate how much we exercise. These women were actually weighed, measured, and to a large extent supervised by researchers, meaning that the data was more accurate. The subjects first dieted for thirty days, eating around 1,200 calories a day and losing six to ten pounds each.

Then they were allowed to eat whatever they wanted for fourteen days, and all of them gained back the weight they'd lost, plus a little more. Next came another thirty-day diet period, during which they didn't lose quite as much as they had the first time around. Finally, they ate freely for the last three and a half months. At the end of the study, the women's weights were around the same as when they started. But their lean body mass had dropped, meaning they had more body fat even though they weighed the same. Their resting metabolic rates had also dropped, meaning they now required fewer calories to sustain the same amount of energy. Finally, their blood pressure and triglycerides rose. They may have looked the same on the outside and on the scale, but weight cycling (typical yo-yo dieting) caused physiological changes that hurt their health and could likely lead to more weight gain and disease down the line.[61]

If you are unhappy with your body for some reason, just know that it is safer and healthier to do nothing compared to going on a restrictive diet and strict exercise regimen because at the end of dieting, when your body is exhausted from eating less and exercising more, you will gain all the weight back plus some more because your metabolism is slower and you've lost a lot of metabolically active muscle tissue and water weight. In addition, you will have problems with increased appetite and binge eating.

After your body survives dieting (read: starvation), its number one priority is protecting us from starving in the future. It does that by storing additional body fat. Researchers call this "fat super accumulation," and they believe it is a primary trigger for "relapsing obesity" – also known as yo-yo dieting. The most disturbing aspect of fat super accumulation is that it does not require us to eat a lot. All we have to do is to go back to eating a normal amount of food.

The Eat Less Group in the study gained a massive amount of body fat quickly while eating the same amount as the Normal Group and the Naturally Skinny Group. Why? The body was trying to make up for past losses. Eating less also slowed the metabolism. If a person with a slow metabolism eats the same food as a person who did not diet and exercise to lose weight, she will gain more body fat than her counterpart who ate normally.

The University of Geneva researchers reported that the Eat Less Group's metabolisms were burning body fat over 500 percent less efficiently and had slowed down metabolism by fifteen percent by the end of the study.

A study conducted by Dr. Rudolph Leibel, director of the Division of Molecular Genetics in the Department of Pediatrics at Columbia University Medical Center, provides another example of starvation's long-term side effects on metabolism.[62]

A group of people weighing an average of 335 pounds starved themselves down to 220 pounds. After the initial period of extreme calorie restriction, researchers wanted to see what impact eating less had on the 220-pound dieters' need to burn body fat. To do this, they brought in people who were the same age but naturally slim. This gave the researchers three groups of people to compare:

1. Nonstarved 335-pound people

2. Formerly 335-pound people who starved themselves down to 220 pounds

3. Nonstarved 138-pound people

Just as a larger car should need more gasoline than a smaller motorcycle, the nonstarved 335-pound people should need more calories than the nonstarved 138-pound people, right? Yes. All things being equal, more body weight means more calories needed per day to maintain and move more mass. So you would think that after losing 115 pounds, the 220-pound people slid right down the graph, right? Not necessarily. It depends on HOW the 115 pounds were lost. After all, we know that starvation burns calorie-hungry muscle while slowing down metabolism. So how many calories did the 220-pound starvation dieters need after having starved away 115 pounds?

Thanks to starvation's side effects, the metabolism of the 220-pound subjects slowed down dramatically. In fact, they needed five percent fewer calories per day than the nonstarved 138-pound people, even though they had eighty-two MORE pounds of mass to move! That is a scary side effect.

How to Get out of Diet Merry-Go-Hell

Next is an excellent testimonial from a woman who explains so beautifully her recovery from an eating disorder following the MinnieMaud guidelines (will explain this in the next chapter!), eating enough calories and whatever she wants. You can find her story in the comment section of this article: http://www.scienceofeds.org/2014/08/15/in-defense-of-eating-junk-food-in-eating-disorder-treatment/

> *I am a 53-year-old woman with a 44-year history of ED, including AN [Anorexia Nervosa], BN [Bulimia Nervosa], orthorexia and anorexia athletica. I have been in recovery for just over a year, and I'm following the MinnieMaud method. My whole life with ED has been spent worrying and panicking about food intake, types of food, and the usual terror about weight gain. By the time I started recovery, I*

was on an extremely rigid, narrow food plan. So the MM [MinnieMaud] approach that takes away ALL judgment regarding food as "good or bad" has been incredibly helpful for me.

A plan that limited or forbade/restricted any food types would have affected me in a similar way to formal restriction, because of the way my anxiety would wrap itself around the 'rules' and turn them into restrictive behaviors. I went from eating mainly junk food at the start to eating pretty standard home-cooked and prepared meals by now, and there is NO FOOD I am scared of and NO FOOD that I consider being "bad" or unhealthy.

The ability to freely eat whatever I feel like at any time has NOT led to me bingeing myself into a coma, or into morbid obesity as some might predict, but rather back to a standard, average body size and weight. It has also reduced my previous 44-year history of panicking about 'what to eat and what not to eat', which has seen me rocket from extreme plan to an alternative extreme plan, ad infinitum. I have a balanced diet, functional bowels, excellent skin, solid deep sleep, strong nails, and dramatically reduced cellulite. My blood results are normal. My mental state is clear, balanced, stable and peaceful – because the main cause – my food fear and obsession – has dissipated.

Gwyneth Olwyn on Your Eatopia accurately predicts this outcome when she speaks of the hierarchy of foods in recovery: 1. highly processed foods; 2. processed foods; 3. some raw foods – and also that as one becomes weight restored and energy-balanced, one's tastes will naturally veer toward a more balanced (in terms of current beliefs about a healthy diet) order 1. processed foods; 2. raw foods; 3. some incidental highly processed foods. http://www.youreatopia.com/blog/2012/12/21/food-family-and-fear.html

Taking the brakes off and allowing free choice with no judgment allows the person in recovery to reduce their fear of food – which ultimately is the root issue needing to be addressed. Practitioners treating people with ED need to practice a form of triage, in that the primary goal is to get the person out of immediate danger, and then to restore weight and energy balance. To restrict food, any food, is counterproductive to that goal – I see many people seeking to recover who are still locked into a state of fear because their therapist or other health professional has warned them not to eat some foods, or to drastically limit their intake of such – this reactivates the drive to restrict and sabotages the recovery.

The people that I know who have made it into remission and stayed there for a number of years are those who did not restrict calorie or junk food intake, rather following the 'free choice, restriction-free' model. The people that I know of who have struggled over and again with relapse are almost always those who are only allowing themselves access to a set number of calories (and then stopping) and/or limiting their 'junk food' (or foods they deem to be 'bad') intake.

HOW DIETS TRIGGER EATING DISORDERS

I literally eat anything I feel like – and that often means that I say no to some foods due to a complete lack of desire. Once they were no longer forbidden to me, they lost their mystique and assumed an ordinary status. I find my taste in food is for nutrient-dense prepared food – basic home cooking – and that I have little or no desire for junk – but when I DO want it, I eat it freely, to satiation, and without anxiety.

The polar opposite of a restrictive eating disorder is restriction-free eating. And the only way to achieve that goal is to create an environment and a set of behaviors that mean the amygdala no longer perceives any food as threatening. Again, therapists need to take the lead in driving such a change – and one of the primary things they need to do is to stop imposing their own fears, or healthy food beliefs, on their clients and instead encourage a return to a state of homeostasis at one's optimal set-point – the point at which the body will manage and monitor energy intake without intervention, in order to keep the body in that stable condition.[63]

I could not have summed up recovery more brilliantly and passionately than she did! As this woman explained, constant dieting and food fears are the ones that keep you obsessed and binge-prone. It is possible to come out of this cycle by eating enough calories and never restricting any types of foods again! You will not become obese by allowing yourself to eat what you want and as much as you want. You will not become a junk food addict if you allow any types of foods you may crave. Actually, by doing just that (eating enough and whatever you want), you will get rid of all your cravings and binge urges! The foods you once thought were "addicting" lose their power over you and become less exciting. That's the #realcovery from an eating disorder and dieting merry-go-hell.

In the next chapter, and in the following ones, I will elaborate upon everything the woman explained about recovery. You will find out in great detail how recovery actually works.

CHAPTER 2

Physical Recovery

Now the actual recovery part begins. Here are some do's and dont's for physical recovery (we will talk about the mental part of recovery in the next chapter!). What works to get over an eating disorder and what doesn't. Remember, this is a huge factor as to whether you succeed in recovery or not. This builds a strong base for your full recovery. Without it, everything can collapse, so pay extra attention!

Road to Recovery – What to Expect

Before we jump right in, I'll give you a little overview of the recovery process so you know what to expect. The length of your recovery really depends on the severity of your eating disorder, how many relapses you have while in recovery, and how quickly you get into the flow of recovery (for some it may take some trial and error to find what works best). Normally, they say recovery can take anywhere from six to eighteen months. Physical recovery might come faster, and complete mental recovery might take a bit longer. But again, everybody is different.

First Stage – Week One to Months One to Two

This is a very crucial part of recovery and most likely the hardest. If you get through this stage, it becomes easier and easier because your body gets used to the new things. Here, you have to make the greatest effort to start changing your habits and the way you do things that used to feed your eating disorder. You change your direction and start to march in an unknown foggy road filled with many obstacles. This road may seem hard at first, but as time goes by, it becomes easier and easier, and the light becomes brighter. When you manage to recover, you will look back on this part of recovery and thank the universe every day that you chose this road. It is likely one of the biggest turning points in your life on the road toward your true happier self. I always look back to these first few months in recovery as something amazing and beautiful because it really saved me!

So what is this first part of recovery about? What can you expect?

You will likely feel overwhelmed by the new information you learn every day. You see the things you must change in your everyday habits in order to recover and get better. You begin eating more food without your usual compensation behaviors. You may feel exhausted, constipated, bloated, and "fat." You can gain quite a lot of weight in a matter of days

PHYSICAL RECOVERY

or weeks (Water retention full on! We will talk about it later!). Most of the weight may seem to go to your stomach and/or thighs – you may feel like you're pregnant! You may have many episodes of bingeing or feeling out of control with food (extreme hunger…will elaborate on this!). You will most likely feel self-conscious, and all your biggest fears may rise to the surface. You will be emotional and have negative thoughts about your body. Many times, you'll think, *It's not working! I'm just going to gain and gain and become overweight! I wanna restrict one last time! Maybe I have to restrict first and THEN start recovery*…and so on.

I want to let you know that these experiences, thoughts, and fears are a very normal part of recovery, BUT they are also things that make some people relapse or stop recovery altogether. So I want you to understand beforehand that it will feel that way, but those thoughts are not your real thoughts – it's your eating disorder wanting you to go back to restriction. Do not listen to it! This is crucial!

Some yo-yo in and out of this phase for many months because every time they gain some weight, have binge episodes, and experience all sorts of common and normal recovery symptoms, they panic and fall back to restriction. They think recovery isn't working, and that's why they keep falling back, but the truth is that this is how our body recovers from an eating disorder. This is to be expected in recovery, and it's normal – you are not any different. You are not the exception, the strange and unusual unicorn – everybody goes through it! You have the power to go on from this phase, and after that, it keeps getting better and better as you get further into recovery. You cannot get past this phase if you go back to restriction – it will only delay your recovery…and doing that cannot work!

There are many positive aspects to this first stage of recovery. You may become stronger thanks to the knowledge you have gained about restriction and how it does not actually work. Many light bulbs are illuminated as you learn more about recovery, and this empowers you! You may realize that the symptoms you have are all a part of recovery, and everybody has them. You also start to feel excited that you will never have to restrict again – all foods are actually allowed! You feel stronger each day that you do not give in to your eating disorder and when you realize you are *actually* on a road to recovery and a major change is slowly taking place!

Second Stage – Month One to Months Two to Three

You still have days of ups and downs. You still have fearful thoughts and still struggle with body image and eating, but it's getting better little by little. You are slowly undoing all the brainwashing and getting better mentally. You have learned how important it is to not restrict and to eat regularly. If you feel urges to restrict or binge, you know why – you were likely triggered by something or fell back to the dieting mindset. You may still have days of extreme hunger, bloating, and feeling negative – but you know it's a necessary part of recovery, and you've learned to kind of accept it. You still may not be quite sure about your hunger or fullness signals,

PHYSICAL RECOVERY

but it's slowly getting better. You have developed some of your own strategies for and knowledge about recovery – you have learned some things that work better than others, and you continue to practice them.

There may still be days when you feel down. You may even want to go back to restriction when the eating disorder thoughts scream at you, but most times, you get through it and keep on pushing forward because you know restriction won't get you anywhere, and you can see it's not worth it!

Third Stage – Months Three to Six

You may feel a lot better at this stage. The bloating may have gotten a lot better, or maybe you don't have it anymore. Most of the water retention has gone away. You feel your health is getting better, and you feel stronger mentally as well.

Your fear of foods is more in the background, and you have started to really enjoy eating and incorporating different foods into your meals. You may even experience signs of normal hunger cues returning – maybe not at every meal, but at least at some meals, you can eat when hungry and stop when full.

You feel you have had your first true successes in recovery, and you can already see the light at the end of the tunnel. You feel so much better in your body.

You still get triggered easily, and your body image may not be the best, but now you're not very likely to act on those thoughts – you know it won't work and will only set you back in recovery. And you don't want that! You know there's no going back now!

Fourth Stage –Months Six to Eight

You may feel mostly recovered by this point. You know what works and what doesn't. You still have some good days and some bad days, but now it doesn't come solely from your weight or body-related fears. Other things have become more important to you. You've started to experience everyday life and want to return to normal living.

You realize that you want to accept your body the way it is and not change it because you know what it will do to you physically and mentally if you do.

You most likely don't have bloating or water retention anymore. You also have more or less recovered your normal hunger cues. You feel you can eat like a normal person for most of your meals. You're still learning new things every day, and having normal hunger cues may still seem a bit weird. But you practice intuitive eating or normal eating by listening to your body and your feelings. You eat when you're hungry – or simply when you feel like it. You don't count calories, and you feel more free around foods than ever! You also enjoy engaging in many other activities that have nothing to do with food.

Fifth Stage –Months Eight to Twelve

You feel recovered! Yay! You finally did it! You feel so much stronger and wiser, and the whole experience has taught you a lot! You have all the knowledge you need to know in order not to relapse or ever go back to restriction or another eating disorder.

You've worked on your body image and self-acceptance, and you feel more at peace with yourself. Now you can see very clearly the mind of an eating disorder and how twisted and sneaky it is – you will never fall for that again!

You no longer have urges to binge or overeat. Your body is nourished, and cravings are fulfilled at every meal. You couldn't make yourself binge even if you wanted to – you've simply lost the ability to think like that because your body is recovered now. You eat when hungry and stop when full, and in between meals or snacks, you can focus living your life free from food obsessions.

This was somewhat how recovery looked like for me and how I experienced it, and also what is to be expected from recovery in general. I had many ups and downs in my recovery, and I relapsed a few times, but I learned from each relapse and went on with my recovery. No matter if your recovery is quicker or takes longer, it's okay and normal – there is no right or wrong way as long as you keep moving forward. If you make mistakes, then I guess they're needed to teach you a lesson – after all, we learn most from our mistakes! Only when you learn from your mistakes can you eventually get past them and move on to the next stage.

Even after recovery, you will continue to learn and grow every day. Even though I have recovered from eating disorder, I still make mistakes, and I still get sad. I still cry sometimes, and I still run into other obstacles in my life. Life will still go on with all of its positives and negatives, but now these things will not be solely related to food or body fears, but other important stuff going on in your life. And I have to say that life will be much easier to take without the eating disorder constantly in the back of your mind.

Should You Recover Under Supervision?

As I do not know your personal history with eating disorders or what condition you are currently in, I strongly advise you to seek professional help. This book is meant for general advice only and should not be taken as something that works for everybody. It worked for me and has worked for many other people who inspired me to try these things in the first place and people I have coached, but every case is different, so be sure to let a specialist monitor you.

To be honest, I recovered on my own by reading and learning about recovery mainly from books and the Internet. I put my own plan together and here, in this book, I will explain how I did it. But in some cases, it might be dangerous to attempt recovery on your own, especially if you have a very low weight, have deficiencies or intolerances, vomit frequently, or take large amounts of laxatives.

PHYSICAL RECOVERY

Also, the refeeding syndrome is rare, but it's very serious if you have it. I will talk about it in the coming pages.

In any case, even when you do feel completely "fine," be sure to check with your doctor.

Do We Need to Count Calories to Recover?

The short answer is yes and no. Firstly, no normal eater counts calories – it's not necessary. However, if you're in recovery, it's beneficial to count calories to make sure you get enough! We have been so conditioned by diets and restrictive habits that we don't know how much we need to eat to recover. Our hunger and fullness signals are so messed up!

I know some people who were not underweight to begin with who simply relied on eating normal portions in recovery. They went through a period of extreme hunger but gradually recovered their normal hunger cues and came out of the eating disorder without counting calories but rather eating however much their body demanded.

I am aware that we are all very different. Some people find calorie counting in recovery lifesaving (as I did!) because it keeps them from restriction and they can be sure they eat enough. But some people find calorie counting very triggering and even unnecessary, and they recover despite not counting calories. In the various stories about full recovery I've read, many people don't think you need to count calories but just follow a normal meal plan, eat regularly, eat until full and satisfied (I personally did not even recognize those signals in recovery), and stop all restriction.

So it can definitely go either way. For the majority of my recovery, I did not count calories but followed my hunger and ate however much it told me to eat. But for a short period, and as a good foundation to achieve full recovery, I counted calories to make sure I get enough. I believe counting calories helped me tremendously to achieve recovery much more quickly.

Counting calories can be a very good – and even crucial – tool to use in recovery to make sure you eat enough and are in *full recovery mode*. By not counting calories, many end up eating too little. They get sidetracked because their eating disorder tells them they should eat less. This prolongs their recovery unnecessarily, can result in more damage to the body, and can even keep them in semi-recovery (meaning: not able to fully recover).

For example, if you have already developed osteopenia (by not having your period), you can immediately start to reverse it by eating enough, but if you let it progress to osteoporosis by still under-eating, you may have to live with the disease forever. In my opinion, it's just not worth the risk! Also, I have to again remind you of the Minnesota Starvation Experiment – the men who received the lowest calorie increase (400-800 calories) in the rehabilitation period saw almost no improvement and still experienced starvation symptoms, but the ones who ate the most calories and responded to their full hunger healed the quickest!

One of the most common things I've noticed when those starting out in recovery do not count calories is that they fall into a trap and still listen to their eating disorder. The disorder tells them, *"Don't eat so much or you'll get fat."* They listen to the eating disorder's false words instead of listening to what their body actually needs! Eating more in recovery is much better than eating too little!

In addition, if you are underweight or have severely restricted your calories, you might not even feel your hunger at all, and if you do eat, you will consume a very low number of calories while feeling completely full. Or you may take normal recovery symptoms like weight gain, bloating, and water retention as indicators that you ate too much and then feel the need to start restricting again. This will not take you to full recovery.

I was never underweight or a low weight, but counting calories and making sure I was getting enough was lifesaving for me. It felt like I was finally making sure my body had the best chance possible for recovery. It was better than guessing and hoping I was eating enough. My hunger and fullness signals were so messed up that I didn't know at all when I was full or when should I stop eating. For me, it was very difficult to trust my hunger and fullness signals because they just felt so wrong and abnormal. It was more reassuring to eat the recommended number of calories for recovery so I could be one hundred percent sure I was doing my best to recover. I didn't want to go through it blindfolded. And that's why, based on my own experience, I recommend counting calories to make sure you have the best chance to recover ASAP.

At the beginning of my recovery, I didn't have a clue how much I needed to eat to recover. I was either bingeing or I was starving myself through purging, overexercising, or participating in occasional fasts. Bulimia (or any other eating disorder) destroys all your normal hunger and fullness signals, so it's understandable that you have no idea how much to eat, what a normal amount of food is, when you are full, when to stop eating, how many calories you need, is it enough for recovery, and so on. I had no idea what I was doing! I wanted to end the bingeing, but I didn't know I needed to eat a little bit more, and do so continually, to get my body out of the restriction and starvation mode to end my urge to binge in the first place. It's like hoping to save more money by constantly spending it!

After discovering MinnieMaud calorie guidelines at Youreatopia.com, I finally felt like I had some structure and some guidance in my recovery. It was something I could rely on rather than just hoping for the best that I was doing it right.

Following these caloric guidelines kept me on my recovery course – and at full speed. I no longer restricted, and I was sure I was eating enough food. And because I was eating enough, my bingeing finally stopped.

If you have a history of any food restriction or dieting, you're most likely afraid to eat enough calories because you're afraid of getting fat. And this is why most people are terrified to follow the MinnieMaud calorie recommendations. But dieting and restricting slows down your bodily functions, and you can actually get fat by not eating enough! And by not eating enough, you will forever stay in this binge-purge cycle if you have bulimia, have constant food obsessions and food fears if you have orthorexia, or suffer badly from malnutrition if you have anorexia.

MinnieMaud Calorie Guidelines[64]

MinnieMaud guidelines are science-based guidelines developed on the Your Eatopia website. "Minnie" refers to the Minnesota Starvation Experiment and "Maud" refers to the only known evidence-based treatment for eating disorders known as The Maudsley protocol.

The calories do not actually provide extra energy as they are based on the amounts that normal, energy-balanced people eat to maintain their health and normal weight. That's why you may experience extreme hunger in your recovery and eat much more on some days in addition to these caloric minimums.

I will not post the exact guidelines here to give full credit to Gwyneth Olwyn for creating them, but you can access them on the Your Eatopia website: http://www.youreatopia.com/blog/2013/3/31/minniemaud-guidelines-for-recovery-from-a-restrictive-eating.html

Go to that page and work out the minimum amount of calories you should be ingesting during recovery. Some people will need 2500, some 3000, and some even 3500 as a minimum. This also includes ceasing from all calorie compensation such as vomiting, exercising, skipping meals, using laxatives or diuretics, etc.

Before discovering MinnieMaud, I had already been in recovery for many months. I followed intuitive eating and tried to recover my normal eating in the first months of recovery, but somehow I still kept overeating and then going back to restriction. I couldn't figure it out. I still had bingeing episodes that came for no apparent reason, and I was kind of stuck in my recovery at that point. I was progressing, for sure, but something was "off" for me. I wanted to eat intuitively, but suppressing and avoiding my binge urges when my body craved bingeing – for whatever reason – didn't seem quite intuitive. Was bingeing maybe somehow necessary for my body to recover?

I learned from the Your Eatopia website that my hunger and fullness signals were not yet synchronized. I learned that there may be an adjustment period before my body returned back to normal after restriction. So this explained for me that my "binge urges" were not something to be suppressed but rather a normal response after dieting and restriction. I learned that I needed to eat enough calories so that my binge urges would subside, and I needed to cease all purging and exercising as well. Prior to that point, I was still overexercising, so it's no wonder I kept having those huge urges to binge. After discovering MinnieMaud and learning about extreme hunger, I thought, *Aha! So I'm not going crazy after all! Everything I'm experiencing is normal, and I should just listen to my hunger!* I had never thought of that! In intuitive eating teachings, they normally urge you to "be mindful," "stop eating on number 6," and other hunger suppressing suggestions.

Before MinnieMaud, I'd always thought that my body didn't need so much food, and if it did, it was a part of my eating disorder and, therefore, unhealthy bingeing. I thought I needed to eliminate that urge. But that approach led to an increased fear of foods and restriction. It did not eliminate my cravings or binge urges – it just made them stronger.

After I read about these caloric guidelines, I was finally able to relax. I saw that 2500 calories for my body was actually not so high. Somehow my body was craving more food than I had given it, so maybe I hadn't allowed enough food after all, I thought.

I also read that the period of "feeling full but still hungry" would pass, and in time I could return back to my normal hunger cues, so I just went for it. And I'm so glad I did because it really helped me to let go of all restriction and the fear of eating "too much." I was able to eventually recover my normal hunger cues.

(Note: There is also a mental aspect of recovering normal hunger cues, we will talk about in Chapter 3 and 5).

I did not follow MinnieMaud for the entire length of my recovery but instead did it for a short period of one to two months. I did it to learn the actual amount of food I should be eating. But I didn't force-feed myself, either. I discovered I was actually hungry for the amount MinnieMaud specified – or even more – when the extreme hunger struck. I hadn't previously allowed myself to eat that much, at least not without guilt, purging, overexercising, or just thinking I was bingeing. When I started to eat enough without any compensation or guilt, my recovery sped up tremendously.

Refeeding Syndrome

There is an exception. If you are severely underweight, you have anorexia, and/or you have decreased calories below 1000 calories a day, you have to be very cautious when starting to eat these recommended amounts. Your body is not used to the number of calories or the amount of food, and it can be very dangerous to start eating larger portions too quickly.

Refeeding syndrome is of particular concern when someone has been eating less than 1000 calories a day for some time and then jumps too quickly to normal levels of intake. It is slightly less of a problem when a patient creates equivalent deficits through excessive exercise, but it's always advised to increase intake incrementally over time to avoid this rare but serious condition.

At a relatively higher risk (keeping in mind this is a rare condition) are patients who purge.

If you have been eating around 1000 calories or less a day, then increase your calories by 200 calories a day every two to three days until you're up to 2000 calories a day. Once you're at 2000 calories a day, it's not common to develop refeeding syndrome from that point, and you can start to eat about 500 calories more each day until you reach the minimum guidelines for daily intake for your recovery (2500, 3000, or 3500 calories a day).

NB! I do not recommend recovering without medical supervision!

People who are at especially high risk of refeeding syndrome are those who:

- are very underweight
- are severely/undernourished malnourished
- have gone without food for more than five days
- have been purging
- have lost weight rapidly

Some of the symptoms of refeeding syndrome are:

- weakness, dizziness, nausea
- rapid and/or irregular heart beat
- abdominal pain, severe constipation, or diarrhea

- electrolyte imbalance
- swelling, water retention
- seizure
- muscle weakness or contractions
- tremors, shaking
- paralysis
- low blood pressure
- paresthesia (a sensation of tingling or burning of a person's skin)
- shortness of breath
- hypokalemia
- and many others

Read more here: http://www.hopkinsmedicine.org/gim/_pdf/consult/refeeding_syndrome.pdf

Should I Eat That Much If I'm Not Underweight?

A lot of people who have a history of bulimia or simply overeating and are not underweight don't think they need as many calories because they "overate constantly." But keep in mind that the binges were most likely followed by some type of calorie compensation – vomiting, overexercising, fasting, "eating clean," cleansing, starting a new diet, calorie restriction, skipping meals, using laxatives or diuretics, and so on. Even when you are at a normal weight or were bingeing a lot, you are very likely restricting or dieting at the same time, and for that reason, your body can still run on a deficit and won't work or recover optimally. Your body will still not trust you, and you need to give it a constant flow of enough calories without any compensation so it can finally gain the stability it needs in order to fully recover. It needs to feel secure that you consistently have enough fuel coming in and there is no more restriction.

I can tell you from my personal experience that I was at a normal weight when I started my recovery. I never lost weight during my eating disorder. But I was still madly hungry because I used to vomit my food and I exercised excessively to compensate. I also restricted a lot of different foods, which made me crave them even more and want to eat them in large amounts. When I allowed myself to have all of the foods I had been restricting in adequate calorie amounts, my abnormal cravings and bingeing faded away.

I did all this without compensating, and that's why I was able to recover. And now my hunger cues are normal, and I do not count calories but just eat when I'm hungry and stop when I'm full. I also did not become addicted to any of the "unhealthy" foods I finally allowed myself to eat. I eat in a balanced way. I did not get fat or gain weight from this in the long run. Bloating and water retention initially, yes. More food in my stomach, yes. But all this went away in time.

What If Counting Calories Triggers Me?

Remember, counting calories is recommended to make sure you eat enough so you will be in full recovery mode! It's not for restrictive reasons anymore. But I know that for some, counting can have a negative effect. So please do what works best for you!

If you feel counting makes your eating disorder worse, the first option is to find a close friend or relative who will help to count calories for you. You can simply write down what you ate, and she/he will tell you if you got enough calories each day. Or you can count calories at the end of the day or week to see if you need to increase your portions. That way it's not so triggering as counting calories at every meal would be.

The second option is to download my 2-day example meal plans (for free!) at my website www.followtheintuition.com. This might help you get an idea of the recommended portion sizes and give you some meal examples. I have a regular meal plan as well as a vegan meal plan available for those who are vegan for ethical reasons (more about being vegan in recovery later on!). I personally did not like to follow a meal plan, and I didn't, but some people find it very helpful.

The third option is to follow a normal eater (a friend or family member) who is healthy and has no food obsessions and mimic their eating. You will see that they eat until satisfied and never restrict. They eat all kinds of foods and don't have unhealthy obsessions. They eat exactly what they crave without even thinking about it. Remember, you are recovering and may need bigger portion sizes, so don't compare the amounts but just try to mimic the overall free behavior around foods.

There are people who fully recovered without counting calories, just by paying attention to their hunger signals and trusting them. They knew that increased hunger in recovery is normal, and they noticed when extreme hunger hit, responded to it, and ate as much as they were hungry for. I did this for most of my recovery after the initial one to two months of MinnieMaud.

My minimum caloric intake based on my age was 2500 calories a day, and I counted calories *roughly* at www.cronometer.com. I never counted *exactly* 2500 calories, but I made sure my intake was somewhere above that number. If I was hungry for more, then I ate more! I do not recommend becoming obsessed with every single calorie consumed. For example, I didn't count veggies, condiments, and some dressings in exact amounts, and I didn't measure my food on a scale – most times, if I didn't know the exact quantity, I just "guesstimated," and that was enough. Counting roughly helps to not make it an obsession. It's not necessary to count every morsel of food you consume but make sure that overall you're eating above your guidelines. This really is the key to not obsessing about counting.

For me, it was not very hard to eat 2500 calorie minimums because, in my eating disorder, calorie restriction was not the main problem. I didn't restrict calories (for most part) but types of foods (orthorexia). I found it quite easy to eat 2500 calories a day, often times even 3000 calories or more when I was hungry or simply craved more food for whatever reason. If you find it hard to eat that much, then simply try to eat more concentrated sources of calories. Eat enough processed carbs (bread, pasta, pastry, starches, cereal, sugary foods, etc.) and add plenty of fat, too (oils, butter, nuts and seeds, avocado, coconut milk, and so on) because this can help you increase calories without making the volume of food too big.

Of course, you don't have to count calories for the rest of your life, but I advise you to do it for at least the first month or so, or until you feel sure you're consuming enough calories, and you're showing constant improvement in your physical and mental health (keeping in mind some uncomfortable recovery symptoms are totally normal, I will elaborate on that one in Chapter 4).

Why Do I Not Feel Hungry?

Coming from a lifestyle of serious calorie restriction (anorexia, extreme dieting), some people might not even feel they're hungry or feel the need to eat. Why is that?

PHYSICAL RECOVERY

Our bodies do not like being denied food. There's a good reason why hunger is so unpleasant. If you are deprived of calories, you want food, and you want it now. Humans evolved to survive when food was scarce. Times of deprivation may have been difficult, but they were survivable – and for years. Survival of semi-starvation is possible because human physiology adjusts quickly to compensate for inadequate food energy. It can even adjust your hunger cues to make sure you survive the famine.

This survival mechanism may even seem to give you "energy" and alertness when you're actually starving. Many people who have gone through anorexia have experienced this. Also, people who have done fasting, myself included, report feeling more "alert" and a decrease in hunger after few days without food. It's basically the same thing.

Due to evolution, if you were starving and lost fifteen percent of your weight, your body would turn off all hunger signals and adapt to the starvation period. Evolutionarily speaking, this was needed so people could migrate to places with more food. Otherwise, they could not have survived.

If you have lost fifteen percent of your weight, your normal hunger signals are turned off so that your body can seek more food. And it's very likely that you're still obsessed about foods every day despite feeling less hungry. So the key here is to start eating enough and gain weight so the starvation signals can be switched off, and you can restore your normal healthy weight and hunger signals.[65]

125

But Normal People Eat 2000 Calories a Day?

The thing is that the 2000-calorie need is self-reported in surveys. Which means 2000 calories was what these people believed they ate during the typical day. When they were monitored later in laboratory settings, they ate around 2500 calories.

> *The measurement of dietary intake by self-report has played a central role in nutritional science for decades... Recently, the doubly labeled water method has been validated for the measurement of total energy expenditure in free-living subjects, and this method can serve as a reference for validating the accuracy of self-reported energy intake. Such comparisons have been made in nine recent studies, and considerable inaccuracy in self-reports of energy intake has been documented. Reported intakes tend to be lower than expenditure and thus are often underestimates of true habitual energy intake. Because the degree of underreporting increases with intake, it is speculated that individuals tend to report intakes that are closer to perceived norms than to actual intake...*

> *Both 7 day or 14 day self-reports trials are all over the map in the actual underreporting that occurs and many researchers will classify trial subjects as failed-dieters, obese, average-weighted etc. etc., which likely removes validity from the trial data as an inherent bias stands that obese individuals are more prone to underreport food intake – a bias that does not stand up to clinical trial scrutiny. And that bias fails to*

address other valid influences such as social desirability and approval as being strong motivators for the underreporting of food intake, as highlighted by JR Hebert and colleagues in 2002.

The underreporting for both men and women can range from 2% to 58%. However, in the one and only trial where two groups of women were identified as either non-restrictors or restrictors of food intake and all were weight-stable, the non-restricting group ate on average 2400 kcal/day and the restricting group eat just shy of 2000 kcal/day.[66]

But why do we see everywhere the recommended average intake of 2000 calories? The truth is that this number was achieved by rounding down some more accurate numbers by twenty percent![67] It was found that it is much easier to use FDA (US Food and Drug Administration) benchmarks for average calorie consumption, even though calorie requirements vary according to body size and other individual characteristics.

In the book *Why Calories Count*, Marion Nestle and Malden Nesheim, explain:

Food package labels and restaurant menus in the United States use diets of 2000 calories a day as the basis for evaluating intake of foods and meals...The FDA originally intended to use 2350 calories as the basis for comparison when it wrote the regulations for Nutrition Facts labels in 1993. This reflected the average number of calories reported as consumed in the USDA's dietary intake surveys of the

BrainwashED

time. But those who commented on the FDA's proposal didn't like this number. They predicted that a 2350 calorie standard would encourage overeating, especially among women...

As an alternative, some advisors of the FDA suggested that the agency list calories in ranges similar to those reported in the USDA's dietary intake surveys. Food labels, they said, should include a statement that "typical intakes for women are 1,600 to 2,200 calories, for men 2,000 to 3,000 calories, and for children (ages 4 to 14), 1,800 to 2,500 calories." Note that these figures are somewhat lower than the estimates for daily calorie needs given in... [the following table]. In any case, the FDA rejected the range idea. Instead, the FDA selected the 2,000-calorie standard and dealt with the range issue by listing diets of 2,000 and 2,500 calories on package labels.

By now it should be evident that 2,000 calories are lower than either measurements or estimates of the total energy needs of all but the smallest and most sedentary people.

The following table is taken from the same book, *Why Calories Count* by Marion Nestle and Malden Nesheim. Nestle is human nutrition professor at New York University and Nesheim a human nutrition professor at Cornell University.

Age in Years	Basal metabolic rate (BMR)	Total energy expenditure (TEE)
Males		
3-8	1,040	1,440
9-13	1,320	2,080
14-18	1,730	3,120
19-30	1,770	3,080
31-50	1,680	3,020
51-70	1,530	2,470
71*+	1,480	3,240
Females		
3-8	1,010	1,490
9-13	1,190	1,910
14-18	1,360	2,300
19-30	1,360	2,440
31-50	1,320	2,310
51-70	1,230	2,070
71+	1,190	1,570

Average basal and total energy expenditures for males and females by age.

(Note: BMR means the calories your body uses just by lying in bed all day and doing absolutely nothing. TEE (total energy expenditure) is calories spent on a normal day while doing typical everyday tasks and activities, which means if you are more active, your calorie requirement increases.)

As you can see, recommending 2500-3000 calories a day based on your age and sex in eating disorder recovery is not necessarily a big number considering that your body has been through starvation and constant restrictive cycles (dieting, calorie restriction, purging, overexercising, etc.). When you are dieting or overexercising, you create a calorie deficit. Your body makes up the deficit by using energy stores in fat, bone, muscles, and organs. But with recovery, you have to provide not only enough energy to replenish fat tissue but also to reverse the pervasive physiological damage. People with a history of restrictive eating habits need plenty of energy (aka calories) to restore their body.

When you dependably eat the minimum (or more) calories every day, you won't get stuck in semi-recovery where you might be weight restored but still have symptoms that indicate you're not fully recovered. You may still feel like bingeing, still have intense cravings, and still have obsessive thoughts about food. Physically, you may have no regular period, feel bloated all the time, easily gain weight, or experience hair loss, brittle nails, fatigue, cold hands and feet, and so on.

If you're still not feeling well, or something seems off, then up your calories! You will not keep gaining and gaining. You need more energy to normalize the neuroendocrine system and metabolic rate.

Once you hit your body's optimal weight set-point, your metabolism will normalize, and that means the extra energy you were taking in for weight restoration and repair will

PHYSICAL RECOVERY

now go to the usual day-to-day bodily functions that stopped when you started restricting calories.

Eating 2500-3000 or more calories a day will not make you fat. You may gain some weight initially if you have a suppressed metabolism and your body is recovering from past disordered eating habits, but if you're eating as much as you want and what you want, your hunger cues and metabolism will normalize in time. After that, you will be able to maintain a healthy weight as long as you do not restrict, overexercise, or adopt any other form of calorie compensation ever again. If your body normalizes, you will eat when hungry, stop when full, and maintain a healthy weight.

I'm adding the following story to illustrate my point. I think it's so clever and true! The link to the full article "Calories Are Not Enemies" is https://www.recoverywarriors.com/calories-not-enemy/

> *A few years ago, when I was nineteen and my sister eight, I was making her a sandwich for lunch. My family always has a few different varieties of sliced bread in the bread bin, and I asked her which she wanted. She climbed onto the worktop and started reading the back of the packet, no doubt as she had seen me do. Panicking and angry at myself that she had noted and was copying my behavior, I let her do so, rather than admonish her for it.*
>
> *"What is a kcal?" she asked.*

I told her the truth. "It's a unit of energy."

"Then I want this one," she said, pointing to the bread with the highest number of calories per slice.

"Why's that?"

"Because I want loads of energy! I've got lots to do!" And she jumped down off the worktop and ran into the garden.

Eating Regularly

Regular eating can mean three meals plus three snacks a day every two to three hours. Again, I don't want to give out "rules," but this guideline has helped people overcome the restrictive cycle in recovery. After recovery, you'll be eating as much and as often as your body tells you, but these tips and suggestions can be very beneficial in the recovery period. Some people, after having an eating disorder, tend to restrict calories in some part of the day and then feel so hungry they have a 3000-calorie meal in one go (restricting first and then bingeing). Or they eat only one banana for breakfast at 9 am, a regular meal for lunch at 1 pm, and then dinner at 9 pm when they are completely famished. Your body desperately needs *a constant and regular flow of energy coming into your body* to recover. To have normal eating and hunger signals, you have to eat normally and regularly.

Regular eating is also promoted by various people who have fully recovered. For example, Ali Kerr from

BulimiaHelpMethod.org and Shaye from Your-Bulimia-Recovery.com.

Different things work for different people. If you feel your eating pattern is messed up and you tend to restrict and let yourself get overly hungry or you feel you have massive binges at nighttime because you didn't eat enough during the day, then this regular eating pattern can help to make eating more normal, regular, and balanced.

However, listen to your body and don't take everything as black and white. There's always room to adjust things to suit you best. I did not count my meals or watch the clock if I can or cannot eat but just tried to eat normal portions more regularly. Regular eating helped me to eat until I was comfortably full. In this way, it didn't trigger bingeing because I wasn't overly hungry at every meal. It was also beneficial mentally because I knew my next meal or snack was just around the corner – I could eat when hungry, stop when full, and then soon I would be able to eat again if I felt like it. If you've been through bulimia, you know what I'm talking about when I mention the constant urge to binge at every meal. It's exhausting and very triggering. For this reason, it's important to not let yourself get too hungry before you eat!

In the first part of your recovery, you will likely have extreme hunger (coming next!) and will feel ravenous – you'll just want to eat, eat, eat because your body thinks the famine isn't over – in your past, the next diet would start immediately after bingeing, and your body remembers that.

If one day you eat 3000 calories and the next day just a few hundred calories, if some days you're starving completely and others you only eat one meal a day, if some days you have massive energy expenditure due to excessive exercising and others the food is magically leaving your system via vomiting…how can your body trust you? How can this ever lead to recovery?

But when your body sees that enough food and nutrition is coming in every single day – three meals and three snacks in between, every two to three hours, seven days a week – it can finally relax and start recovering. The famine period is finally over, and binge urges will be eliminated. There is simply no need for bingeing anymore.

I hope you can see now why ingesting enough food and eating regularly are two of the most important things in physical recovery!

Extreme Hunger that Feels Like Bingeing

You will most likely experience extreme hunger in your recovery. You eat, eat, and eat but never seem to get full. You may be physically full, but you still feel like you want to eat more! You feel like that crazy Foodzilla we talked about earlier. A normal amount of food (even 2500-3000 calories) doesn't seem to satisfy you, and you think it's a binge eating disorder. You feel hungry…but not hungry. You feel "empty," but you know you're physically full. You feel like a bottomless pit.

Like you could literally inhale all of the food in your sight! BAM! Gone!

If you are beginning recovery from any kind of eating disorder or just have a history of dieting and restriction, extreme hunger is normal, and *it will pass!*

Extreme hunger is your body's response to starvation and restriction. Remember the Minnesota Starvation Experiment where men consumed 4000, 7000, or even 11,500 calories in a day in their rehabilitation period. Urges to "binge" are our body's normal and healthy reaction to dieting. It's an "adaptive response"[68] to compensate for food restriction. Laboratory experiments with rats show that previously food-deprived animals that were then allowed to eat to satiety and normal weight will binge eat when presented with highly palatable (tasty) food.[69] This extreme hunger in recovery is your survival instinct kicking in! It's there to overcome your under-eating and caloric compensation.

Extreme hunger will pass as long as you continue to eat an adequate amount of food and forego any form of calorie compensation.

How Long Will Extreme Hunger Last?

This varies from person to person. It can last for one day, it can last for the entire period of recovery, or it can come and go – it's all normal. For me, it came and it went throughout my recovery. At first, I experienced it more frequently, but in time, it came less and less. By six to eight months into my recovery, it was maybe only once or twice a month. Keep in mind I had many setbacks in my recovery as well, so that might be the reason it lasted that length of time.

Even now, as a normal eater, my hunger level varies from day to day. I don't eat the same amount of food every day. Some days I might feel hungrier and some days not as much. If I'm more active, I want more food. When I'm less active, my hunger decreases. It's important to always follow your hunger and not overanalyze everything. Most importantly, don't restrict or compensate, no matter what!

Extreme hunger may cause panic for pretty much everyone with a restrictive eating disorder. They lock in on the incorrect assumption that they're just "bingeing" and it will never end.

People who are underweight (anorexics) need to follow their extreme hunger in order to gain weight and emerge from the starvation mode.

But what about people who are not underweight? Maybe these people are even overweight. Do they also need to eat that much?

This is a concern for people who have had bulimia. Bingeing was the hardest thing to overcome in their eating disorder, so they don't understand how listening to their extreme hunger – in their eyes "bingeing" – is necessary in recovery.

You need to understand that during your bulimia, you were also purging or restricting in some way between your binges. Restricting is why you were bingeing in the first place. Bingeing is our body's response to restriction. Not only calorie restriction but food restriction (as we see in orthorexia).

If you stop restricting and start to eat normal amounts of foods, bingeing won't stop overnight because your body doesn't trust you, and your brain is strongly wired to your eating disorder habits (I'll explain this in Chapter 3).

In order to break these habits, it's important to let go of restriction and then listen to your hunger. If on some days, your hunger leads you to 4000+ calories (extreme hunger), then so be it. But if you start to resist this hunger, your body becomes wary that it can't restore its lost calories and thinks the period of famine is not yet over.

Eventually, as you eat enough and regularly, extreme hunger will rear its head less and less. Slowly but surely, it will fade away, just like the men's extreme hunger did in the Minnesota Starvation Experiment.

For example, if you've been underwater and holding your breath, you become deprived of oxygen. When you finally get to the surface, you'll gasp for air for quite some time. So should you restrict your oxygen to make sure you don't "over-breathe"? Of course not. Well, it's the same with restriction and extreme hunger. If your body hasn't been getting enough calories, you will eventually binge or "overeat." That's a normal response, just like gasping for air after oxygen deprivation. After your body has restored the oxygen levels in your lungs, your breathing eventually normalizes just as when your body finally gets enough calories and restores itself, the extreme hunger phase passes. Your body simply needs an adjustment and recovery period.

In all the recovery stories I've read, nobody ever said that they started their recovery and there was no bingeing or binge urges (extreme hunger). Every single one of them still "binged" in the beginning stages of recovery, whether they did MinnieMaud or not (and most of them did not). But as time passed, and they ate enough food, they binged less and less frequently until their body finally accepted that there would be no restriction forthcoming, and hence, no binge signal initiated. The famine was over.

So my point is that I don't want you to see this extreme hunger as a threat, as something abnormal, or as something you want to anxiously suppress. Rather, see it as your body's way of coming out of the restriction – like gasping for air after oxygen deprivation.

Your Thoughts Can Affect Extreme Hunger

The mental part of recovery is also very important for full recovery. I will discuss the mental part more thoroughly in the next chapter, but I want to quickly address it here.

This might not be of interest to everybody, but my experience during recovery and in talking to the people I've coached is you have to think about extreme hunger differently than bingeing. If you think about it in the same way as bingeing (as something negative), it can hinder your recovery. This is why some people feel like they're stuck with bingeing while others feel they're actually progressing.

Example #1: Do not act on it with fear. *OMG! I'm eating so much! I'm getting fat!* This attitude will only affirm to your brain that your eating disorder is still full on. Mentally, you are still in the restrictive mindset (*I will have to restrict later to compensate!*).

Instead, if you have this extreme hunger, try to see it as a part of recovery. Be present and actually enjoy your food. Give yourself the freedom to follow your hunger.

Example #2: When you binged while in the throes of your past eating disorder, you were thinking, *I'd better eat it all now while I can because tomorrow I'm gonna start this new diet program. So this is the last time I'm gonna eat that much – I promise!* This kind of thinking will feed your eating disorder.

Instead, you should think like this: *Okay, I'm hungrier today, and that's okay! My body is still coming out of restriction, and I'm going to finally show it that there's no restriction or diet coming ever again! Food will always be available to me! If I'm hungry, I'll eat! My body will learn to trust me and know that food is not going anywhere and the extreme hunger can fade away in time!* This kind of attitude will affect your recovery in a positive way.

I hope you can see the difference between these mental approaches – you can either foster your old eating-disordered way or actually make a positive impact and move toward recovery.

Just Eat and Don't Overanalyze!

If you've had disordered eating for any length of time, your true hunger cues are messed up. You don't have clear signals about when you're hungry and when you're full. This will normalize over time if you *always* eat when you're hungry – or even when you feel like eating. You always have to respond. Just eat and try not to overanalyze.

I will repeat: If you feel hungry for whatever reason – whether it be physical or mental – just *eat*. This is what I did, and it was much easier than overanalyzing. *Should I eat or not? Is it the right time? I'm hungry, but I know I ate already. OMG!*

Stop overthinking and eat when you want food or feel like eating! If not eating makes you anxious and causes you to obsess about food, then eat! Don't get into the trap of overanalyzing your hunger signals and obsessing – just eat the food! Don't worry, the uneasy feeling about hunger cues will pass. It won't last forever. And after recovery, it will become automatic and natural!

But keep in mind that every time you eat, you *cannot* purge. Don't do anything to compensate for the calories you've eaten– no throwing up, no exercising, no eating less the next day, no skipping meals, no eating "clean," no using laxatives or diuretics. Nothing. Only in this way can your hunger cues recover. (I will elaborate on how to listen and relearn your hunger cues in Chapter 5.)

Worshipping Purity

I think one of the biggest things holding me back from achieving full recovery from my eating disorder was my worship of purity. It may not be like that for everyone, but for me, it was the final thing I had to let go of in order to start healing from bulimia.

I found out that I did not binge because food was "addicting" (as I'd thought previously!) but because I had an unhealthy obsession with eating healthy or "clean" and not allowing myself to have other foods I craved. I had orthorexia.

Worshipping purity made me binge on junk foods and overeat in general because my cravings weren't satisfied. The more I restricted something, the more I craved it. The more control I wanted to have over food and eating, the more out of control I felt.

I thought that being 100% raw was the only way to be healthy. I studied whole foods nutrition. Particularly raw foods. I even got certified as a Natural Health Practitioner. I still think our bodies need plenty of whole foods for health and nutrition, but developing an eating disorder as a result of following an obsessively "healthy" diet is much more damaging to your body and mind than any "unhealthy" food!

I used to think orthorexia was a manipulative way of forcing healthy people to eat crappy food and a way for society make excuses for their bad eating habits. I was sure that the people who didn't eat healthy were lazy and didn't have the willpower or the right "knowledge." I thought orthorexia wasn't real and was just something people made up.

But it is real because I had it.

In my own words, I would define orthorexia as trying to eat only healthy, clean, and pure foods for the benefit of your health but feeling miserable and unhealthy as a result. It makes you obsess about food, restrict your foods, and it creates anxiety around food. It impacts your personal life and your social life. You develop disordered eating habits and have constant food cravings, binge episodes and you generally feel obsessed with foods, what you can and cannot eat. Orthorexia isn't necessarily about restricting calories but more about restricting foods. It can also be mixed with bulimic or anorexic tendencies.

Orthorexia is a term coined by Steven Bratman, MD, to describe his own experience with food and eating. It's similar to other eating disorders in that those with anorexia or bulimia obsess about calories and weight while orthorexics obsess about healthy eating. Weight loss can represent one of the goals, but it's not only about being "thin" and losing weight.

I want to stress that not every person who eats healthy has orthorexia or an unhealthy obsession with foods. Also, it can be tricky to identify whether or not someone has orthorexia because many people don't see anything wrong with eating healthy. And those doing the healthy eating also think they're just trying to do what's best for their body and health, and therefore, they see nothing wrong with it. However, there are symptoms to look out for.

These are some of the symptoms of orthorexics:

- Feelings of guilt when failing to follow diet guidelines.

- Increased amount of time spent thinking about food.

- Regular advance planning of meals for the next meal or day.

- Thinking critical thoughts about others who don't follow the same diet or have the same eating beliefs as you.

- Fear that eating away from home will make it impossible to follow the diet or "clean" eating.

- Distancing from friends or family members who don't share similar views about food.

- Avoidance of food bought or prepared by others. You cannot enjoy meals prepared by loved ones because they may contain some foods you cannot eat.

- Obsession about foods. *Is it healthy? Is it clean?*

- Sometimes wishing you could just eat normally and not worry about food.

- Your other life and hobbies take a back seat because your newfound healthy diet or lifestyle is all you care about. Everything seems to be affected by it.

- Consistently looking and researching about foods and whether they are healthy or unhealthy. It sometimes seems you can't eat anything anymore.

- You react very badly to foods you used to eat – even foods you once thought were healthy. Your digestion and body have become ultra sensitive.

- You feel guilty when you eat something "not pure enough" and try to compensate for it by following the diet more religiously from then on. You are constantly starting "tomorrow."

- You constantly wonder how others can eat SO unhealthy and not have a care in the world. You are preoccupied with what you eat and also by what other people eat around you.

- You seem to have lost the ability to eat intuitively. You don't know when you should eat or when you should stop eating. You don't have normal hunger and fullness cues, or you ignore them.

- You do not intuitively eat what you truly want but instead eat only what you think you should and what is considered "healthy" by the diet you follow.

- You worry that you aren't getting results like other "gurus" because you are not doing the diet "correctly."

- You keep "falling off the wagon."

And the list goes on. There is a huge difference between eating healthy for a good outcome and eating healthy in a way that makes you crazy and miserable.

Notice how similar all these symptoms are with other diets? You can't follow a diet that has a list of rules, tells you what you can and cannot eat and when and how much and just call it a "lifestyle." A lifestyle, in my humble opinion, is a very personal thing. It's not about following what other people eat and what works for them. It's about making your own choices and doing what works for *you*.

I know we don't need processed food or junk food to get nutrition and that they can actually be harmful to our bodies when consumed in large amounts over a long period of time. And I'm sure there are numerous studies you can show me that prove it. But from my experience, eating junk food occasionally was necessary for me to completely recover from my eating disorder. It helped me let go of my food obsessions and my fear of eating. It helped me to achieve complete freedom. Not so much physically, but definitely mentally.

My own knowledge of health and what we should eat to be healthy was a major reason why I had an eating disorder and couldn't get better. I thought that eating only healthy foods would somehow be the way to get rid of my bulimia. I was wrong. It was much more complex than that.

Just recently, I read my diary entries from the time when I had the most severe bulimia episodes. I was so desperate to find a solution and wrote: *"maybe I just need to let go of the control and eat whatever I want."* Those were my exact words. But I didn't believe back then that this was what would help me recover because I had the mindset of purity. I instinctively knew what I *should* do, but I was so scared to eat unhealthy foods because of all the things I had learned about them. I thought the reason I still craved them was because I was simply addicted.

The first time I read *Recover from Eating Disorders* by Nina V, the message in the book didn't convince me. She recommended letting go of the fear of eating junk foods in order to recover. I was too focused on being pure and still believed only healthy foods would cure me – somehow, someday.

When I read her book the second time, about one year later, I was willing to actually try it. By then, I was just so desperate to find an answer and would do anything to get over my eating disorder. I was at rock bottom and felt I had nothing else to lose. I had seen numerous times that being pure was not helping me and slowly started to realize that maybe it was part of the problem.

Now I'm so happy I listened to Nina and let go of purity and trying to be raw and eating only healthy foods. Letting go of purity and eating what I craved was a big part of why I started to recover and get better.

I won't lie – it was very hard at first to eat the foods I thought were unhealthy and even "dangerous." It was difficult to do something completely opposite to my former beliefs. But slowly, the fear faded away, and now I can honestly say I don't have any fear foods. I take all food as being equal. All that matters is what I crave and don't crave, what I feel like eating and don't feel like eating. I listen to my body and not my fears.

I'm not saying that everybody who eats raw or healthy foods has an eating disorder. The fact is that eating disorders can occur with any kind of diet or big lifestyle change where you restrict something you're not ready to let go of. And it's no coincidence that the majority of people who follow these diets have already had eating disorders. It is just another way to restrict and control food. To lose weight and control weight.

It can happen when you're on the Paleo diet or the Mediterranean diet or any other diet. The problem is the *restriction* of foods, not the exact diet or "lifestyle" one follows. If you don't crave some foods, then fine – you don't have to eat them (I don't like some foods, and I don't eat them!). But if you *do* crave it and restrict until you eventually binge out, then you have a problem.

Restriction is one of the biggest reasons we develop eating disorders. So in order to recover, we have to let go of those restrictions and the fear of eating certain foods. The problem wasn't that I was eating raw fruits and vegetables. The problem was that I forbid myself from eating foods I still craved. Those foods were the main source of fear for me during my eating disorder. The more I tried to restrict them, the more they fueled my obsession and pulled me deeper into misery.

Eating fruits and veggies or healthy foods does *not* directly cause the eating disorder, but the mindset of "follow 100% or die trying" and being obsessed if some ingredient is not "optimal" paves a direct path to an eating disorder.

Letting go of all the restrictions and eating exactly what I wanted is what allowed me to recover completely. I needed to eat junk foods – not because my body needed some nutrients found in them or because junk foods are natural and we should eat them, but to let go of the *mental* obsession about being pure and eating "clean." I needed to undo the brainwash of "if I eat anything unhealthy, it will make me more addicted." Actually, my experience shows it can heal the addictive symptoms!

Also, the feeling of deprivation my body and mind always felt when I said "No!" when I actually craved some unhealthy foods, was very damaging. I needed to show my body it can have everything it wants! And this healed all addictions and cravings.

Eating junk foods healed my mind and body because I ended the war of unhealthy vs. healthy foods. I ended the battle between "good" and "bad" foods – and stopped putting myself in the middle of it. I ended the obsession and guilt that always surrounded it. I surrendered to my body's cravings and signals, and suddenly there was no battle anymore. I won.

I ate what I craved without guilt, and for the first time, I didn't try to fight against those cravings. My body learned slowly that I will not deprive myself of anything anymore, and the weird thing is that *the more I let myself eat anything I wanted, the less I had cravings. The more intuitively I ate, the more balanced and healthy my eating was.*

Right now, I can say I don't have any cravings. If I crave something, it feels totally different than in my eating-disordered days. It's not a terrible, scary, all-consuming fear or a feeling that I need to binge on the foods I crave. It doesn't develop into this big, lurking monster that keeps me up all night and thinking about food all day. I eat what I want, when I want, and in the quantities I want – and then I'm done with it. The rest of the time, I do whatever other stuff interests me and don't think about food until my next meal or snack.

So please let go of all restrictions and eat whatever you want. If you have a craving for candy, chocolate, pizza, a burrito or whatever, then eat it. Trust your body…it knows what it's doing.

Letting go of the obsession and allowing myself to eat whatever I craved no matter whether it was "healthy" or "unhealthy" was what allowed me to recover and – surprise, surprise! – led me to more healthful and balanced eating.

How to Not Obsess About Eating Healthy?

We may think that we need sooooo many vitamins and minerals every day, and the more some foods have, the better. We think we have to make sure we're "loaded up" with them every day, every single meal. This is very common thinking, but do you know what and how much our bodies actually need?

The following is taken from the book Your Natural Diet: *Alive Raw Foods* by Dr. T. C. Fry & David Klein.[70]

What does our body need?

1. *About **ninety percent of our body's nutrient needs, besides water, are caloric needs** the body uses for energy and heat. All caloric values are used as sugars (if not, fat is used): fructose and glucose.*

2. ***Four to five percent of our body's needs (aside from water) are for amino acids** (high protein foods).*

3. ***Three percent of our body's nutrient needs, aside from water, are for mineral matter.***

4. ***One to two percent, aside from water, is for essential fatty acids.*** *The body can synthesize all fatty acids except linoleic (omega-3) because it is available abundantly in our natural foods.*

5. ***One percent of our body's needs is for vitamins.*** *The need is small, but they are vital for human health and nutrition.*

6. *Also, many kinds of nutrients called hormones and auxones.*

As you can see from the above, our bodies' basic needs – 90%!!! – are just pure needs for energy. And every food that has calories provides energy for our body!

And you see that only 1% of our bodies need is for vitamins! ONE freaking percent! If you look at the health and diet industry, they want you to believe that 99% of our bodies' needs are for vitamins. At least, it seems like it.

And also, the other needs like minerals, amino acids, and essential fatty acids are so much smaller than we would normally think.

I just want to show you that the body is very clever. We don't have to consume tons and tons of vitamins and minerals just to be healthy. Our major and most basic need is for the calories and energy our body gets from foods.

I don't want to say that you can eat junk food only and be healthy, but I want to stress that you don't have to worry about not getting enough nutrients when you do eat some processed or junk food when you crave it. As long as you eat whole foods, too, you don't have to worry about it.

Yes, we can say that vitamins and minerals and other nutrients are essential for our body – that's completely true – but when we look at how much our body actually needs, then we see we can meet this criterion easily by having fresh whole foods in our diet. We don't have to eat 100% clean-pure-whole-food-diet 100% of the time!

I once strongly disagreed with that, but through my recovery and personal experience, I learned that stress-free eating, truly enjoying what you eat, having your cravings satisfied, and not going crazy over every ingredient is way better than eating a 100% #riperaworganic diet which only made my eating disorder worse.

And let me remind you – having an eating disorder, starving, purging, obsessing, and constantly worrying and stressing about foods is NOT physically or mentally healthy no matter how much nutritious food you eat. An eating disorder is much worse than eating some "unhealthy" foods.

If you are in starvation mode, then it doesn't matter how many nutrient dense salads and protein shakes you consume. If you don't eat enough calories, your body will not be healthy. Some people think that by eating healthier foods, they can eat fewer calories, still recover and be healthy! This is not true.

PHYSICAL RECOVERY

Let's refer to the Minnesota Starvation Experiment once again:

> *After six months the rehabilitation period started. Keys divided men into four groups, which received 400, 800, 1200 or 1600 more calories than they had in starvation. He did this to observe the optimum amount of calories for them. But the men in lowest calorie groups still saw almost no improvement, they still felt hungry all the time and had no signs of recovery.* **Even after providing them with extra vitamin and protein supplements they didn't improve, they just needed more calories!**) *He eventually concluded that in order to recover from starvation, a person needs around 4000 calories a day to rebuild their strength [emphasis added].*[71]

Your body cannot give you healthy metabolism, a balanced hormonal system, or well-functioning organs if it doesn't have enough calories, no matter what amount of nutrient-dense foods you eat for your "health."

So first, get out of starvation mode by eating enough. After you're recovered, you can think about including healthier foods (you will start to crave them naturally if you don't restrict anything in recovery). Don't worry about "eating healthy" in recovery! Your most prominent need in recovery is for energy (aka calories!). Don't make the mistake of trying to fill up on low-calorie, "healthy" foods that don't provide the energy your body needs. This will only add to bloating and abdominal pain (which you will experience anyway in recovery, so why make it worse?).

The number one reason high-calorie processed foods are recommended in recovery is that they are pre-processed, making them easier for your body to digest and, therefore, easy to get energy from.

Eating Fear Foods

As I've said already, making peace with all kinds of foods is a big part of mental recovery. Many people make the mistake of eating only foods that are "safe" in recovery. Don't get me wrong, even if you eat only your "safe" foods but eat enough calories and stop compensating, it's a *big* step toward recovery. Eating enough is a huge accomplishment by itself. But it's too easy to stay in that comfort zone, and it won't lead to a full recovery where you feel complete freedom and have no obsession about food. If you still fear some foods, that's the zone in which your eating disorder wants to keep you. It wants you to continue to restrict. It wants you to be stuck there. It sits in the back of your brain and whispers to you, telling you to restrict the "unhealthy" foods that will make you "fat." You have to realize that this is your eating disorder talking. It's the fear talking. This is not full recovery.

Eating your fear foods is the best way to eventually eliminate *all* your cravings. I don't know about you, but when I had an eating disorder, I thought it wasn't possible to not have cravings. To me, that was something unimaginable. It was a nice fairy tale but certainly not believable. But now, it's part of my everyday life. I have found freedom!

PHYSICAL RECOVERY

If you endured years of deprivation, you may go through a period where you will want to eat large quantities of *only* the foods you restricted, your fear foods – maybe even for breakfast, lunch, *and* dinner. For many days in a row. It's a common misconception that you will eat *only* those "unhealthy" foods – forever – if you actually allow yourself to eat them. But I promise you – if you let go of guilt and truly enjoy yourself while eating these foods, your cravings will be satisfied, and you will eventually be bored by those foods. You will soon want something else to eat. So many people have written to me describing their experiences with this exact thing.

Ali and Richard Kerr describe this phenomenon in their book *Bulimia Help Method: A Revolutionary New Approach That Works!*:

> *Just because you may have felt like eating chocolate all day long before recovery doesn't mean that it will happen now. Food habituation research shows that the more a person is exposed and allowed to eat a food, the less desirable it becomes to them over time. Food habituation has been demonstrated in many species (including humans) and with many foods, including pizza, chocolate, and potato chips. If you can have something anytime you want, it stops being so special. If a kid can play with any toy except a blue truck, have a guess as to which toy he will want to play with. Whereas if the kid plays with the blue truck every day, he won't find it as special. If you can have chocolate whenever you want it, eventually it will become about as exciting as an apple.*[72]

Once you go through this period of I-only-want-to-eat-junk-24/7, you will start to crave other foods as well, and in time, all foods will become equal to you. That's exactly what happened to me and what many fully recovered people confirm. If I want a bowl of fruit, I'll eat it. If I want a thick slice of cake, I'll eat that, too. There is no difference between those foods. There are no "good" or "bad" foods. If I crave it, it's always the best food to eat. And if I allow myself to eat everything, I get fewer cravings.

I know eating your fear foods can be hard in recovery, but trust me, you will get your freedom back by doing it, even if it might be very challenging at first.

I started eliminating my fear foods one by one. I went to the shop and said to myself, *I can eat whatever food I want from now on. So Elisa, what do you feel like eating?* And then I chose whatever I wanted and ate it. And, I tried to enjoy the food, rather than just inhale it in one go without even thinking. Even when I had extreme hunger, I still tried to enjoy myself and feel happy while eating. Remember, the mindset is important!

At first, when I ate those foods every day, I was afraid. *What if I only eat these foods from now on? Will I get sick, get fat, feel miserable?* I had a huge fear of eating those "unhealthy" foods. But as time went on, my cravings were satisfied, and I noticed I was eating all kinds of foods during the week. And nothing bad happened!

In time, my cravings grew smaller and smaller because I was not restricting anything anymore. I knew I could have any kind of food whenever I wanted it. So no, I did not become a junk food addict or get obese or die!

Self-Love – Eat What Your Body Wants

Next is a great article about self-love and letting yourself eat whatever your body wants without guilt. I thought I'd include it here because I find it to be very true and inspiring. You can read the whole article here: http://www.monicarodriguez.com/2014/07/07/the-health-benefits-of-junk-food/

For many years of my life, I used to be obsessed with eating only wholesome, healthy, alkaline, "clean" food. I got myself to a place of such fear and restriction around food that I stopped enjoying my life. I lost my menses, and I felt sad and depressed....

I lost myself in the process of trying to find the perfect diet, and I was giving my power away to outer experts. I got to a point of so much stress, anxiety, and fear around food that I completely surrendered, as this "problem" was just too big for my small self....

While listening to various spiritual leaders' lectures, there were several times in which I heard comments like: "Eating healthy, wholesome foods is an act of self-love." However, in my case, I had another voice within my own heart that was telling me to go a different route. "How on Earth could my heart be leading me in a different direction?" I thought. "How could I challenge and question the teachings of such powerful spiritual leaders?"

After I had the courage to listen to my heart's promptings, I realized that the most self-loving thing I could do for myself at that time would be to fully enjoy and give myself permission to eat the foods I had deprived myself of.

All of a sudden, I started coming across the stories of MANY people (mostly through the work of the amazing nutrition researcher Matt Stone) that eating what is labeled "junk food" had helped them overcome many health issues they had dealt with while eating a puritan, obsessively healthy diet.

I started having the inspiration of following the actions that seemed more life-enhancing for me, which included eating ALL FOODS with such ease and enjoyment that I could not believe it was ME eating like this. I can truly say that a force with such strength, love, compassion, and conviction was acting through me because there was no way in the world that I could have done this with my limiting beliefs, previous knowledge, and fear that kept me engaged.

The results were amazing; my menses came back, my body started stabilizing, and my cravings and obsession diminished! My mind started opening to a new awareness *around food. I now deeply know that what seems to be the most self-loving way of eating for a particular person may be the total opposite for another. And this will always evolve forever.*[73]

I really hope this helped you to see things more clearly and not obsess about eating healthy or eating the purest foods possible. Give yourself true self-love and eat what you want! The body is designed to be very efficient. It's good to eat wholesome foods, but there is no reason why you should stress about eating all the foods you crave. Eating in a balanced way will come as you heal your obsession, cravings, and years of restriction.

The Trap of Perfectionism in Recovery

This is an interesting thing I have seen happen in recovery. Myself included. Some people look at recovery as kind of another diet with rules. Many people with eating disorders are perfectionists. They're an all-or-nothing kind of people. I was, too! They obsess when a day isn't a "perfect" recovery day. If they ate something they didn't enjoy or ate too little, or if they feel crappy or there's some other kind of unusual situation, they automatically think something is dreadfully wrong. *I walked fifteen minutes with my dog today. Did I just do a compensation?* or *OMG! I was busy and only ate 2000 calories today. I'm back to restriction!* And so on.

I'm not saying this to make fun of anybody –it's an actual problem. I had those fears, too, and I had to get some perspective to stop myself from falling into this trap of perfectionism in recovery.

Yes, you will have many questions arise in recovery. A lot of fears and doubts. These worries can be legitimate, and they show that recovery is important to you! But sometimes we can focus too much on the details and not see the bigger picture.

Don't fall into the obsessive trap of trying to be perfect each day. There is no such thing as perfection. Always remember that trying to be "perfect" in recovery or in eating was a part of your eating disorder. It's very important not to succumb to that when you get to recovery.

There will be (lots of) times in recovery – and in your life – when you cannot eat the exact foods you want or crave. Life can be very chaotic and unpredictable, and situations may occur when you have to just eat and not think about it. And it may not be the perfect choice every time or even what you craved at that moment. Or you are busy, or have flu and you don't get to eat enough calories.

For example, when traveling, you might eat some delicious foods you normally don't eat – and some crappy foods you may not even like. But you need to eat something if you're hungry. You make the best choice you can. Choose the least crappy thing! You might go out with your friends, and there's nothing you particularly like or crave on the restaurant's menu. Maybe you'd prefer to go somewhere else, but sometimes it's best to just choose something and enjoy the company rather than stress out about the perfect meal. You may end up eating something that gives you a bloated stomach and constipation. Or you may not have any appealing food in your house because you forgot to go shopping, so you have to eat the "same old" macaroni to prevent going to bed hungry. Sometimes you might not crave anything or have no appetite because you have the flu. Or maybe you feel you could eat a potful of food because you're close to your period.

All this is a part of normal eating! Normal or intuitive eating is *not* perfect all the time. You can't be perfect all of the time. It doesn't mean that when you don't get the exact foods you crave, you're not eating intuitively. It doesn't mean that when you're ravenous before your period and eat three slices of cheesecake, you're "bingeing" and have tumbled back into your eating disorder. In normal life, different situations will happen. You can't control life. You have to let go of your perfectionism in eating and just accept that oddities are a part of life, and all of it is a part of being free from the rules surrounding food and your eating.

Exercise As a Way to Restrict

"In general, exercise will make a healthy person healthier and a sick person sicker"[74] – Matt Stone, a renowned metabolism expert.

If you're trying to recover from an eating disorder, it is absolutely essential to skip exercising! When I first started my recovery and committed to eating enough every day and eating whatever I wanted without purging, I fell into the trap of exercising.

When I started to recover and eat my former fear foods I felt scared, and I felt dirty. I wondered what would happen to my body if I didn't do anything to burn off the calories or pump my lymphatic system to get rid of the "toxins." I was so sure that exercising was essential for my health. I thought if I didn't exercise, I would gain weight and automatically become unhealthy.

But the truth is that when you have an eating disorder in your past, exercising will keep you from full recovery! I didn't realize that purging wasn't only vomiting, but it can take a variety of forms. Exercising to burn off calories is also purging. I wasn't aware that I was slowly turning to another form of bulimia – bulimia athletica.

I ran, and I went to the gym several times a week. Some days, I burned off 1000 calories! I was overdoing it big time, and it wasn't healthy at all! There is no way that you can successfully recover from an eating disorder while exercising this much.

My real recovery started when I began to skip exercise completely. My bloating subsided (by that time, I was already many months into my recovery, so this played a role, too!), and I felt the restrictive mindset get better and better. I used to obsess overexercising, and if I didn't exercise for many days, I felt extremely guilty. But everything seemed to speed up in a positive way when I stopped exercising.

It is absolutely necessary to skip all exercise when you are in recovery. Exercising is a form of restriction, and it won't help you at all. Just the mental aspect of exercising can keep you in your eating-disordered mindset – you are still obsessing about eating, about foods and calories, and about whether you need to "burn it off." It's still all about unhealthy control.

Maddy Moon is a famous health blogger who helps people to restore their healthy relationships with food. She was doing cardio many times a week, fearing weight gain, but one day she decided to stop, and here's what she has to say about her experience:

About a year ago, I gave up cardio, hoping and trusting that nothing terribly bad would happen. I was praying that I wouldn't wake up with a different body than the one I was used to, [and] that I would still be the same Maddy Moon I always was. But deep down, I just wasn't sure.

Every Pinterest "fitspo" picture, every Instagram running meme, every self-righteous "clean eating" Facebook group invite kept trying to reel me back into my old ways.

At first, it was difficult to ignore pictures like this, but deep down I knew there was something phony and fake about them.

I knew that many girls in fitspo photos have most likely 1. Been photoshopped, 2. Lost their period, 3. Wanted to stop doing cardio, too!

So I pushed on.

And years later, I still look the exact same as I did when I was doing cardio…if not better. I look better in my eyes, at least....

In fact, my eating habits didn't become out of control, either. I actually got my period back, too! I even quit my job and became a full-time entrepreneur. Hmmm, I also wrote a book! I made a coaching program as well. I flew to Hawaii and spent two weeks there (not running). I scheduled photo shoots confidently with my favorite photographer. I ate yummy delicious food without any consequences at all.[75]

I think moving your body is very natural and doing activities you enjoy is healthy, but you should never exercise to lose weight or do it because of a fear of weight gain or to compensate for calories. If you do it for these reasons, it's a form of restriction, and it's just like any other diet.

Signs that you exercise too much:

- Feeling guilty and anxious when you skip a day, a week, or a month of exercise.

- Exercising despite being tired or injured.

- When unable to exercise, becoming irritable, anxious, or worrying about weight gain.

- Needing to push harder and longer to see "results."

- Family or loved ones think you exercise too much.

- You think you have a problem with exercise.

It can be hard to let go of exercising because in a health industry, or in any diet, exercise is believed to be healthy and absolutely necessary. I'm not saying that exercise is unhealthy, but it really depends on the state of your body and mind. If you have a past history or present experience with dieting or an eating disorder, if your hormones are out of balance or your metabolism is suppressed, if you do not have your period, or if you feel cold all the time, exercise will slow down your healing or even stop it from happening! A broken bone takes time to heal, and it's important in that time of healing not to put unnecessary stress on it. And the more severe the break, the longer the healing will take. Eating disorder recovery is the same. You have a lot of things to restore in your body. You can't heal things by adding even more stress. Exercise is a huge stressor to a "broken" body.

> *If you have the kind of metabolic damage I've described above, the worst thing you can do is "add cardio" to try to burn fat. To attempt to tap into the aerobic energy system when it is damaged this way is likely to further metabolic damage and hormonal disruption on several other fronts as well. For example, a metabolism slowed by 15% could easily become 20-25% if you add extra damage on top of it. –Scott Abel, Understanding Metabolism*[76]

But If I Don't Exercise, I Will Gain Weight

Many people exercise because they are extremely afraid they'll gain weight if they don't. But exercising isn't healthy when you're sick, and it won't give you the results you want in recovery – to be eating disorder free. It will just delay the process, and recovery might never even happen!

Also, you need to know that you don't have to exercise aggressively to lose weight if you're overweight. For example, let's look at a study on overweight women conducted by Timothy Church. In the study, Church worked with college-aged, overweight women and had them burn 2000 calories per week through exercise for eighteen months (1.5 years!). What happened? These women experienced no weight loss even though they were burning 2000 calories a week through exercise. If you do the calorie math, over the one-and-a-half-year period, they should have lost an average of 44.5 pounds. But they didn't. They lost *nothing*.[77]

The International Journal of Sports Nutrition found that twelve weeks of forty-five minutes a day of aerobic training had no effect on body composition, relative to just dieting alone for the same period of time.[78]

But calories in, calories out equals weight loss, right? NOT!

That has also been my personal experience with exercise. I was running very consistently for about two to three years. I experienced no weight loss whatsoever. None. Nada. Zero. Talk about frustration! But thanks to that, I now don't waste my time on aggressive exercise. I just do what I enjoy. I move my body by doing my regular activities. And I haven't gained any weight since I stopped running like a crazy person.

Moving your body is healthy in terms of walking in nature, cleaning the house, playing a game, gardening, etc. This is normal and healthy activity. It's not heart-stopping, breath-gulping, P90X-type exercise, and that's not needed to be healthy or maintain a normal weight. If you enjoy it and you are healthy, by all means, do it! But if are trying to recover, it's a definite *"No!"*

If you eat enough calories, trust your hunger, start to eat intuitively, and never fall into restrictive or compensatory behaviors, you *will* heal your body, your metabolism, your muscle mass (even with no exercise), and your hunger cues. Your weight will then take care of itself.

After recovery, you won't have extreme hunger, you won't feel like bingeing, you will naturally eat when hungry and stop when full, you'll eat enough, and you'll feel normal around foods – and that's the whole point of recovery. If you do this, it's very hard to become overweight, so stop worrying about it!

Female Athlete Triad

Female athlete triad is a combination of three conditions: disordered eating, amenorrhea (loss of menstruation – will talk about it in Chapter 4) and osteoporosis (low bone density).[79] A female athlete can have one, two, or all three parts of the triad.

People with disordered eating are trying to use exercise as a way to compensate for calories and control their weight. But when you don't eat an adequate amount of calories to make up for the exercise, it leads to a decrease in the hormones that keep your reproductive organs healthy and regulate your menstruation cycle. As a result, your period becomes weak or irregular, or you lose it altogether.

Then, as a result of poor nutrition and energy-burning through excessive exercise, there is a decrease in estrogen and the nutrients in your body that are essential for good bone health – and your bones start to deteriorate. When the illness is in the beginning stage (osteopenia), it can be curable, and you can reverse the damage if you start recovering as soon as possible. But if you wait too long, it can progress to a much more serious illness (osteoporosis), and at that stage, it becomes incurable.

Even when you increase your calories to compensate for the calories lost in exercise, your menstruation and bones cannot recover if you continue to exercise. You have to completely refrain from any exercise and continue to eat enough calories to recover your menstruation and bone health.

But Can I Ever Exercise Again?

You can exercise after your recovery, but you can never exercise for weight loss or to burn calories. Moving your body and doing things you enjoy is healthy, but if it's for weight loss, then you're motivated by restrictive reasons.

Not everybody who exercises and does it regularly has an unhealthy obsession. There are people who exercise to feel good or keep strong. Perhaps they're personal trainers, competitive athletes or just people who genuinely love to move their body. Some like to ride a bike to work instead of driving a car, some jog with their dogs to get some fresh air, some take dance lessons because it excites them and gives them pure joy, and some do yoga to relieve stress.

But if you come from an eating disordered past where exercise was a part of your restriction, or even if in the present you feel it helps relieve the guilt of eating some foods, then it raises a red flag.

I cannot give you a clear green light and tell you when and how it is safe to start exercising. You just have to recover and figure it out. When you feel mentally strong, and you have a healthy body image, you will know the best activities for you and the right amount of exercise you need to feel good.

The best reason to exercise is because it makes you feel good or you enjoy doing it. It's right when you eat enough calories, you aren't trying to restrict your eating after exercising to "see results" (aka to lose weight), and you eat enough calories to restore your body's energy requirements.

Give your body enough time to recover and rest. Never exercise when you're tired or injured. Of course, all of this can be very subjective, and even someone who has a problem with overexercising can feel that they're exercising to "feel good," but I hope you can use your common sense here. Don't take it lightly.

I think a healthy way of exercising is more about finding fun ways to move your body and enjoying the activity. It's about moving your body as a part of your daily activity, something you do without seeing it as "exercise," something you would have done anyway, no matter if it burns calories or not.

If something bores you, why do it? Do only the things you really enjoy doing. People tell me that when they do gym exercises, it's very triggering, but when they play basketball, for example, it's not triggering at all because they truly enjoy it and would have done it anyway. The gym exercises were more like something they had to do to stay fit, not something they truly enjoyed doing. It was driven by restriction.

So you can use that example to determine whether the exercise you do is restrictive or not. If the exercise had absolutely no physical effect on your body (no weight loss, no calories burned, etc.), would you still do it? Or would you rather do something else?

Be very honest with yourself. Some days, you may feel that you truly just want to go out and move your body. And on those days, you can do just that, and it's healthy. But if on other days you feel you want to exercise out of guilt or because you're afraid of gaining weight, you know you have to skip exercising on those days. Just wait and rest and do something else you enjoy. People with eating disorders may tell themselves, *Exercise boosts my mood, and it's my me time!* But honestly, there are plenty of other ways to boost your mood and have some "me time" other than exercising, so don't use that as an excuse.

I hope you now have some great insights on what it takes to recover physically. But please take into account that each individual must do some tweaking here and there to make recovery suitable for them. Keep in mind that I'm not a doctor, and I always advise seeking professional help for recovery. I can only talk about my own experiences and things I find to be personally true. I didn't follow only one recovery method but learned from things I read and put together a recovery program that worked for me. So I hope you gain a lot of useful tips from my experience and suggestions, but please don't take it as a "one size fits all." Ultimately, I want you to be able to think for yourself as an individual.

Now you have all the tools to start your physical recovery. That makes a huge difference and gets you out of diet prison. But physical recovery is just one part of full recovery. You have to recover your mind as well. Destructive thoughts and negative self-talk have become so automatic and so easy to believe and act on that it may seem hard to break free. But I did it, and I will show you how you can do the same in the next chapter!

CHAPTER 3

Mental Recovery

Restriction Affects Your Mental State

There is a clear connection between dieting and the worsening state of your mental health. It did not happen because your brain suddenly started working against you or because some mysterious illness overtook your brain. The altered brain function has more to do with a chemical and biological response to restriction and deprivation. The brain needs adequate nutrition, and if it does not get it, you will experience a decline in mental health.

Let's go back to the Minnesota Starvation Experiment for a moment. Those men were perfectly stable mentally when eating their daily average of 3200 calories. But when put on a 1570-calorie, semi-starvation diet, they developed common mental eating disorder symptoms.

They became obsessed with foods. They didn't think about anything other than eating. There was no interest in politics or sex or everyday problems. They just talked and thought about food all day.

They also developed body dysmorphic symptoms. They saw themselves as being too fat, and they became fearful of weight gain. They saw themselves (skeletal as they were) as being at a normal weight but saw others (the normal people) as being too fat. Their body images became skewed.

They also developed the need to binge and purge. They overate and then felt like failures, totally disgusted by what they had done. They developed addictive behaviors around foods. Some even ate from dumpsters.

One man had vivid dreams about cannibalism and threatened to kill himself if not let out. One chopped off his finger. Talk about being mentally unstable! But this didn't happen because something was wrong with their brains but because they were being deprived of food.[80]

All of these mental symptoms developed thanks to a sparse diet of 1570 calories a day. Once they stared to eat enough again, their mental states returned to normal. There were some lingering mental side effects even after their physical recovery – like the fear that food was going to be taken away from them again – but most of the mental symptoms went away just by receiving adequate nutrition and not restricting foods again. It was concluded that on the average, a person needs about 4000 calories a day to recover.

MENTAL RECOVERY

If you don't commit to eating enough and don't skip all compensatory behaviors, you can't just "think" yourself better. A starved brain is a profoundly malfunctioning organ. Eating-disordered behaviors, such as starving or purging, alter the brain chemistry. A lot of the mental issues seen in those with eating disorders are triggered by the body being physically starved. That's why I dedicated the first two chapters to how to stop restricting and how to recover your body physically. Recovering physically will partially recover your mental health as well!

There's another part of your brain that reacts to the mere idea of restriction. When you eat normally but are always thinking about new diets, food fears, obsessions with weight, and so on, it can trigger eating disordered behaviors! It's the mental stress over food and body that makes you crazy! Our body can physically react to our thoughts!

I do believe that something more mental triggered the need to diet, restrict, and control your weight in the first place. Something made you think you aren't as good as you are. Something made you think you need to change it by controlling your eating and/or your weight.

So let's say you're now eating enough, and your body is physically recovering. Now it's time to deal with the mental aspect of recovery. You need to heal the obsession, your body image, and all of the other mental aspects of your eating disorder.

For full recovery, it is absolutely necessary for you to identify your triggers and eliminate them. Remember, these are the things that made you restrict and diet in the first place.

Triggers

What triggers a person to have an eating disorder is different in every case. I'm going to give you several examples of things that can lead to eating disorders. By understanding where it all began and making peace with your past, you can actually start your mental recovery and not make the same mistakes again.

1. **Reaching Puberty**

   Some would call me a late bloomer. I didn't hit my growth spurt till sophomore year in high school, and suddenly I went from being the shortest of my friends to being the tallest at 5'9". My body had a hard time with my rapid growth, and at my new height, I was struggling to gain weight.... When my body finally started to fill out and catch up with me, which was all completely normal, I rejected it. So many people had told me that I needed to gain weight, but at the same time, I received so much praise for being so thin. People told me they were jealous. Or that I should model. Such opposing views didn't help with my body image.[81]

This is actually a common trigger for eating disorders at a young age – gaining weight in puberty. The body develops the most in that time, and many are not prepared for that and don't know that it's completely normal. Some gain more weight than others, and some may even lose weight after the period is over. You can't look like a young child forever – you have to grow up and adopt a fully developed body.

However, this can't happen naturally and healthfully when we interfere with the system by dieting or trying to control our weight. Some may lose their period or not even get it, some won't develop physically, some will intentionally lose weight and become skinny and sick, some will gain unnecessary weight as a rebound effect thanks to dieting, and some will have eating disorders for years thanks to the interruption of normal body development and hunger cues.

I gained weight in puberty and developed much quicker than other girls. This made me insecure and uncomfortable. And that was when my weight and food struggles began. Now I know that what was happening to my body was normal and healthy, and what I did in reaction was not. When I understood what happened, I could let it go. It wasn't my body working against me, but it was me working against my body.

2. **Industries with Unnatural Body Standards**

When I entered the eighth grade in 2010, I was turning age thirteen, and it was then I wanted to start furthering my ballet education. My dream was to perform with the top companies in New York City, and to do that, I had to attend a competitive ballet high school, which would be within the next year or two when I was of age. I did everything I could to try to ensure my acceptance: I took extra ballet classes, my teachers who graduated from these schools would mentor me, and I found myself researching online what to do. The majority of what I found on the Internet stated specific body proportions: long arms, legs, and neck, small head, perfect arches and turnout...I didn't know it was that specific. But the majority of what these ballet blogs told me was that I needed to be thin; stick thin with no curves at all. So I made it happen; I began by simply eating healthy at first, but before I knew it, my body was eating itself away, and at my worst, I couldn't breathe properly. My parents took me to a local counselor and nutritionist who worked together, and within three months, I was on my way to treatment in a different state.[82]

As in ballet, modeling and competitive sports have unnatural body standards you have to follow to be accepted as a "professional." In these industries, eating disorders are common – perhaps not full-blown eating disorders in all cases but disordered behaviors around food and body for sure. Some may be naturally skinny and thin, but this is a minuscule amount of people. For the majority, achieving these body standards means you have to alter your health. In the long run, your body and mind will burn out. This is not you "lacking professional attitude" or having zero willpower...it is unnatural and dangerous!

"Not fitting in" or not being accepted in the industry you want to be a part of can be mentally hard to face. You're told you need to lose X amount of weight and have measurements that are this and that much. And despite all your efforts, they're still not happy with you. You might see that maintaining that low weight is quite impossible and not sustainable. It's a trap, and you need to get out of it.

3. **Hurtful Comments**

> *When I was in the sixth grade, an incident that I now know to be a start of my eating disorder occurred. I was in a school play with some of my friends. My best friend at the time behind my back said that I looked fat in my dress. When I heard her say this, it crushed me. I had never looked in a mirror and thought that I was fat in my entire life. I had always been comfortable with my weight and was considered healthy for my tall figure. But in that moment, I made an irrational connection.... That summer I made the decision that I was going to lose weight. I did not realize how much this was going to change my life forever. No matter what it was going to take, I was determined, and I put all of my time and energy into becoming thinner.*[83]

A hurtful comment about your appearance can instantly trigger the need to change yourself physically. To look better, be thinner, feel "normal," and fit in. To be accepted. To prove to the other person that she was wrong, and to make sure nobody can ever say these things to us again. Comments like this can come from anybody – from a stranger or even a close family member. The closer the person is to you, the more authority he/she has, and the more significant his/her role in your life, the more it can affect you.

You have to realize that the comment comes from the other person's insecurity, jealousy, or issues. It was not about *you*; it was about *them*. Nobody who is genuinely happy and at peace with themselves says things like this to others – ever. It's always the ones who are unhappy themselves. Or the ones who have been treated badly. And this is one way they let out their frustration, often unknowingly.

They most often have no idea about the impact their words have and may even think they are "helping" you by being honest. Forgive them for their ignorance and unknowingness, and move on.

4. **Peer Pressure**

According to research conducted by Dr. Christopher J. Ferguson of the Texas A&M University, young girls are easily influenced by their peers especially when it comes to dissatisfaction with their bodies. Published in the Journal of Youth and Adolescence, the research further states that "peer culture" develops eating disorders in teenagers, particularly young girls, to a point where they feel pressured to keep up with the perfect body image portrayed in the media. Girls indirectly feel the need to compete with their close friends when they witness them follow a diet regimen to get that perfect look. In order to avoid feelings of inferiority for not having the perfect physique like their friends, adolescent girls push their bodies to the limit, which is when they start to develop symptoms of anorexia. Teenagers suffering from anorexia are prone to develop further disorders like genetic disposition, low self-esteem, and high levels of perceived stress.[84]

We will talk more about body image and the rise of diet-induced eating disorders because of media and the culture we live in. Again, here you can identify the cause and see that you are not genetically destined to have an eating disorder but are pressured by your peers, today's society or by the media to look a certain way.

5. **Family and Upbringing**

About ten years ago, a call came in from the parents of an eight-year-old girl [Michelle] seeking help for her overeating. They were concerned about her weight and worried about potential health issues. The parents reported that they were both dieters but knew that a diet was the wrong approach for their daughter....

Michele revealed that she often ate too many desserts at parties. She'd eat so much, especially chocolate, that she would end up having "a very bad tummy ache" and would have to leave the party. When asked why she thought that she ate enough dessert to make her feel sick when she was at her friends' houses, she said that her parents wouldn't allow any desserts at home, unless they were low in calories. She didn't like the diet desserts, so in order to get what she liked, she felt the need to eat as much as she could at her friends' homes....

> *Michele's parents followed up on their promise to bring previously restricted foods into the house. Over time, Michele started trusting that she would have sweets at home when and if she wanted. As a result, her feelings of deprivation vanished, and she found that she only needed moderate amounts to satisfy her. She stopped overeating at parties, talked about balancing her nutritious foods with her play foods, and grew into a tall, athletic young woman.*[85]

This is just one of many examples showing how the eating habits we were taught at a very young age can affect us. Sometimes we don't even realize how unnatural the common eating behaviors were in our household and how this resulted in all sorts of problems with eating later in life. Food may have been restricted or forced *(Finish your plate!)*, or maybe eyes were rolled when we took that second scoop of ice cream. Or perhaps someone in the family told you how much weight you'd gained or how you should *watch your eating!*

Kids who are led to dieting at a young age can be affected in the same way – or even more detrimentally – than grown-ups. Kids and teens who diet are linked to long-term weight gain and have patterns of dangerously disordered eating that can last a lifetime.[86] Dianne Neumark-Sztainer, a professor of public health and epidemiology at the University of Minnesota, has found that the younger kids are when they start to diet, the heavier they tend to become and the higher risk they have of developing eating disordered behaviors like purging, abusing laxatives, bingeing, and overexercising.[87] Children and teens who diet are significantly heavier ten years later than those who don't, even if they weren't fat to begin with![88]

If our intuitive eating was interfered with in any way at a young age, it can have a negative impact on our eating later in life. As we see in the previous example, the more we are deprived of a particular food, the more anxiety and unnatural behavior we have around it and the more desirable it becomes to us. Once the food is made available, the restriction and pressure are removed, and eating can go back to normal. Please read more about children and healthy eating habits in the book *Intuitive Eating* by Evelyn Tribole and Elyse Resch.

6. Trauma

Sometimes a very traumatic past event will cause a person to get an eating disorder. For years, scientists have been reporting a link between bingeing and post-traumatic stress disorder (PTSD), which can happen after you've seen or gone through a violent or life-threatening event.

> *People with PTSD have such a hard time focusing on the present and future because they are preoccupied with traumatic memories or trying to avoid traumatic reminders," says Rachel Yehuda, Ph.D. She's the director of the traumatic stress studies division at the Icahn School of Medicine at Mount Sinai in New York. "Sometimes that means they don't plan well for future meals, and [as a result], they may get very hungry and overeat or overeat compulsively.*

> *Many people who binge eat have negative thoughts about their bodies. This poor body image is worse if the person also has PTSD, research shows. Sometimes, these feelings are the result of a trauma, and they spark the eating disorder. For example, a woman who's been sexually abused might think that if she gains weight by overeating, her attackers won't hurt her in the future. (Research shows that 35% of women with binge eating disorder have been raped or sexually assaulted.)*[89]

7. **Health Problems**

For me, bulimia and orthorexia began slowly developing when I started to change my diet to eat healthfully in order to heal my acne. It definitely started with a good purpose – to heal my skin naturally and not have to take drugs with serious side effects. You can definitely have good intentions when you start eating healthy, and it can have a positive impact, but it can also be taken too far. It can get to the point where you start to fear even the foods you formerly thought were healthy. You realize that you can hardly eat anything because your body has become so hypersensitive thanks to all your restrictive behaviors. It can really be a trap. In your mind, you're just trying to be healthy and correct your health problems, but in reality, you're becoming trapped in the "what to eat and what not to eat" rules and growing physically and mentally unhealthier.

Changing your diet if you have a serious health issue can be a positive thing, but in terms of an eating disorder, some don't know when to stop and where to draw the line.

MENTAL RECOVERY

My 30-[year-old] son was muscular, trim, and fit being 6 feet tall and 200 [pounds]. He always ate a healthy, balanced diet until about a year ago when he gradually became obsessed with food purity. His diet became more and more restrictive. He couldn't eat at restaurants or at other people's houses. If invited somewhere, he brought his own food. Only organic foods, specific combination regimens, not this, not that, etc.... He spent hours everyday shopping, chopping, preparing, making mega messes in the kitchen, and thinking about food. That's all he talked about. He lost most of his friends over this compulsive, purist behavior, and he gradually became more and more isolated....

He rapidly lost weight. He lost all his muscles and became severely emaciated. Literally just skin and bones. He looked like a Holocaust survivor, all the while believing he was doing great and was healthy. He didn't see himself as too thin. He had trouble moving, walking, lifting his arms. He fell asleep at the wheel several times. He went down to 109 lbs. His speech slowed as well as his mental functioning. His hands turned blue. His nails got deformed. His legs swelled. He was dying.[90]

From my own experience, I want to say that if you are at a normal weight and eat enough calories, it does not mean you don't have an eating problem like orthorexia. I did not restrict calories, and I was at a normal weight while having orthorexia. I was eating tons of healthy food. Seems like there was no problem, right?

But at the same time, I was restricting foods I craved, and it frequently turned into a bingeing session on the exact foods I regularly tried to restrict. Then the guilt was inevitable, and I purged or overexercised to "undo the damage." I thought about food all the time, obsessed about what to eat and what to avoid, and missed many events with friends when I could not control what food I would be able to eat there. Bingeing and purging took a big toll on my physical health, and the obsession and worry and stress about food were damaging my mental health as well. I thought I was just trying to eat healthy, but it went way too far.

Above, I've mentioned some of the triggers for an eating disorder. There are plenty of other examples – like being a perfectionist, having an all-or-nothing mindset, or turning to an eating disorder in response to a stressful period – but those I've discussed above are some common ones to look out for.

Body Image

You may commit to eating enough food, and you may stop restricting. You may even recover your normal hunger cues and normal eating. But if you still have a bad body image and still think your body needs to change for you to be happy, then it can be very easy to fall back to your eating disorder behaviors or stay in a destructive mindset, one that never lets you enjoy a full recovery and the true freedom of being and feeling normal around foods and your body.

In one study of college students, 74.4% of normal-weight women stated that they thought about their weight or appearance "all the time" or "frequently." But the women weren't alone because the study also found that 46% of the normal-weight men surveyed responded the same way.[91] That's an alarmingly large number of people.

Poor body image increases the risk for extreme weight/body control behaviors. Researchers have found that increased preoccupation with appearance and body dissatisfaction put people at greater risk for engaging in dangerous practices to control weight and size. Extreme dieting, overexercising, laxative abuse, vomiting, smoking, and use of anabolic steroids have all been associated with negative body image.[92]

Most often, people with eating disorders focus on having a skinny body. They look at "thinspiration" pictures on Pinterest, watch YouTube videos with different diet gurus, search #thighgap on Instagram, and so on. This frequent participation in social media (and media in general) may lead to a distorted and unrealistic body image.

People Magazine asked 1,000 women about their bodies and how the images of Hollywood's stars influence their self-esteem. The results? Only ten percent of respondents said they were completely satisfied with their bodies, and eighty percent said images of women on TV and in movies, fashion magazines, and advertising make them feel insecure about their looks. This insecurity can easily lead to a distorted view of one's body. If the media doesn't revise its ideal standard of beauty, more and more women could end up as victims of media-triggered eating disorders.[93] According to the authors of *The Adonis Complex*, *"There's often a vicious circle here: the more a person focuses on his body, the worse he tends to feel about how he looks – obsession breeds discontent."*[94]

The more we live in an artificial world of media – either through TV, magazines, Instagram, Facebook, or YouTube – the more distorted our image of the real world and real bodies is. We might think we know how media tries to manipulate us and that we're just too aware to be fooled into that, but studies show otherwise.

German neuroscientist Dennis Hummel showed young women photographs of themselves that had been digitally manipulated to make their bodies look subtly heavier or thinner. Then he put the women through a series of visual tasks that asked them how realistic they thought their bodies looked in a series of photographs that were also subtly altered. Hummel found that after the women had been exposed to a thinner image of their bodies, they judged everything else they saw during the test as fatter, and vice versa. When they looked at images of other women's bodies, they then judged their own differently. In other words, what they got used to seeing all around them influenced their sense of their own bodies and other people's. That's how media skews our body image. It is all about chronic suggestions that change our view and understanding of reality.

A famous study of teenage girls in Fiji examined their attitudes around eating and body image just after television was introduced to the country and then again three years later. Psychiatrist and anthropologist Anne Becker, currently a professor at Harvard, chose Fiji for several reasons: large bodies were considered aesthetically pleasing there, dieting and disordered eating were relatively unknown (there'd been only one documented case of anorexia in Fiji), and the advent of television in 1995 offered a unique chance to explore its effects.

Becker and her colleagues saw profound differences in teen girls after Western television was introduced. Before TV, no girls vomited to control their weight, and few reported dieting or body dissatisfaction. Only three years later, eleven percent of the girls said they vomited for weight loss; sixty-nine percent acknowledged dieting at some point, and a full three-quarters of them said they felt too big or too fat at least some of the time. As one 1998 study subject told researchers, *"The actresses and all those girls, especially those European girls, I just admire them and I want to be like them. I want their size. Because Fijians are, many of us, I can say most, we are brought up with those heavy foods, and we are getting fat. And now, we feel that it is bad to have this huge body. We have to have those thin, slim bodies [on TV]."*[96]

The female ideal these days is not even genetically achievable to most women. The ideal is not only biologically unattainable but downright dangerous to achieve as well. Skinny does not automatically mean healthy. As we talked in the first chapter, your body has a natural set-point weight where it feels it's best – if your weight fluctuates a lot from that point, it's unhealthy, and you will face some consequences such as loss of menstruation, osteoporosis, heart failure, and so on – your body will have to work overtime to bring your body back to balance, back to its set-point.

Did you know that if Barbie were life-sized, she'd be at seventy-six percent of a healthy body weight – a weight consistent with acute hospitalization? *"The same thing goes for [six]-pack abs and the 'ripped' look being promoted to men; the ability to have very defined abdominal muscles is genetically endowed, and the hyper-muscled physique of action figures and male fitness models is impossible to achieve without illegal anabolic steroids."*[97]

About fifty years ago, the media's portrayal of "the ideal" female figure was drastically different than it is today. At that time, mannequins and models more or less reflected the average woman's size. Mannequins and models have grown thinner by the year, straying further and further away from the average woman's physical form. Not only do most runway models currently meet the BMI for anorexia, but even the median plus-size model has shrunk several dress sizes over the past decade.[98]

But there is hope! One study shows that the more we are exposed to body diversity, the more we tolerate, accept, and even prefer different body types.[99] The more we see one kind of body (either bigger or smaller), the more we like that kind of body. So the more you come out of the magazine-skinny-photoshopped-model-body-idealization bubble, the better your body image and the more supportive you become toward all kinds of different body types, including your own.

And some may think, "But the obesity epidemic is also real and dangerous!" Yes, I understand that, but from my point of view, criticizing our own bodies does not help the obesity epidemic! Body image issues don't help – they can actually be one of the causes of obesity! If obese people go on restrictive diets, they get trapped even more! Their body will shut down normal functioning as we discussed in the first chapter. In fact, too many people have actually become overweight and obese thanks to being labeled fat, ugly, disgusting, lazy, and so forth, as that leads to dieting and restriction, which leads to even more weight gain long term.

For many obese people, their body image issues started when they were still at a normal weight because society accepts only "skinny" and "lean." Society forces us to diet and restrict, and that in turn can end up being one of the leading causes of obesity!

Sometimes even a well-intentioned comment suggesting weight loss for health reasons can spiral into even more overeating and anxiety about our bodies. Harriet Brown, who writes, researches, and teaches about eating disorders, writes about her own experience in her book *Body of Truth*.

> *She didn't, for example, refuse to treat me until I'd lost weight, or write "noncompliant" on my medical chart, or*

> *try to sell me a carton of Medifast or a Weight Watchers membership. But she did make it perfectly clear that I would never be healthy until I lost weight.... Ironically (but predictably), her well-meant lecture had the opposite effect from what she'd intended. I went into such an anxious tailspin over the next few weeks that I wound up stress eating and gaining weight.*[100]

If this can happen because a medical professional tells you to lose weight, imagine what happens when bombarded with these messages on a daily basis, which most overweight and obese people are. It can spiral into even more self-hatred and onward into unsustainable dieting. In the long run, it's doing way more harm than good.

Some may think that telling an overweight person to lose weight doesn't seem like a negative thing. But I bet if people accepted them as they are and gave encouragement, love, and support instead of criticizing them or "helping" them by suggesting they drop the pounds, they would be much better off. Negativity breeds negativity. Support and love give a lot more!

If overweight already, the best a person can do for her body is stop dieting and restricting and work on body image. Start eating more whole foods and home-cooked meals, also, respond to cravings, develop a healthy relationship with foods in general, be moderately active (take the stairs instead of an elevator, play with your kids, go on a hike –mindful activity that isn't strenuous), and recover from dieting and eating disordered behaviors. No matter our situation or eating disorder, we must find our way back to intuitive eating so our bodies can start to function normally again. In this way, we can be healthy regardless of the number on the scale.

If you still want to diet and push hard in the gym, then by all means, it's your life and your decision! In my opinion, however, it will only feed the problem, and you'll risk adding more fuel to your eating disordered fire – you'll lower your metabolism, destroy your hormones and forget how to eat intuitively, none of which will provide you a long-term way to manage a healthy weight.

To prove I'm not the only one thinking this way, there is a study that actually proves that intuitive eating is a better, healthier, and much more sustainable way to achieve normal weight compared to standard dieting.

> *A similar approach was piloted as part of a California study. The study compared changes in weight, lab work, eating behavior, eating attitudes, and psychology (self-esteem, depression, body image) between two groups of women receiving 6 months of weekly group education. The first group received behavior-based weight loss education that included nutrition information, moderate calorie and fat restriction, keeping a food diary, and monitoring weight. The second group used a Health At Every Size (HAES) approach that focused on body acceptance, decreasing restrictive eating, increasing attendance to internal cues for hunger and satiety, nutrition information, and addressing barriers to enjoyable physical activity.*

The results were pretty striking. At the two-year follow-up point, the HAES group showed sustained and significant improvements in total cholesterol, LDL, blood pressure, moderate physical activity, restricted eating, susceptibility to hunger, body dissatisfaction, and self-esteem. The diet group did not sustain positive changes in any of these areas, and in fact, self-esteem was shown to be significantly worse at the two-year follow-up point. Fifty-three per cent of the diet participants expressed feelings of failure, compared with 0% of the HAES group.[101]

Self-care works better than self-hate and is so much more sustainable!

Body Positive Exercises

Since positive body talk doesn't seem to happen naturally, it's good to practice it. Practice it every day! Write it down, and put it somewhere you can see it – on the mirror, fridge door, in your wallet. This will help to un-brainwash you from your negative self-view.

Positivity Lists

#1 Write a list of things you like about your body (write at least five to ten things):

Here's an example list:

I like:

1. My womanly figure
2. My long hair
3. My cute little toes
4. My natural breasts
5. My beautifully shaped eyebrows
6. …

Now write a list of some of the positive qualities you like about yourself (write at least five to ten things):

My positive qualities:

1. I am a good listener
2. I appreciate things I have
3. I am sincere
4. I am funny
5. I am a good friend
6. …

And write another list about what are you good at (write at least five to ten things):

Things I am good at:

1. I can draw
2. I can dance
3. I am very creative
4. I have good intuition
5. I can easily relate to people
6. ...

I really hope you actually did this exercise since it will affect you positively! When I first did this, I was actually amazed at what an awesome person I am! Ha-ha, just kidding! But yes, it did show me that I have worth and that negativity will not help me!

As you can see, having a positive body image is not only about your body. It's about the full spectrum of who you are – the body, mind, and soul.

We have been conditioned to believe that only people who are "full of themselves" talk positively about themselves. Positivity about ourselves and having a good body image is confused with arrogance. But this is not true. You can be a very modest and humble person but still have a positive body image and love yourself as you are! Loving yourself is not the same as the "oh-I-am-so-faaabulous-and-you-are-not" kind of arrogance. It's about loving yourself unconditionally, just the way you are.

Apology Letter to My Body

It can be very good to let out the feelings you have felt toward your body and to ask for its forgiveness- forgiveness from all the negative things you have done to it, said to it, and thought about it. Just like you would say sorry to your close friend if you know you hurt her. Please take your time with this exercise as it's very personal and important message to your body and will help you recover.

Example:

Dear Body,

I want to apologize for all the days I blamed you for everything bad that happened. I didn't know that what I was doing was not realistic or fair. Now I see that you were always just doing your best with the conditions I gave you. I am truly amazed that you are still here, still working, and still the same amazing body. I'm amazed that you could go through such hell but still stand by me and still work toward repairing yourself and offering me the best conditions you can given the situation. Now I see that you were never against me but always there for me. Now I finally see you for what you are and take you exactly as you are, with no conditions. I do not expect you to be anything you are not, and I love you exactly as you are!

Love Letter to Myself

Next you can write a love letter to yourself – to your soul! The body is nothing without the soul. Our soul is where the real hurt lies, so it's important to speak to that part of you and make peace with it.

Example:

> *I accept myself with all my good and bad – all my uniqueness and all my flaws and imperfections. I can see that these little flaws are part of me and are the things that actually make me who I am. I do not need to be "perfect" in order to love myself or receive love. I am good as I am now, right here and now. I would never expect a good friend to change in order for me to love them, so I will not expect that from myself. I would not give my loved one conditions under which I would love them, so I will also love myself unconditionally, no matter what.*

These letters might seem stupid or useless at first, but they can actually be very powerful. Don't worry – nobody has to see them if you don't want them to – they're just for you and for your recovery!

Do Not Compare

Comparing your body to people around you – your classmates, your friends, your family – is kind of the same as comparing your body to pictures in magazines, famous people on TV, and so on. It's just not realistic to have someone else's body type or size. Whether it be smaller or bigger, it is not your natural set-point and is not healthy or sustainable – trying to achieve that weight will only cause you physical and mental suffering.

Researchers at the University of South Florida-Tampa, who published a study on body image and social comparison, think it's important to broaden the field, so to speak.[102] They suggest you go out in a public place and watch people passing by. In that way you will notice all kinds of different bodies. Not only the skinny ones we often see on television, in magazines and those perfect Instagram accounts. This will train your brain and your inner beauty detector to start accepting all kinds of different body types. Your own included.

Instead of comparing, start to embrace the variety of bodies and the individuality around you. Instead of looking at other people's bodies with criticism, judgment, or in comparison, look at people for their uniqueness. And I mean real people from the streets, not people from the media. Notice the many different shapes and sizes there are and yes, even the beauty "flaws," according to today's beauty standards.

By doing this kind of "exercise" in my recovery, I started to see value in all different body sizes, and it helped me feel more accepting of my own body. I also regretted having wasted a part of my life constantly thinking about my flaws and focusing on my "imperfect" body. I looked at women on the streets, and I started to see beauty in every single one of them, in their own personal struggles and stories. And through all of that, I saw myself as just being one of them, a person with my own unique appearance, attitude, and character, all of which stretched far beyond my physical weight and body.

This is how I woke up from the illusion that life was about having a perfect weight and size. It was just a superficial, meaningless programming. A brainwash. Superficiality was not a part of the person I wanted to be, so I quit believing in it and worshipping it.

I am fully aware that curing negative body image is a big task considering how much programming we have to undo. Negative body image is rooted much deeper than our eating disorder, and it's a real bitch to dig it out. It takes a lot of time, practice, patience, learning, and repeating to undo the negative image and self-perception. It's not an overnight thing. But is it possible to have a healthy body image after an eating disorder? Yes, I absolutely believe it's possible!

> *If you can accept your natural body weight – the weight that is easy for you to maintain, or your "set-point" – and not force it to beneath your body's natural, healthy weight, then you can live your life free of dieting, of restriction, of feeling guilty every time you eat a slice of your kid's birthday cake. But the key is to accept your body just as it is. Just as I have had to learn to accept that I have thighs that are a little bigger than I'd like, you may have to accept that your arms*

are naturally a little thicker or your hips are a little wider. In other words, accept yourself. Love your body the way it is, and feel grateful for it. Most important[ly], in order to find real happiness, you must learn to love yourself for the totality of who you are and not just what you look like." – *Portia de Rossi, Unbearable Lightness*

Eating Disorder Thoughts

Eating disorder thoughts (for simplicity from now on, ED thoughts) are not hallucinations like in schizophrenia. It's not an invisible voice or person telling you to do crazy stuff. Rather it is an internal chatter where you talk to yourself in a negative way, and it affects your body image, eating habits, and self-worth. It will keep you stuck thinking you have to follow a particular diet to be healthy or skinny. It will keep you hiding and lying, stuck in mental self-hatred, and obsessed with your body and food.

If you have experienced an eating disorder, then you probably know what I mean. Everyone has different thoughts, and they can depend a lot on your personal background and what your biggest triggers are, but they generally go something like this:

I'm so lazy and useless! All I do is eat, eat, eat! No wonder I'm fat! I don't deserve to eat!

If I could only be 100% raw or follow {insert type of diet}, I would have a perfect body and I'd be happy!

I hate my thighs and stomach! If I could only lose X pounds, I would be happy!

OMG! I just ate all my daily calories in one meal! I'd better skip dinner and go for a run instead.

I feel so fat and bloated. I can't believe I have no self-control. I feel so disgusting. I need to purge!

These are all very negative and self-destructive thoughts. These thoughts keep you restricting and cement you firmly in your eating disorder.

Some say it's impossible to not act on these thoughts as the fear is so real. And the action that comes afterward is automatic. It's out of your control. The restriction, bingeing, purging, doing XYZ-thing seems like the only solution to make these thoughts stop, even if it's just for one second.

How Eating Disorder Thoughts Develop

Let's take a young girl who is very happy in general and doesn't think about her body or eating at all. She has friends, and she loves to play games, climb in trees, walk her dog, swim in the ocean, and do other stuff normal kids do.

But one day, some kid comes up to her and out of the blue tells her she's fat (even when she might not be!). At first, the little girl is puzzled. She runs to her mom, who says the boy was just rude and not to worry about it. But suddenly, the girl becomes very aware of her body, and she feels very conscious about her appearance when she goes to play with other children. She even starts to notice other girls' bodies, and she compares herself to them. She fears that maybe this boy was right and there's something wrong with her. She thinks that maybe she isn't normal after all.

Before the boy's comment, she didn't care about her body because everybody loved her for who she was, and nobody had said anything hurtful to her before. But all of a sudden, she's very aware of her body and tries to eat less because "food makes you fat!" as her aunt said last weekend at the Christmas party. She had never paid attention to comments like that before, but now she starts to hear and become aware of those things because her focus has changed.

(Note: The more you focus on something, the more you start to see it everywhere! And if you believe it, your brain actually starts to look for evidence to support your belief that you are fat, not normal, too big, etc.)

She notices how her big sister says no to desserts, and she sees how beautiful but skinny the girls on the *Seventeen Magazine* cover are – and she decides she will be like that, too, so nobody will call her fat again. She constantly worries about her weight and her looks, and unfortunately, she is soon caught up in an eating disorder.

She would have grown up to be a beautiful woman with a healthy body, but one comment changed her views on weight, on what she eats, and on what is normal – and she now thinks she has to control her weight by dieting. She wanted to be loved and accepted but got the message that the way she looked was not okay and she should change it.

Before the boy's comment, she never thought about her weight and didn't care, but after, she began to have a new thought pattern in her brain that slowly grew stronger and stronger by repetition until it became very subconscious. She started to see the thoughts as part of her true self. Even when she later had anorexia and was very underweight, she still heard that voice in her head telling her she was still fat and needed to lose more weight.

That's how scary, upsetting, and ridiculous those thoughts are. They make us act in destructive ways. This is one way eating disorder thoughts develop – one little comment can turn into an eating disorder.

Unfortunately, there are many thousands of stories like that, each a little different and unique, but the bottom line is the same. Nobody is born with an eating disorder. Nobody just "gets" an eating disorder out of the blue. There is always a reason behind it. A trigger. Even when you are genetically disposed to have it, it does not mean you will, unless there is a trigger. Something happens to us that changes our thoughts, and then those thoughts change our behavior, and the behavior spirals into an eating disorder when we keep making these negative neural connections strong enough by repetition.

Somewhere we have learned that the way we look or the way we are is not okay. We think we have to change it or control it, and we start to teach our brain destructive ways to think – ED thoughts, body dysmorphic thoughts, self-blaming and hurtful thoughts that keep us stuck in a downward spiral. The thoughts make us restrict, feel guilty when we eat, and tell us we are not good enough and we have to change ourselves to be accepted.

You teach your brain to follow a particular path of thinking. And as time goes by, it becomes harder and harder to change that thinking. You are refueling your negative thoughts by repetition – you are creating strong neural pathways.

You create these negative thoughts by repetition and by acting on them. You tell yourself you don't deserve to eat, so you starve or restrict food and binge because you're overly hungry and feel out of control. Then you purge and start restricting again to compensate and get back control. It's an endless cycle. You have these thoughts, and you affirm them by acting on them either physically or mentally! This is how they develop into a strong, automatic behavior.

How to Change Eating Disorder Thoughts

When you come from many months or even years of having an eating disorder, those constant thoughts of restriction and body shaming have become very normal and automatic in your mind. They have become a very strong part of you. It is a *bad habit* that at first seems kind of hard to break.

You create these destructive thoughts in your head the first time you start to see yourself and/or your body as abnormal, fat, or unhealthy. You repeat those thoughts to yourself again and again until they become subconscious and very "real" – you get brainwashed! The thoughts become part of you, and that's why you think they are actually you, but I want you to see that these thoughts are not you! You created them in your head and then gave them life by repeating and acting on them until it became normal and logical to think or act that way!

Following different diets and eating rules, reading diet-related websites and magazines, watching videos or TV programs that refuel your restrictive thoughts and behaviors, and following people who tell you what foods you should and should not eat brainwashes you! I was brainwashed to believe that "cooked food is poison," "the fat you eat is the fat you wear," "eating XYZ food is an addiction," "if I'm not skinny, I'm unhealthy," and so on and so on.

Also, the more you affirm in your mind that some food is harmful, you can get physically sick only thanks to your belief, not because of the food itself. It's the placebo effect of conditioning – this is the powerful example of our thoughts and how it can manifest physically if you believe something to be true, even if it might not be: https://www.youtube.com/watch?v=O2hO4_UEe-4

If you repeat something to yourself time and time again, it will brainwash you! It's the social influence of different dieting groups, media, and so forth that make you think that weight loss and being skinny is the only way to health and happiness.

> *In psychology, the study of brainwashing, often referred to as thought reform, falls into the sphere of "social influence." Social influence happens every minute of every day. It's the collection of ways in which people can change other people's attitudes, beliefs, and behaviors.*[105]

But the truth is, it's only the conditioning and the brainwash that keeps you stuck. It's not the real you – it's the self-imposed beliefs planted in your mind. It's planted by those dieting groups, and it's planted by following today's body/beauty standards and listening to someone else's advice about what and how much you should/shouldn't eat to achieve that "perfect" body and be accepted as "healthy."

I'm not saying that having knowledge about health and well-being is entirely wrong. Or that someone who promotes a healthy lifestyle is brainwashing you into becoming their puppet. There is some very good advice out there for sure. But I want you to be able to eliminate the messages that will keep you stuck in your eating disorder and keep you feeling guilty and shameful!

It can be hard, at first, to see and realize what the negative thoughts are and what the eating disorder is leading you to believe, but once you know, you can change them! You can rewire your brain to think differently and escape from the old, destructive thought patterns!

Logically, you may know that those thoughts are bad and destructive, but somehow it's hard to break free. It's because your brain had become very well-adjusted to these thoughts – you have affirmed them to be true by repetition for many months or years or even decades. It's like being hypnotized to act in a certain way. You don't know why you do it, and you may even realize that it is harmful on some level, but you do it anyway. It's the conditioning!

That's also why some eating disordered people don't want to recover and prefer to stay in the eating disorder, even if it means they'll die or suffer badly. There was a guy who was brainwashed in a Korean death camp to betray his own family and have them killed, all the while believing he was doing the right thing![106] This is an extreme example, but I want you to see what the mind is capable of if it's brainwashed. It loses the ability to separate right from wrong, and as a result, we can get caught up and believe something is normal when it's actually not.

Someone with an eating disorder has conditioned their brain to think that these thoughts and behaviors are normal and safe. Trying to eliminate these patterns creates a lot of fear, and they feel threatened because they believe having the eating disorder is the only way to live. They believe they're doing the right thing and think it's their safe reality when in actuality it's merely an illusion!

Human beings are very adaptive. Women stay in abusive relationships because their partners brainwash them to

MENTAL RECOVERY

believe they deserve it, it's their fault, or they're not good wives and need to be punished to behave. It's crazy, but it happens. I don't mean to sound like a conspiracy theorist, but being brainwashed is the best illustration I can find to explain the disturbing relationship between your healthy, realistic thoughts and your delusional, destructive ED thoughts.

The eating disorder is like an abusive relationship. It wants you to be stuck forever and never come out of it. But you *can* come out of it one hundred percent. You just need to start changing your thoughts and not acting on them. Your brain will forget how to have an eating disorder when you deprogram yourself and get rid of the destructive beliefs!

Every time you repeat something to your brain, you make a neurological connection. You make something true even if it might not be. Your brain doesn't know the difference between the actual truth and self-imposed truth.

So what are you teaching your brain every day, time after time? I'm assuming that if you're reading this book, you're probably not feeding your brain nourishing, loving, and kind thoughts about yourself, right? But you can change that! Once you realize that your brain is very adjustable, you can actually change your thinking by positive repetition. You can change your brain to think differently until that becomes your new normality.

For example, I had depression many years ago, and I have to admit it wasn't easy to be in that situation. My thinking back then was much different than it is today. I told myself how miserable I was and how I was failing at everything in my life. But I made a conscious effort to change my thinking to get out of that life-sucking habit of negative thoughts that only fed my depression. I read numerous self-help books and did a lot of mind-exercises, and little by little, my thoughts changed, and I came out of the depression. Change your thoughts… change your reality!

I still have negative thoughts – I'm only human – but I know how to change them and not let them pull me down. And now positive thoughts are more dominant in my mind than negative ones. Positive thinking can become a habit.

Thoughts in your brain are like muscles – the more you pump one kind of muscle, the easier it is to use that muscle, and the less you give power to another muscle, the less you can use it because it's just too weak. Similarly, the more you feed one thought pattern, the stronger it will get, and the less you feed another, the weaker it gets.

I also had to change my eating disorder thoughts by making an effort, and it wasn't easy at first because the neurological connections in my brain were very strong, but the more I started to build new thought patterns – positive ones – the weaker my negative thoughts got because I wasn't feeding them and giving them strength over me anymore.

I rewired my brain to thinking in a different way, and I stepped away from my old destructive path and started to make my way to a new path. And now the old path is forgotten, and the new path is the easiest way to go for me. It's very automatic now.

How to Separate Yourself from the Eating Disorder

To get out of the negative thinking pattern and the mindset of "I do not want to recover or get better" is to separate yourself from the ED thoughts. These negative thoughts are not the real you! They represent your eating disorder, the conditioning, the brainwash, the negative neurological connections that have become so strong in your brain by constant repetition. You and the eating disorder are *two different things*!

Many people can't tell what the ED thoughts are and what their real thoughts are. Think about it this way – every negative thought that makes you feel worthless, makes you want to restrict, or makes you act in any eating disordered way is an ED thought! And conversely, every loving, caring, realistic, and positive thought is a real thought that comes from your heart – from the place that will help you recover and get better!

The action you must take is to write down every negative thought you typically get from your eating disorder and then replace it with a positive and realistic one. It's very important to replace them with positive but realistic thoughts – something that is actually true and believable. Don't write overly idealistic things like *I will be forever happy and free and get back to my ideal weight very soon!* because it might be too much for you to believe in at this point, too much of a head-in-the-clouds type ideal. That's not how real life works. It's best to keep things realistic and achievable – *If I restrict now, it will only make me binge later, so I won't do it!* or *If I recover my normal hunger cues, the weight will take care of itself! I trust my body!*

I will give you some practical examples of how to change your negative thoughts and patterns to new ones and rewire your brain. It will take some practice, but it is possible! Doing this kind of mind-exercise helped me a lot!

#1 Replace negative thoughts with positive and realistic ones

1. ED thought: *I am so lazy and useless! All I do is eat, eat, eat! No wonder I'm fat!*

Replace it with a positive thought: *I eat so much because I've been restricting, and it's only a normal response from my body. I need to eat to get better. I will never restrict again so my hunger cues can normalize. I am good enough just the way I am!*

2. ED thought: *If I could only follow {insert type of diet}, I would have a perfect body, and I would be happy!*

Replace it with a positive thought: *Trying to follow any kind of diet is only keeping me stuck in my eating disorder and is actually a part of my eating disorder! This "perfect diet" is just an illusion. If it could solve my problems, it wouldn't need so much of my willpower and restriction to follow it. It's NOT natural at all! It's clearly just a destructive behavior and conditioned thinking!*

3. ED thought: *I hate my thighs and stomach. If I could only lose X pounds, then I would be happy!*

Replace it with a positive thought: *Negative thoughts and restriction will only make me more miserable. The restriction will make me binge and gain even more weight in the long run. It's not worth it! I will eat when hungry and stop when full, and then my body can decide whatever weight is best for it!*

Do not skip this exercise as it comes in handy when you have those overwhelming negative thoughts. If you are struggling, you can take out this list and repeat the positive thoughts to remind yourself of your positive and logical answers to your eating disorder thoughts so you won't act on them!

Which brings me to the next point...

#2 Do not act or react to your ED thoughts

Acting on ED thoughts makes the neurological connection stronger, so don't do it!

An action is very powerful. You keep your eating disorder alive by acting on your negative thoughts. By acting on your ED thoughts, your brain continues strengthening the neural connections and pathways.

For example: If the ED tells you to restrict, you go on a diet. If the ED tells you to not eat, you listen to it and skip meals.

If the ED tells you *you're fat!*, you repeat it to yourself and believe it.

By "acting on your thoughts," I mean two things: the real action you take physically after having these thoughts and the mental *reaction* you have after these thoughts.

Physical action: If the ED says you don't deserve to eat, you act by skipping dinner.

Mental reaction: If your ED tells you, *you're fat!*, you believe it and repeat it in your mind or look at yourself in the mirror with disgust and tell yourself you don't deserve to eat.

The mental reaction is *very* important in recovery. Even when people don't act on their ED thoughts in a physical way – they continue to eat enough food, they don't purge, they stop exercising, etc. – something is still keeping them stuck. In this case, it can be that in their mind, they're still very actively reacting to ED thoughts, and this will actually keep them from recovery!

Even if they eat until full, they may still react in their mind with shameful and destructive thoughts like *You ate so much, you're gonna get fat!* or *If you keep eating and not exercising you'll just keep on gaining and gaining!* This kind of mental reaction will keep you stuck even if you are not physically acting on your ED thoughts.

The good news is that when it comes to your brain, it's true that "what you don't use, you lose." If you don't refuel your negative thinking patterns, the ED thoughts will lose their strength, and you will forget them as time goes by. Our brain is a very efficient organ. It builds and refuels the neural connections and pathways that are frequently used, and it weakens the ones that aren't. When you stop performing a behavior, the neural connections that support that behavior simply fade away.

Next you will learn how to not act or react on those thoughts so you can build new positive neural connections.

Examples of Acting on Your ED Thoughts and How to Change Them

1. **Purging** – Vomiting, using laxatives, diuretics, overexercising, skipping meals, etc.

What to do: Whatever you do, even when you feel completely stuffed and uncomfortable, do not purge! If you do, the cycle cannot stop. Purging creates an even bigger appetite and keeps your body in starvation mode. Purging refuels the next binge. Just wait it out! Sleep, watch a movie, or distract yourself in any way necessary until the uncomfortable feeling passes. It always does! By not purging, your appetite will be able to go back to normal.

2. **Restricting** - Restricting calories or types of foods, dieting or following someone else's rules about what, how much, and when you should eat.

What to do: Do not restrict in any way. Eat when you are hungry or crave more food, and stop when you're full. If you don't know your fullness signals, have a history of serious caloric restriction, or are very susceptible to restriction, I recommend following the MinnieMaud caloric guidelines for a period of time until you feel more recovered. Start to eat your fear foods to get over the "good" and "bad" food mindset.

3. **Engaging in triggering things** - Watching "thinspo"/"fitspo" pictures, reading diet websites/magazines, reading food labels, and connecting with people who follow diets or who are eating disordered. Anything that triggers your ED thoughts and behaviors.

What to do: Recognize – or even better, write down – all the things that trigger you to relapse and keep you stuck in an eating disorder, and then eliminate them from your life! Replace them with new positive activities. Start to connect with your friends who are normal eaters, take an interesting class and learn something new, go to exciting meet-ups, read books on different subjects, watch inspirational movies, paint your nails, do a different hairstyle, take a bubble bath, draw or paint, or do whatever else you can think of – start to do and experience different things!

4. **Fueling your negative body image** – Weighing and measuring yourself, body-checking, talking about yourself badly, comparing your body with someone else's, focusing on your flaws, and shaming yourself if you do something "bad."

What to do: Acknowledge that you are enough as you are, just the way you are. Your flaws are a part of *you*, things that make you unique. Start to notice how different people's body shapes and sizes are in the real world. Notice how media brainwashes us to believe only one body type is "right" or "healthy," and start to distance yourself from that unrealistic standard. Stop all ED behaviors that fuel your body-focus such as weighing, measuring, and comparing. Buy comfortable clothes that sit well on your body.

5. **Mentally reacting to triggers** – From skinny pictures in magazines to a friend who asks, *Are you really gonna eat all of that by yourself?* – anything that triggers you back to ED thoughts and makes you want to restrict again.

What to do: Realize what's happening, and acknowledge your trigger. You don't necessarily have to fight the thoughts but try to see them as an outside observer – separate yourself from the ED thoughts and just watch them flow by as a cloud. Recognize that they're something created by your previous conditioning, brainwashing, and neurological thought patterns, and they cannot harm you in any way or make you act on them. They can just float by because you have created for yourself a new way of thinking and don't want to participate in your old habits anymore. They have absolutely no power over you.

By recognizing the old negative neural connections and action patterns, you can start to rewire your brain and really recover mentally from your eating disorder. Your previous habits and thought patterns will start to weaken and change. This is what happens to someone in eating disorder recovery as they work on their mind – they start to build new positive neural connections, and the old negative ED thoughts just get weaker and weaker until it's quite hard to remember what it was like to have an eating disorder.

Many people who still have an eating disorder or who are just starting their recovery don't believe it's possible to achieve a full mental recovery. They don't think recovery from the destructive thoughts is possible because the thoughts in their brain are simply too strong, and it seems insurmountable to overcome them (I didn't believe it, either!). Some will say, *maybe you'll manage it better after recovery, but the thoughts will still be there or you just have to learn to cope with it.*

But rewiring your brain is not something I invented; it's a scientifically proven fact. There are numerous books you can find about how our brain works. We can teach our brain new habits – either positive or negative – by repetition, and we can change bad habits by repeating new ones and not fueling the old ones. So it's totally possible to fully recover mentally from your eating disorder!

What If I Do Not Want to Recover?

You feel this way because the mental conditioning of the eating disorder is very dominant in your mind. You got to this point by continuous negative behavioral and thought repetition. This is how our brain works! The more you repeat something to yourself, the more you start to believe it, no matter if it's good or bad for you. Your brain doesn't know the difference. The more you act and think in eating disordered ways, the more "normal" it seems to you, the more automatic it becomes, and the stronger the neural connections are.

On the other hand, you know there's also another voice in your mind, the one that doesn't want to have an eating disorder and wants you to recover. This is your *true* authentic voice. This is *you*!

You have to separate yourself from the ED thoughts just as a person in an abusive relationship has to realize that she/he is not the bad one, but the abusive partner is. I've already said, the eating disorder is your abusive relationship!

Separate yourself from the ED voice and see it as being outside of you, see it from a distance. Then start to replace these negative ED thoughts with true, positive thoughts that come from you!

You have to take responsibility for your own recovery. Only you can help yourself! If you don't believe in it, then no recovery effort will last. If you give all the responsibility for your recovery to your parents, to the recovery team, or to anybody else without committing to it yourself and understanding why you need it, it won't last!

And lastly, you have to ask yourself *why* you want to recover. Why is it important to you? What will happen if you choose not to recover? How will it affect your family, your children, and the people you care about? What will happen to the dreams you once wanted to pursue? Write down why recovery is a must for you, and then use it as a motivation every time you want to give up.

It's Not Working!

Everybody who goes through recovery has felt this fear or screamed this thought internally many times.

You feel that you're doing everything right, and it has been so long already, but nothing seems to be working or getting better, and maybe it even seems to be getting worse. Or maybe you've had so many relapses back to restriction that you feel it's just too hard to overcome the relapses and stop them from happening – maybe even impossible.

You feel like surrendering to your eating disorder. It sure seems like an easier way to go sometimes. *Just one last time!* – you may have said it a hundred times already. But deep down, you know it's only the sneaky ED voice tricking you into another relapse. And it won't end unless you choose to fight back.

I want to remind you that having these negative thoughts and doubts in recovery is very normal. It's part of the recovery process. But do you really want to relapse and just give up?

No, you might say, *but it's not working!* And this is when your eating disorder screams at you the loudest because it's afraid the recovery *will* work, and it realizes you're finally trying to take charge of your life. That's why it fights back so hard! It's intimidated!

Remember this quote when you're dealing with situations like these: *"Eat. Get up whenever you happen to get up in the day and eat. Keep eating. Cry. Eat. Sleep. Eat. Have a bath. Cry some more. Call a friend. See a friend. Eat with a friend. Eat when you can't sleep. Sleep when you can."* [107]

In other words, try to not overthink it, but just do it. Continue on the recovery path no matter what the ED tries to tell you. That negative, threatening, and scary voice in recovery is *not* the real you speaking – it is still your eating disorder in its nasty disguise trying to convince you to go back to those negative habits. Do not trust that voice!

Emotional Eating

Emotional eating is the practice of consuming large quantities of food – usually "comfort" or junk foods – in response to feelings instead of hunger. Experts estimate that 75% of overeating is caused by emotions.[108]

In my opinion, before we give someone, or ourselves, the label of an emotional eater, we have to first look for a few other critical factors. I do not believe all people who think they eat emotionally are actually emotional eaters.

A while back, even before my eating disorder started, I thought I was an emotional eater. I ate when I wasn't hungry or ate when I was stressed. Not always, but sometimes. I didn't know what caused this need to eat when I wasn't hungry. From all the explanations I could find in my research, the label of emotional eater fit perfectly. I seemed to have every symptom of emotional eating.

When I was younger, I never cared about food. I didn't think about food in my spare time or obsess over it. I ate when I was hungry. I ate what I liked and how much I liked. Sometimes I took a second helping, sometimes I left food on my plate, and sometimes I forgot to eat when I was doing something exciting.

But when I became a teenager, I somehow started to eat emotionally. I had no idea when or how it started, but it was just there all of a sudden. For me, I think the main factor was that my body changed. As with any normal teenager going through puberty, my body started to look different – bigger, fatter, more uncomfortable. For the first time in my life, I started to notice my figure and pay attention to what I ate.

I thought I just needed to "watch my intake" from then on. And that was the first time I tried dieting. That was the time I started to care about what I ate and how I looked.

Do you see where I am going with this?

From the time I began to control my food and my body, I started to develop this "emotional eating" behavior. What I'm saying is that emotional eating has triggers similar to those of eating disorders and disordered eating – dieting and restriction. When we start to artificially control our natural instincts, such as eating, we start to drift away from normal, intuitive eating, and we develop all sorts of difficulties and abnormal behaviors around food (such as emotional eating, stress eating, eating from boredom, overeating, eating disorders, and so on).

Now that I have recovered from emotional eating and an eating disorder, I don't eat for any reasons other than hunger. I actually lost the ability to eat when I'm not hungry. Now, eating more when not hungry feels very unnatural to me, and it's something I just can't do anymore. I lost the ability to overeat. Sometimes I may feel hungrier, and sometimes not so hungry, but I never feel I eat abnormally. So what changed?

I chose to give up all the diets and restrictive behaviors and restore my natural hunger and fullness signals. I also restored my mental health by changing my thought patterns. I unbrainwashed myself and stopped thinking I needed to be skinny or follow a diet to be "healthy." This is exactly what this book is about. And it's why I don't "eat emotionally" anymore. My own experience showed me that my problem was not purely emotional – it all started because of the physical things I did to my body. It started by my dieting and restricting.

Researcher Janet Tomiyama has found that dieters tend to be more emotional and react more strongly than non-dieters to upsetting events, maybe because dieting itself creates so much stress. Dieters tend to have higher levels of cortisol, sometimes called "the stress hormone," and free fatty acids, both of which signal stress.[109]

When I used to diet, I was definitely more stressed out by it, so it's no wonder every little thing made me overeat or turn to food. But now, without the stress of dieting and fully recovered, I do not turn to food no matter how emotional the event. It just does not happen. I used to eat like an emotional eater, but I am now completely free from it.

Have you had a history of dieting? Did you try to lose weight? Have you done "cleanses" or fasting? Did you follow any diet or lifestyle that restricted foods you ate before? Have you restricted calories? Do you obsess about foods or eating healthy? Do you exercise for weight loss?

I think if you can answer yes to all or some of them, it's very likely that you are not an emotional eater. It's scientifically proven that when we restrict foods, we develop all sorts of problems as we discussed already in the first chapter.

I still have my bad days. It's not like I recovered from my eating disorder and no longer have emotions. Sometimes I cry and feel like the world is ending. I have lows, and I sometimes feel negative emotions. I get stressed out. I get bored. But do I turn to food? No! I changed the unnatural things I used to do around food, and I don't have an eating disorder anymore. I didn't delve into my childhood memories or try to fill an "emotional void." I just stopped restricting and feeling guilty about what I ate, and I got cured.

MENTAL RECOVERY

I still have all sorts of negative emotions in me that surface from time to time, and I need to work on my self-esteem and my ability to forgive, but what I want to say to you is that you can work on those things after you have recovered from your eating disorder. It doesn't have to hold you back. I'm not saying that mental healing from our past is not important, because it definitely is. You just don't need to fix all of your emotions before you recover.

When I tried to fix my emotional problems while still in the middle of an eating disorder, it was incredibly hard, and I still ended up "eating emotionally." It's important to recover from the eating disorder as soon as possible. Digging into your childhood to look for "the emotional root" of the problem doesn't help – it just delays your recovery. I'm not saying it's not beneficial, but you don't have to do it if you feel it's too overwhelming. You can recover despite your emotions and despite what may have happened to you. It's important to know that mental recovery cannot happen when you are physically still restricting.

In conventional eating disorder treatments, it has been stated that recovery from eating disorders can take years. And often it's not even full recovery but more about *managing and coping* with the problem. And that's because many eating disorder recovery programs focus first on digging into the underlying emotional stuff and "filling the void" and so on. But you will always live in fear that the eating disorder might come back at any time.

Many authors who have fully recovered from eating disorders, like Kathryn Hansen in her book Brain Over Binge, have indicated the same thing I experienced.

> *The false assumption that my binge eating was a coping mechanism formed the basis of my therapy and most traditional therapies. Since my therapist believed I was binge eating in order to cope with emotions and problems, an important goal of my therapy was to find and practice healthy ways to cope. In therapy, I was told that once I found and implemented healthy coping, I wouldn't want to binge eat anymore; but until I did this, I would continue needing to binge. As I've said before: not only was this approach ineffective, it gave me plenty of excuses to binge. Finding healthy ways to cope was a worthwhile life goal, but it wasn't necessary for complete recovery from bulimia.... When I stopped binge eating [once I was recovered] – that was it. There was nothing special I had to do to cope with the life after bulimia, just as there was nothing special I needed to do to cope with life before bulimia.*[110]

Nina V says the same in her e-book *Recover from Eating Disorders*:

> *We don't eat over stress – it's the stress of eating that makes us eat! I always believed that if I could just manage my emotions better, I wouldn't binge or starve. But the fact was that I ate whether I was happy, sad, or indifferent! It really had nothing to do with the stress in my life, but it was the disordered eating that was causing me massive stress, and*

the only way that I could numb myself was through MORE EATING.[111]

Or read the awesome article "What If Everything Media Told You About Bulimia Nervosa Was Wrong" by Richard Karr from bulimiahelpmethod.org:

Chances are, if you had never restricted your food intake, you would never have felt compelled to binge on food in the first place and you wouldn't have bulimia. It's a bit shocking, isn't it? Keep in mind, this has nothing to do with your upbringing, personality, or emotional state. If the healthiest, happiest person on the planet restricted their food intake, they would make themselves susceptible to becoming bulimic. This isn't conjectured, this is a scientifically proven fact.... Shockingly, there is no scientific evidence supporting the idea that resolving underlying psychological problems leads to recovery. Despite this lack of evidence, many people remain absolutely convinced that bulimia can be healed by focusing on the mental aspects alone. This also might help to explain why traditional treatments that focus only on the mental aspects of eating disorders aren't very effective. If bulimia is mostly a physical condition, you cannot possibly "think yourself" better. Try "thinking" a broken leg better. It won't get you very far.[112]

I made a big shift toward getting better when I finally realized that my problem was the restriction, not some particular emotional baggage or whatever. It was the physical restriction that made me suffer mentally as well. I was trying to follow a perfect raw food diet. I constantly failed, but my goal was always to be one hundred percent raw someday. I thought it would cure all my problems. I thought eating cooked food and junk food was bad and fat in my diet was the devil's work. I didn't want to listen to my body – I thought it was stupid and didn't know what it wanted. I believed that eating only "clean foods" was the best for my body, and if I just kept pushing through it, I would get to the other side. But I never did. My eating disorder just got worse. You cannot cure your "emotional eating" if you still restrict, diet, or have an eating disorder.

Only after I let go of all the restrictions and all of my guilt about food did I recover and completely stop "eating emotionally." Trusting my body and what it wanted took some time, but when I realized the simple truth that I had to let go of the restriction and guilt, I took a big step toward being recovered.

So before you assume you have an emotional eating problem, think about your past. Have you been dieting, restricting calories, or avoiding particular foods? Do you overexercise to compensate for your eating or to lose weight? Do you avoid foods even though you crave them? If yes, then your problem is not "emotional eating."

I still have all of my emotions – I cry, feel pain and sadness, get stressed, and feel insecure and helpless – but I never overeat or feel an emotional need to eat when I'm not hungry, and that's because I don't restrict, I don't diet, and I don't have any rules about eating. All my previous "emotional eating" was just a side effect of restriction, following rules, and dieting.

How to Relieve Stress/Negative Emotions in Recovery

Recovery is tough, and you will have some emotional breakdowns and moments of despair. I know I did. So I want to give you some tips that helped me to relieve stress and lessen negative emotions. I used these things in my recovery, but I still use them today to deal with any negative life situations. Everyone will find unique things to help them manage stress and negative thoughts, but I'll share some of my own here.

1. **Your thoughts are powerful!**

Stress is actually created in your head, in your thoughts. That explains why different people act very differently in stressful situations. Thoughts can't actually hurt you unless you let them. The more you repeat something in your head, the more power it gets. The more you repeat any negative thing to yourself, the stronger the connections with that thing become in your brain, and then the same pattern becomes easier for you to follow. Similarly, when you repeat something positive, it will start to make new neurological pathways that make your life easier and happier – the same way we already talked about changing your ED thoughts. And this new, more positive way of thinking can become a natural thing for you. You can teach your brain how to act differently and positively in stressful situations.

Let's use public speaking as an example. Some people find it very stressful, but others enjoy it and feel empowered instead. Same situation, but very different reactions. So what's the difference?

I used to get extremely stressed when I had to speak in front of people. I had a panic attack every time, no kidding. It wasn't just a feeling of "butterflies" in my stomach, but it was an all-consuming fear. My heart would pound, I couldn't breathe, my vision blurred, thoughts raced through my head, my hands would sweat, and my legs shook – no fun at all! I got attacks like this for over ten years, and it was one of the most difficult things for me to overcome. I tried every method I could find to suppress this fear and stress, but nothing worked until I discovered it was all created in my head. It existed in my thoughts, and those thoughts didn't have any power over me. They couldn't harm me. But the more I repeated my fearful thoughts, the more power I gave my fear and the more automatic it became. I had made such a strong neurological connection in my brain that it seemed impossible to reverse, but I did it.

I stopped following the thoughts and fears and started to look at them as an outside observer instead. I still heard the voices of those thoughts and fears, but I separated myself from them and started to hear them from a distance, like they were coming from outside me, not from within me. I stopped trying to eliminate the fears, stopped trying to make them go away, but let them come, watching them as if they were just a cloud drifting by overhead. Something that's there, but not attached to me.

The key here was that I didn't give power to my thoughts by acting on them or letting them affect me emotionally. I knew that they were just thoughts, and they weren't harmful. And the less I acted on them, the less power they had. Eventually, they started to fade away and got smaller and smaller. I stopped believing my fears and started to look at them as neurological junk, something created in my head. That's how I got over my fear of public speaking.

The more you repeat negative thoughts and think you don't have power over them, the more you actually let them sink in and take hold of you. But the more you look at them as an outside observer and don't act on them, the less power they have.

In my past, I had depression for three years. My thoughts were very negative, and I felt sorry for myself. But learning about my thought patterns and how powerful my mind is helped me get out of the depression and see that life was not too cruel, too bad, too hard, or too pointless – it was only my thoughts that made it so. I have the ability to control how good or bad my life is. And thanks to my experiences overcoming my fear of public speaking and beating depression, I knew that I would conquer my eating disorder, too! I knew I had the power to do it. I just had to keep searching for solutions and take the focus off feeling sorry for myself. Even in the midst of my eating disorder, I managed to stay positive and hopeful in hard times, and that's why I was able to finally find out how to recover – my mind was focused on the solution, and I wasn't feeding my misery with negativity.

2. Attitude of gratitude

The number one thing that helps me to feel better about my life and the things that stress me out or make me feel sad is thinking about other stuff going on in the world and about other people and what their lives are like. There are people who have lost their homes in natural disasters, people who have lost families and friends, people who were born with unique conditions that make their lives more difficult and give them additional challenges. There are people with no arms and legs who can still walk and swim and people who have no money and live in a one-room home with no water and no electricity but are still smiling and happy with love in their hearts. There are people with incurable diseases who still find something positive in each day that they have left to live.

These are the people who truly inspire me. These are the people we should look up to. And how silly I feel when I think about my own problems. I have cellulite? Why do I care about cellulite when I still have my legs? I'm fat? I'm worried about that when 870 million people in the world are suffering from malnourishment? I have bad skin? Across the globe, 780 million people don't have access to water, and 2.5 billion people don't have access to a toilet, basic sanitary things we take for granted. And the list goes on and on.

I don't mean to make you feel better only because some people have it worse than you do, but I just want you to have a healthy perspective. Open your eyes and see what you have, and realize that most people don't have that. So many people would do anything to have it as good as you do! When I think like this, I suddenly feel like the richest and most fortunate person in the world.

An attitude of gratitude is a powerful thing. Every week, I take some time to remember the things I'm grateful for. I've done it for many years, and it works! I accept myself and am thankful for the things I have so much more by practicing gratitude. I can notice beauty in the little things and in everyday moments.

I have had dark times in my life. I have had numerous big challenges to overcome. And every time I accomplished something, I gave my thanks to the universe. I made sure that every time I overcame a challenge, I was grateful for it. And I think if you're grateful, it starts to have a snowball effect, and you will bring to your life even more great things. At least, that's what it has been like for me.

It's important to be grateful for things you have accomplished, but it's also important to be grateful for the things you already have and the things that are already good in your life. For example, when I am being grateful, I think about things that truly make me happy and things I maybe don't notice in my everyday life. I am grateful for my boyfriend who is the best person I've ever met. I'm grateful for my parents who have supported me no matter what. I'm grateful for my few but truly close friends. I am grateful I have a place to live and a place I can call home. I am grateful I have overcome many big challenges in my life. I am grateful I have the opportunity to travel and see the world. I am grateful I can breathe, walk, smile, love, and write this book to share my experience and help someone with the same struggles. There are so many things to be grateful for.

I think the biggest problem is that we often concentrate only on the negative and not so much on the positive. And what we concentrate our thoughts on is what we get. If we concentrate only on the things that are wrong in our lives, we will give more power to the negative and invite similar things into our lives. I know it's a cliché, but you have to think positive! For me, it's a habit. I have the ability to always see something good in the bad things that happen.

For example, when something bad happens to me, I ask myself why it was necessary and how it can be useful. If I don't have an answer, I make something up! There are no negatives without positives, I believe. Things happen for a reason – even my bulimia and all the other challenges I've had. When I had bulimia and was desperate and unhappy, I always knew I would get over it, and I knew I would help other people to recover thanks to my experience. This kind of positive attitude – even in darker times – is a good practice.

3. **Let your stress out**

The most effective way for me to let stress out is to just cry. I let myself be sad, vulnerable, and emotional. Emotions should never be suppressed. They need to be let out one way or another. When I cry, I tell myself, *It's okay, let it out. You're sad, and it's okay to cry. I love you.* I try not to talk negatively about myself – I never say I'm weak, worthless, pathetic, or any of that. Instead, I take care of myself the same way my best friend would – by allowing myself to be vulnerable and by supporting myself in the hard times. In this way, I feel loved and cared for, and the crying actually makes it better, not worse.

Also, it's sometimes good and healthy to be angry or disappointed or feel helpless or sad. It's okay to let yourself feel these emotions – they can't harm you. You are only human, and you don't have to be strong, know all the answers all the time, or feel "amaaazzing" all the freakin' time! It's okay to feel bad sometimes!

4. **Look for solutions**

Now that you've let your stress out in a physical way and found some relief, you can start to focus on looking for solutions.

What can you do to make the situation better? If you have an eating disorder that makes your life miserable and unhappy, is there something you can do to find a solution for the problem? Reading this book, for example, is a good start! Can you now start to implement some of the things you learned here in your real life so you can start to feel better and begin the recovery process?

Do something every day that takes you out of the negative situation and makes your life better. Even if it's something small, just a baby step. Feeding the negative emotions won't help. Without action, nothing changes.

5. **Look for support**

You do not have to go through it alone – and you shouldn't. It's okay to ask for help and support. Talk with your family. Meet up with a friend. Sometimes it helps just to share your worries and what's bothering you. It's good to get things off your chest and feel some support from others.

Sometimes it isn't possible to talk with someone, or you feel you don't want to. In that case, you may still need to clear your head by letting your thoughts out some way. And here it might be helpful to write it down.

When we worry, feel sad or depressed, or something is bothering us, the thoughts tend to spiral in our head and get very messy. You don't know what to do and may feel helpless.

I have kept a diary for many years, and it has helped me a lot. I've found that if I write my thoughts in my diary, everything becomes clearer and I can breathe again. Sometimes if something feels like it's weighing on my chest, I just write it out, and it relieves some of my worries. I may even forget and let go of the problem altogether! I don't keep it locked inside of me, but instead let it out in writing. Some say that writing is a form of meditation, and I agree. In times when nobody was there for me or I didn't feel comfortable talking to anyone, writing helped me a lot. It gave me support. It was like therapy because my emotions didn't have a chance to pile up and overwhelm me.

6. **Distract**

Sometimes there are situations where we just have to wait it out and see where life takes us. Some things are just out of our control, and there's not much we can do about it. At these times, negative thinking and worry don't help. I know that these negative thoughts are sometimes so hard to avoid, so it's helpful if you can find an interesting distraction, something to get your mind off the things that bother you.

I like to watch inspirational movies based on true stories, documentaries, or funny TV shows. I also like to talk to my friends or family or read a book. Meditation is another great alternative to calm your mind and let you relax. And sleeping when you feel stressed can also be very beneficial.

You can do anything you enjoy – paint, take a bath, go out with a friend, listen to positive music and dance with it, and so on. Make up a list of things you can do, and then start doing them!

7. Create a positive, healthy environment

Look around you and see if there's a lot of negativity around you. It doesn't necessarily have to be coming from you. Maybe you listen to dark, melancholic music or watch a lot of violent movies. These things can affect you at a subconscious level. Maybe you have a lot of negative and energy-draining people in your life. If you have things or people in your environment that negatively affect your mental state, find ways to change those things.

Right Mindset in Recovery

Having the right mindset is important in recovery. It's why some people succeed, but others keep on crashing. In the following pages, I will teach you some of the things I did so that my mindset sped up the recovery process rather than slowing it down.

#1 The power of your subconscious mind

You can attract almost anything you want to your life. You can choose to be happy or sad. Many people do not realize that they have this power. There is amazing power in our subconscious mind.

I read *The Power of Your Subconscious Mind* by Joseph Murphy when I was about eighteen years old, and it opened up a new perspective for me. Later when I struggled with depression, I already knew I had the power to change my life by changing my thoughts. I read the book again many times – it gave me hope and affirmed that there was no point in blaming anybody for what was happening to me. I had to take all responsibility for my life and change my attitude and thoughts. I had all the power I needed to change my life already within me.

I started to work on my thoughts, my mindset, and my view of life. I decided not to be a victim or feel sorry for myself anymore but to do something about it – to be active and work toward solutions. I started to implement the knowledge I'd learned about how the subconscious mind works into my everyday life, and little by little, I started to see some amazing changes. Now I can see that learning about my subconscious mind and how my thoughts affect my life fundamentally changed me. It transformed me into a better, happier person and someone who finds positive things in every life experience and always works toward solutions rather than getting caught up in negative thinking.

#2 Believe in recovery, and believe that you can do it

I have had many obstacles in my life (who hasn't, right?), and I've overcome many of them. Some of them seemed quite impossible to overcome at the beginning. There were things I thought I would never be able to fix, and sometimes I felt I was destined to always have those troubles.

But I have always had a sense of determination and hope in me, and somehow I pushed through. Each time I overcame something, I made it a point to stamp it into my core belief that

I can overcome *anything* if I put my mind to it. I'd tell myself, *You see? I did it again! I can achieve anything!* I believe this kind of attitude carries you more easily over life's hurdles. Every time I felt completely defeated, low, and miserable or had a major binge and purging session, I reminded myself that I *would* get through it!

No matter how bad it is today, tomorrow it will be better. I know this because it always is. If it's hard for you to believe that, then search for people who have fully recovered. Read their stories. This will show you that it is possible.

#3 Be a realistic optimist

It is vital to be confident that you will succeed in your journey toward complete freedom from food obsessions and eating disorders. That's very important. But it is equally important to admit that you will have some difficult stumbles along the way. People are most successful in reaching their goals when they couple optimistic goal-attaining confidence with realistic expectations of a bumpy path along the way. In other words, you have to become a realistic optimist!

It's important not to overestimate how easy or smooth the recovery will be. You have to be realistic or you will just be disappointed, and then if you have a relapse, you will find it very hard to get back on track. Know that you will absolutely be eating disorder free, but at the same time, proactively and realistically assess the obstacles you will face. That way you spare yourself the unnecessary anguish of misinterpreting the inevitable challenges you'll face as signs of failure and will instead focus on learning from your mistakes and doing what you can do to make sure it never happens again.

You have to accept that recovery won't be an easy ride. You will have some days when you feel you could have done better. It isn't realistic to expect to go from the start of your recovery to remission in a perfectly ordered, neat, and tidy fashion. It is vital when learning a new skill – or unlearning an old one like dieting and restricting – to know that change is not linear.

How to Bring Recovery to Your Life

This is not only for your eating disorder recovery but generally for anything you may want to achieve. I will show you how you can accomplish anything you want. Maybe you've heard about the Law of Attraction?

1. **What do you want to achieve?**

The first step is to dream. Have a wish. What do you want? Pretend you are in a big, endless supermarket of the universe, and you can choose anything that you want from the aisles. If you're reading this book, I have to believe you want to get over your eating disorder, food obsessions, binge eating, or something like that, right? So ask for it! *I want to get rid of my binge eating and be free from my eating disorder.*

Great! Now on to the next step…

2. **Imagine you already have what you want**

It's great to know what you want, but asking for what you want is not enough. You are telling the universe that you actually do not have what you want. So the next step is to imagine that you already *have* what you want.

This might seem like a difficult step because it is hard to imagine something that doesn't exist yet...but this is how you get it. To attract something, you need to radiate the right kind of energy, and you have to visualize having what you really want every morning and every night from this moment on. Our subconscious mind is most open and receptive right before we fall asleep and right after we wake up. So use that time to really soak in that thought of already having what you want.

Imagine how you'll feel when you are recovered from your eating disorder. What are you eating, and how does your body feel? Where are you going, and what are you doing? How good does it feel to be eating disorder free and have complete freedom from any food obsession? How does it feel to eat intuitively and without restriction.

This leads to the next step...

3. **Be thankful for already having what you desire**

This will really make your dream more real. Normally, you are thankful for what you already have, aren't you? So if you are thankful for your full recovery, your brain starts to think that

MENTAL RECOVERY

you are actually recovered – and it will speed things up. By thinking in this way, you will resonate at the right frequency.

When I was imagining myself recovered, I imagined something like this: I saw and felt very happy inside, and I said to myself, *I did it! I am now fully recovered. Thank you so much!* And I actually felt the feeling of being recovered.

While writing this book, I discovered something really cool, something I had forgotten completely. I was looking through my old diary entries, and right before I started my recovery, I had written:

"All my cravings have completely disappeared. I do not binge or eat emotionally anymore. I am completely free from [my] eating disorder. It feels so amazing! Thank you!"

Keep in mind, at the time I wrote this, I still did not have a clue of how I was going to recover. I was still regularly bingeing, restricting, and believing that raw food would cure me. All I knew was that I had to have a clear vision of where I wanted to be and then the universe would somehow lead me there. And it did. One month after writing this down, I had read again the Nina V recovery book *Recover from Eating Disorders* and finally realized what I had to do, and this started my recovery path! One year after writing this in my diary, I was fully recovered! This is the power of visualization and belief.

The moral of this story of mine is that you don't necessarily have to know how to do something – all you need is a clear vision in your head of where you want to be in the end. Leave

243

the rest to something far greater and more powerful – the universe, God, angels, higher spirits, or whatever it is that you believe in.

And the last step…

4. **Take action!**

You cannot wait and expect things to just fall into your lap without making an effort. You have to take action! Some people may say, But *I dunno what I should do or where to begin.* And the answer is simple – don't worry about it too much, and just start with something. Start with anything you can do even if you're not sure if it's right or wrong. Eventually, every little step leads us somewhere. We need to be alert and adjust our direction when needed. We need to be open minded and not afraid to try new things. And look for the signs – listen to your intuition. If you practice all the steps above, the right people and the right answers will come to you. This is the real "Law of Attraction" in action. Trust that it will happen, but take action!

For example, I searched the internet for answers about how to recover from an eating disorder. I read a lot, and I tried many things. Some things didn't work, but some drove me closer to the answers I was looking for. It was literally trial and error for me. I started with *something* and learned along the way, and it eventually led me to full recovery.

Start implementing the Law of Attraction in your life. This will put you in the right mindset for your recovery. You need to be optimistic and believe in your recovery. To speed things up, you can do daily visualizations where you see yourself already recovered and being thankful for it. This will keep everything moving in the right direction and your mindset focused on success. But remember to take action! Start with anything! It's important to take the first step and start moving. Trust the Law of Attraction, but be realistic about it, too. Having some bumps in the road does not mean you are a failure or that it doesn't work. Just wipe off the dust, and keep on going!

In the next chapter, we will talk about recovery issues. When you start your recovery, you will have all kinds of symptoms – bloating, water retention, night sweats, digestion issues, etc. Your body will go through a metamorphosis. You have to know what's ahead of you so you won't get discouraged or fall back to the eating disordered mindset and behaviors. My recovery was so much easier once I learned about everything that can happen in recovery. It all made much more sense!

CHAPTER 4

Recovery Issues

"Recovery feels like shit. It didn't feel like I was doing something good; it felt like I was giving up. It feels like having to learn how to walk all over again."[113] –Portia de Rossi

In this chapter, we will talk about all the issues that can come up in recovery – bingeing, cravings, bloating, water retention, digestive issues, weight gain, sweating, feeling tired, and many others – and what to do or not to do.

When you struggle with an eating disorder, you may think your body is working against you. You hate your body and don't see all of the amazing things it's doing to keep you alive and repair itself!

I believe our bodies never work against us. They do everything they can to keep us alive and healthy. If we get a headache, we think, *Oh no, not that again!* and automatically take a drug. We think we have to suppress this bad sensation, but actually, it's there for a reason. It's there to show you that something is wrong. It's there to tell you to rest and give your body time to recover.

It's the same with eating disorder recovery. You will feel bad in recovery. Your body is aching, or it's swollen up. You will feel panicky and want to do something to make it go away. You might even want to go back to your eating disorder habits because negative issues in recovery make you extremely anxious. It's something you haven't experienced, and you may be too afraid to just let it happen and trust that it will pass.

First and foremost – give your body time to recover. Rest, and trust your body. It knows what it's doing! The bad and uncomfortable symptoms happen so that you will listen, rest, and provide the right tools to support your body's healing! The body is an amazing system, and it's smarter than you think, so let it do its job!

Digestive Issues

It's very common to have a lot of digestive issues and food sensitivity problems in recovery. Sometimes you can have real issues with food intolerances (such as lactose or gluten intolerance), and you can always take a test to make sure, but if you come from an eating disorder, it's very unlikely you have an actual intolerance. More likely, you've been avoiding so many foods for so long that your body has lost the ability to properly digest them! But you can overcome this in recovery. You can heal your digestion.

It's very normal to experience bloating, constipation, diarrhea, gas, acid reflux, indigestion, stomach pain, and many other digestion troubles in recovery. These things can be very scary when you experience them, and you may think, *Will this ever end? Is my digestion ruined completely? Will I ever have normal digestion again?*

Most of those recovering from eating disorders fear their problem is different and their body won't be able to overcome these issues. Often these problems cause a relapse because they're convinced they need to use laxatives, "cleanse," leave out food groups, or eat less to ease their stomach problems.

But it's important to understand that the eating disorder has made it so that the stomach is not used to dealing with the proper amounts of food. It's not used to digesting the kinds of foods you've been avoiding and, in addition, has most likely gone through many binge/purge sessions, a lot of calorie restriction, and avoidance of particular foods for days, weeks, and even months.

Your eating habits have been very inconsistent and confusing to your body. After eliminating some foods or food groups from the diet, your body has to get used to them and learn how to digest them properly when you start to eat them again. There is nothing mysterious about it – it's how our body works and adjusts.

I restricted a lot of different foods, and when I introduced them back into my diet on a regular basis, I thought my body had completely lost its ability to digest these foods. I was constipated for days and had lots of gas and indigestion. I felt like the food was just "sitting there" and not going through my body as it should. I thought I would have to eliminate those foods completely if I ever wanted my digestion to return to normal again.

But then I read about other people's experiences in recovery, and a lot of them had similar issues. Every one of those people said that it would pass – we have to give our body some time to adjust.

And they were right – my body did find balance again, and I can digest foods normally now.

The Clean Eating Digestion Disaster

If you have tried to be raw for any period of time (or have otherwise been on a very "clean and pure" diet) and then went back to eating cooked food or more processed foods, you can have a lot of digestive issues arise. You may feel like your body has become so pure that it simply cannot digest those "toxic" foods anymore. Frederic Patenaude has discussed this issue in his book *Raw Controversies,* calling it the "raw curse." I think the same concept applies to any "clean" eating or eating style where you leave out different foods for long periods of time.

RECOVERY ISSUES

Frederic Patenaude writes:

Many raw foodists tend to yo-yo back and forth between 100% raw and cooked food binges, only to return to more cleansing and detox and an even stricter raw food diet. They find that whenever they eat cooked food, it totally "destroys" them. A bowl of rice will make them pass out as if they ate a big Thanksgiving dinner, and eating out at the restaurant causes them to feel so sick that they'll spend a week recovering from it....

Raw foodists incorrectly think that their bodies have become so pure (as in "super healthy") that it now rejects the toxic cooked foods that most people are habituated to (like a drug).

In reality, what's really going on is that the "raw food" body has simply stopped producing the right mix of digestive enzymes, that they simply can't properly digest more complex foods now. By eating only foods that require almost no digestion (like fruit and greens), their digestion has "dumbed down" to the point it can't handle anything much more complex.

Some people even take this to an extreme, making their diets even stricter with time, eliminating fatty foods like nuts and seeds entirely, for example. This leads them to become even more sensitive.

The same phenomenon happens in reverse. Someone eating a junk food diet, devoid of fiber with lots of meat, white bread,

> *and few vegetables can experience some serious digestive discomfort when they start eating lots of fiber-rich foods, like beans or fruits and vegetables. It can take them weeks or months to adapt to this new healthy diet....*
>
> *The trick to avoid the "raw curse" is to retrain your body to digest certain foods. You can do it for almost anything. And eventually, eating a bowl of brown rice won't put you in a coma, and having a little bit of garlic in your stir-fry won't cause you to have nightmares all night!*[114]

As Frederic said, this kind of thing can happen with any kind of food you have eliminated from your diet. It does not mean that the reason you cannot digest the "toxic" foods anymore is that your previous diet was so "pure."

For example, if you've eaten a lot of processed foods all your life and then decide to eat more fiber and water rich foods, it can cause digestive problems. A lot of raw food newbies experience digestion issues when they start to eat more fruits and vegetables. But does that mean that the previous diet with lots of processed foods was more "pure" and they simply cannot digest the "toxic" fruits and veggies anymore? Of course not!

I have experienced the raw curse many times. Every time I eliminated some foods from my diet, and the purer and cleaner I got with my eating, the fewer foods I could digest. Every little thing seemed to cause trouble, and I thought if it continued like that, then soon I wouldn't be able to eat anything without problems. And I have seen so many people in the raw food movement experience the same thing. They have trouble digesting some of the foods most of us would consider healthy.

What you should do when starting to eat previously avoided foods is start with a very small amount every day so your body can get used to it. I restricted many foods when I was raw or mostly raw, and when I finally gave in and ate them, I felt incredibly bad physically. I thought this was proof that cooked food is, indeed, poisonous to my body and addicting as well. But my body was simply not used to eating those foods and had lost the ability to properly digest them.

Your body needs time to adapt to the foods that were previously eliminated. I'm not saying that junk foods are perfect for digestion or that you have to eliminate healthy foods from your diet, but I am saying that your body still has the ability to digest cooked foods and processed foods if you eat them. They do not have to put you in a coma, and they are not "toxic."

Food Intolerances

The most common intolerance is probably lactose intolerance. The primary form of lactose intolerance is when our body just stops producing lactase, an enzyme necessary to digest lactose. This normally happens at a very young age.

A secondary type of lactose intolerance occurs in many people with restrictive eating disorders. Their bodies are so energy compromised that they cannot produce enough lactase to digest lactose. However, when they recover, they can again produce the lactase.

> *An intolerance to a food item will mean that the body is unable to produce enough digestive enzymes to handle the food breakdown effectively and the result will be various gastrointestinal symptoms: gas, bloating, pain, acid reflux, possibly diarrhea and/or constipation, and occasionally skin rashes as well.*
>
> *When food intolerances appear and the patient has an eating disorder, then the primary reason for failing to tolerate these foods will be too little energy within the body available to produce adequate amounts of digestive enzymes.*
>
> *It's a catch-22: you have to eat to provide enough energy for the digestive system to get back up to speed, but the digestive system is how you transform food into energy and it's not yet up to speed.*[115]

It's a similar scenario thing with gluten intolerance. I was so sure I had gluten intolerance when I started my recovery. I had previously avoided gluten-containing products as much as possible for many years. Whenever I tried to consume them, they seemed to not digest properly and caused digestive troubles.

In recovery, I started to eat many things I had been restricting like white bread, pizza, pasta, pastry, and many other white flour and gluten-containing foods. I developed such bad stomach and indigestion problems that I had to go on a gluten-free diet for a month in my recovery to get some relief.

But after about three or four months, I planned to travel to Italy, and as you probably know, Italy is famous for pasta, pizza, and pastry products. The whole trip was *full* of gluten! Yes, at first, my stomach didn't handle it very well, and I was constipated. But after that trip, I slowly started to add more gluten to my diet since I liked those foods, and now I can say I do not have any symptoms of gluten intolerance. My body got used to digesting it again.

Reintroducing Foods

Please do not attempt to reintroduce foods without medical supervision. I am in no way saying that intolerances are not real. I'm just saying that you may have the symptoms of a food intolerance because of your eating disorder. Leaving out those foods may have caused your body to lose its normal ability to digest them, but this can be restored over time.

It is best to introduce the formerly absent foods into your diet in a rotation over time. This goes along with upping your calories and eating consistently. Every day or every week, you can choose a few foods to introduce back into your diet. At first, they can be lower amounts in terms of your overall daily calories, but gradually increase the quantity and frequency of these foods in your diet.

This will probably not be the most comfortable thing for you – physically or mentally. Being bloated, constipated, exhausted, and in pain is just plain miserable. And there is also the fear and doubt that goes along with it. Just keep in mind that all those symptoms are a part of the recovery process.

Also, know that this short-term, uncomfortable period is all done for long-term, positive results. For example, after knee surgery, the patient is encouraged to get out of bed and start working on the knee. It might be uncomfortable and even painful at first, but it will help the recovery of that knee. The same goes with healing the digestive system after an eating disorder. Recovery is a rehabilitation period, and it is not completely devoid of uncomfortable recovery symptoms.

Tips to Relieve Stomach Problems

#1 Probiotics

I personally do not have experience with taking probiotic capsules. Some say it helps in recovery, and others say it's best to wait for your stomach to rebalance itself. I do not believe in taking laxatives or medication for indigestion as it does not help to restore your normal digestion and might only delay the healing or even make it worse. But every case is different, so it's best to consult your doctor.

I do believe, however, that it can be good to include some probiotic-containing foods to your diet – things like fermented foods. If you feel it helps, then great. If you don't like them, that's okay, too. Try whatever works for you!

Good probiotic foods that help restore your gut bacteria are kefir, yogurt, sauerkraut, pickles, and Kombucha. You can find recipes online or look for these foods in your local shops or health food stores. Don't overdo it, though. Use them only as a small part of your daily foods.

#2 High Fiber or Processed Foods?

Here the lines get little blurry. Some say processed foods are much easier to digest in recovery because they're already pre-processed and are more calorie dense, so it's not necessary to eat them in large volumes to get enough calories. Some find fruits and veggies good for digestion, added into the diet in moderate amounts. I do not, however, recommend eating fruits and low-calorie veggies as the base of your meals because they can make you feel bloated and give you an overly full sensation with a too-low amount of calories.

Try what works for you. I balanced myself somewhere between these two options – eating whole foods but also including processed foods. I would say the most important thing is to eat enough calories and not restrict, and in time, your stomach problems will pass.

Processed foods are not necessarily junk food. Processed foods are also things like yogurt, whole grain breakfast cereals, canned beans, nut butters, and even frozen vegetables. So when I tell you to eat processed foods, I don't necessarily mean only candy, cookies, pizza, fries, and hamburgers, even though it is okay to eat those, too!

#3 Eat Enough Calories, Eat Frequently, and Eat Calorie Dense Foods!

If you don't eat enough calories, your metabolism will remain slow, your digestion won't speed up, and your body will not be able to restore itself. Many people find that after eating enough calories consistently for a while, they suddenly start to go to the toilet much more frequently. The body understands that enough food is coming in on a regular basis and doesn't feel the need to hold on to the food in your stomach. More food coming in pushes the old food out. One girl who recovered from anorexia was so happy to write to me to tell me that she was now going to toilet consistently – she just needed to eat more food to alleviate her constipation.

Make sure you eat frequently: three meals + three snacks a day on average. This is very good for digestion and healing. If you eat a big breakfast and skip lunch altogether and then maybe have a small dinner, it's not good for digestion when you're still healing – even when you're eating enough calories. Frequent food intake will help your stomach and digestion get back to normal!

Even though high-fiber foods can help you to digest, don't fill up your stomach with low-calorie, water-rich veggies. This will only balloon you up because you have to eat too much to feel satiated and get enough calories. Eat more high-carb foods (bread, pasta, rice, potatoes) and add fats to make food calorie dense (oils, avocado, nuts, nut butters.) And if fiber bloats you, then choose regular pasta instead of whole wheat and white rice instead of brown rice – or just generally eat more processed foods.

#4 Wear Comfortable Clothes and Relax!

Sometimes we just have to wait it out – there's no way to make things quicker artificially when our stomach just needs some time to figure things out. You will be your stomach's best friend if you support its work by giving it the time and rest it needs.

Wear comfortable clothes that aren't too tight and don't make you feel uncomfortable. Wear stretchy and floaty clothes that expand when needed, such as leggings or yoga pants and comfy tops. Other great items are harem pants and peplum-style skirts or tops. If you feel bloated, constipated, and gassy, the last thing you need is a pair of tight jeans and a small shirt that presses on your stomach.

To further help in this uncomfortable phase, it's best to lie down and sleep as much as possible. Distract yourself with a good positive movie or book!

There are many other things you can do that will help you feel better when stomach issues arise in recovery. You can drink warm water or herbal tea and try some yoga poses that are especially helpful for digestion. Find what works for you!

It will definitely take some time for your digestion to go back to normal. To make sure it happens as fast as it can, eat enough calories so your metabolism can reach optimal speed. Allow some time for your body to adapt and for the gut bacteria in the intestines to go back to normal. You cannot cut corners here, so just accept the process. Recovery takes time and patience!

Water Retention

Water retention (edema) is a very common symptom in eating disorder recovery. Even if you have dieted or restricted for only a short period of time, you can gain many pounds of water weight quite fast. It will make you feel bloated and uncomfortable, and it will make you put on weight.

At the beginning of this book, I told you the story about how I gained several pounds of water weight after fasting for three days. This weight came off over time when I stopped restricting. My body just needed time to heal.

Water retention is often the number one reason people relapse. Recovering from an eating disorder – or from any dieting and restriction – is scary because of the fear of putting on weight. Most people are afraid the weight gain is all fat and don't realize it's mostly water.

For example, you can easily put on ten to fifteen pounds or more of water weight in a matter of weeks (or even days!) when you start to eat normally again. People who recover from anorexia will gain real weight (muscle, bone, fat, organ tissue, etc.), but there will also be more water weight and generally more food in the system. People recovering from bulimia and binge-purge cycles can also gain several pounds in just days after quitting their restrictive habits.

> *It is normal to see an increase of 8-16 lbs. (3.6 to 7.3 kg) within days of starting to eat to the minimum guidelines every day. It is equally common to see 20-40 lbs. (9-18 kg) within 1-2 weeks. The increase is almost entirely attributable to water retention and it is necessary for cellular repair.*[116]

To ease your worry and to show you that you are not the only person this has happened to, you can read how Shaye, from Your Bulimia Recovery, gained eleven pounds of water weight in just one week of her bulimia recovery. By purging, you become very dehydrated. When recovering, it's understandable that you would gain water weight: http://www.your-bulimia-recovery.com/Your_Bulimia_Recovery-weight-gain-in-bulimia-recovery.html

The amount of water weight you can put on really depends on your individual background and body. You may temporarily shoot up from your normal set-point weight, and it may seem like you're just gaining and gaining and it will never stop. You'll have episodes of extreme hunger, and you'll put on real weight, too, if you need it. But don't worry – you will not become obese by eating enough calories. Over time, your body will relax when it sees that the famine is over, and it will let go of the excess weight if there is any.

Once your body heals, your hunger cues will normalize, and you will be back at your normal weight. This will differ for everybody – we have different shapes and sizes. Just remember that you are not the one who decides your goal weight or the weight you want to be. It's all up to your body!

And there is no way to say how long this period will last for you. It varies from person to person. The only thing you can do to make it as quick as possible is to make sure you eat enough calories, never restrict again, and, as your recovery progresses, eventually return back to intuitive eating.

Why does water retention happen?

Water retention is a sign of healing. When you walk with uncomfortable shoes, you can get a blister that might be full of water and swollen up. The body gathers fluid where healing is taking place. And the swelling and aching are the body's ways of making you sedentary so that you allow time for rest and recovery.

You don't want to interfere with this process and artificially make the water retention go away by, for example, taking a diuretic pill or starving yourself, because with that, the healing process will stop. Trust that once the healing is done, your body will release the excess water and return back to its normal state. You have to wait it out.

How can you tell it's water retention?

Many people in recovery want to know if it is really water retention and not real weight. So look out for these signs:

- When you started eating more, you gained several pounds in a matter of days.

- Your face and eyes look puffy and swollen up.

- Your skin might hurt in different places just like when you have bruises.

- You may have pillow and sheet prints on your face and skin when you wake up and also imprints from your socks on your legs.

- You gained most of the weight on your stomach and thighs. You may also see increased cellulite.

- You feel six months pregnant, and your belly is like a balloon (also a sign of bloating/gas).

- You feel very heavy and uncomfortable.

- Real weight gain happens very gradually, but you notice this weight gain immediately.

How to feel more comfortable with water retention/bloating

When you gain water weight, it can feel very uncomfortable. Your body may ache and be swollen.

- This is a sign that you should relax. Rest as much as you can. Sit and lie down as often as you need to. Sleep and take naps.

- To make sure the process will end as quickly as possible and the weight will even out, you have to eat enough. Always respond to hunger and/or cravings. This will help your body recover and give it the extra energy it needs for repairs. It will also speed up your metabolism.

- Wear very comfortable clothes. Wear things that are stretchy and floaty.

- Do not use diuretics to lose water weight. It will mess up the process, and then you'll have to start all over again. It will not speed things up!

- Do not weigh or measure yourself. Stay away from triggering websites or social media. Use this time for doing something else – watch a movie, be with your friends, read a book, enjoy your favorite foods, or do anything that you love that is not triggering or upsetting.

Drinking Water

It is okay to drink enough water when you're thirsty. But don't overdo it. It's not good to drink too much because it can make your electrolytes go out of balance and can even be dangerous. The best idea is to drink when thirsty. I would say one to two liters a day is okay. Drink more in hot weather or when you're involved in physical activity and are sweating more (but remember to rest from exercise!) or when you're spending a lot of time in artificially heated rooms or traveling on planes. But again – drink when thirsty and don't force yourself to drink water just for the sake of doing it. And by the way, it's okay if your pee is yellow – it doesn't have to be completely clear!

It's also very good to drink water with some calories in it so you're not consuming zero calories and getting bloated with no added energy.

Avoid drinking before meals, with meals, and right after meals since this can dilute your digestive juices and make digestion sluggish, which adds to the bloating. Drink between meals and about thirty minutes to an hour before and after meals. If you need to sip on water during a meal, then go ahead. Do not drink big amounts in one go but rather drink one sip and one glass at a time or just sip throughout the day.

Listen to your body and find out what amount of water works best for you. These are just suggestions for you to try, not rules!

Weight Gain

The reason I talk about weight so much in this book is because it's one of the most common reasons people relapse or don't want to recover. Weight gain frightens people, and because of that, they may never recover. So my goal is to show you why weight gain happens and how to not be afraid of it. I want you to know that you will not become obese just by eating enough.

Most people who go through eating disorder recovery inevitably gain weight at some point. Some of it can be water weight as we talked about before, but some of it will be real weight gain.

People who are recovering from anorexia and serious calorie restriction gain weight because they are underweight and need more weight to be healthy.

Even bulimics and people who have gone through bingeing and purging will gain weight despite being a normal weight because they are stopping all restrictions and compensation, and their normal weight was being maintained thanks to those restrictive habits. It may not be sustainable after those habits stop.

A person who had an eating disorder during puberty may have had a delay in growth and body development, and now that they are reaching young adulthood, weight gain is understandable and healthy. You can't stay looking like a young child forever!

If you are overweight, you can, temporarily, gain more weight because your body is not functioning optimally. Once things speed up and you recover normal hunger cues you may lose some weight naturally.

If you come from restriction, then your body's systems are not functioning optimally compared to people who have never restricted or dieted. Your metabolism is suppressed, and you've likely lost some metabolically active muscle tissue and also an amount of necessary water weight. So when you stop restricting, it's very easy for your body to gain weight rapidly. Go back and read the first chapter again if you have to.

When your body is recovering, it will store water weight for healing purposes. You will also have more food in your system and may feel more bloated and constipated because your stomach is not yet working optimally. All this will make you gain weight, but this is not real weight gain – it's just water, bloating, constipation, slowed metabolism, and digestion. It will heal in time and balance out!

Many people freak out about the weight gain in recovery and go back to restricting or compensating. But this is the worst thing you can do! It will keep you in your eating disorder, and you will have to go through the recovery symptoms all over again when you finally tire of restricting (and you will!).

The best way to overcome weight gain in recovery and let your weight stabilize is *consistency*. Consistency along with eating enough and ceasing all compensations.

You cannot eat enough on one day and not restrict but the next day go back to purging and then say recovery is not working for you! Some girls write to me that they have been recovering for many months now (or even one to two years!) but still have no signs of recovery and ask me why that is. But then I find out that they still restrict on some days, they have kept up their rigid exercise regimen, and they even purge *"just a few times a week."* This is not recovery!

Relapses happen in recovery and they are part of the process, but as long as you engage in restrictive eating disordered behaviors, you cannot recover. You have to give yourself enough time. If you keep going back and forth between eating enough and purging or restricting, you are not progressing. You are stuck in the eating disorder. Recovery cannot happen this way!

The biggest motivation for me in my recovery was that I did not want to go through the weight gain and bloating and water retention hundreds of times. I realized that if I purged or restricted again, I would have to do it all over again, so I decided I'd better just wait it out. I knew it would pass in time – and it did! The ones who are now fully recovered are the same ones who did not continue the purging, overexercising, and restrictive behaviors in their recovery. You will never meet a fully recovered person who kept up restricting and purging *"just a few times a week."*

You can also gain real weight in recovery – body fat, muscle mass, organ tissue, bone mass, a healthy amount of water in your tissues, etc. Your body has a healthy set-point weight where you feel the best and healthiest. It strives to restore itself to its normal optimal weight. Some people are naturally bigger, and some are smaller – we all have different body types and sizes. Your body will return to the weight it's naturally set to be, and that may be different from what's right for somebody else's body.

Negative self-image and stress about your weight can actually keep the weight on. Keep that in mind and make sure you work on your body image as we already talked about in the last chapter. Matt Stone writes, *"Negative self-image is a powerful stressor, and stress prevents fat loss – even encourages fat gain. If you aren't upset and ashamed of how you look, you're much more likely to actually lose fat. Thus, it's important to resolve body image issues BEFORE losing weight."*[117] The reason why negative self-image and stress about your weight makes you gain weight is because of hormone cortisol – "the stress hormone." It actually encourages your body to store more fat.

People may overshoot their set-point weight because that is how the body recovers. Men in the Minnesota Starvation Experiment overshot their previous weight by ten percent, but after about a year, they started to gradually go back to their previous weight when they didn't restrict. This is how our body recovers, and we can't change this natural system. You can make this phase as brief as possible by stopping all purging and restriction, eating enough calories every day, resting and relaxing, working on your body image, and being consistent.

Weight Redistribution

You may notice that all the weight you gain seems to go straight to your stomach and/or thighs. This is also a normal part of recovery. The fastest weight gain happens on your stomach area because that is where the most valuable organs that need protection are located. Having more weight and water in this area assures faster nutrient circulation and provides protection from further damage.

> *Researchers have shown there is a significant increase in trunk adiposity (fat deposits around the midsection of the body) in recovery ... and this fat mass is evenly redistributed in the optimization period after weight restoration only if the patient continues to eat in an unrestricted fashion.*
>
> *In other words, the initial trunk adiposity and disproportionate fat mass ratio in the early period of re-feeding may not resolve unless and until a patient successfully supports the period of hyperphagia [extreme hunger] that is part and parcel of the process of reaching a healthy remission. We also know that trunk adiposity, in particular, is correlated with cardiovascular disease in older men and women ... which is all the more reason to encourage those in recovery to allow their bodies to complete the re-feeding process fully to allow for a return to optimal fat mass to fat-free mass ratios.*
>
> *The overshoot in weight during a re-feeding process is not present for all patients, but it is assuredly temporary for those who do experience it.*[118]

Uneven weight gain in recovery is expected. It can be fat gain, organs being repaired, or restoration of muscle mass, but it can also be bloating, water retention, and more food in your system, especially if it happens very fast in a matter of days.

Julia, from the recovery blog Lord Still Loves Me, writes:

> *Initially, I was astounded by the amount of bloating I would experience each day. On some occasions, I could have passed for a pregnant lady! To make matters worse, no weight was going to my arms, specifically my shoulder blades. Though, I do need to be mindful that my clouded mind probably made it out to be worse than it actually was. Either way, it was difficult for me to continue to eat at least 3,000 calories a day knowing that my stomach was going to expand.*

> *The distribution of the weight I was rapidly gaining was uneven, and it completely infuriated me. My mom had to constantly remind me that I was beautiful and that what I was doing was right. She told me it would go away and everything would balance out. I would nod my head and wipe the tears away, but there was still a little demonized thought stuck in the back of my head that thought it was all a lie.*

> *My mind would play tricks on me to get me to think that I would forever look this way. Many nights were spent crying over my new body that had come to me during recovery, and I could not stand to think about gaining, even more, weight. However, I kept going on this path and decided to*

give recovery my all. After all, I could already focus more, clothes were actually beginning to fit (though I was not pleased with what I looked like), and I was eating many more types of food.[119]

You can continue reading the quoted story here: http://www.lord-still-loves-me.com/weight-redistribution/

Even myself, after coming from bulimia, bingeing, purging, and overexercising have seen on the pictures I took at that time how different my figure was. I had a much rounder stomach and increased cellulite even though I exercised a lot and I wasn't overweight. I also had bloating and digestion issues. Now I have more definition even without having to exercise! The body will rebalance once it gets healthy!

Feeling Tired

When you were actively starving and maybe felt more "energetic," the fact is that your body was just in fight-or-flight mode, an evolutionary protective mechanism to keep you from starving and a way to give you "energy" to search for food. Without it, humans would easily die from starvation. But this protective mechanism keeps you going, even when you're in big danger.

When you finally start to eat more, your body can put all of its energy into repairing. Your body doesn't want to give you extra energy to do everyday stuff but instead wants to put everything toward recovery. Once it has restored what it needs, you will have more energy to function in everyday life.

> *It is a good sign if you are exhausted because it suggests your body is finally able to communicate its needs for recuperation and energy in a way that was not happening during active restriction.*[120]

Tiredness in recovery is your body telling you to rest as much as possible. Some people feel incredibly sleepy all the time, and it's okay to sleep more and lie down as much as you need to. When your body is sick with the flu, you feel more tired and want to sleep more. That is what restores your body. An eating disorder recovery is the same. Your body has been sick with an eating disorder, and now that you are giving it the right conditions to do so, it needs rest and time to heal.

Night Sweats

I had such bad night sweats that I seriously thought I was experiencing menopause! I would wake up in the middle of the night totally soaked with sweat. I had to turn my pillow over or put a clean towel between my sheets because they were so damp. I often woke up and had to go dry myself off or take a quick shower. Sweat was dripping off my skin.

I learned that these night sweats are just another sign of recovery – it was my metabolism speeding up, which was good! It can also happen because of all the hormonal changes during recovery.

It's very uncomfortable and annoying, but I kept reminding myself that it was actually a good sign and learned to celebrate it!

In time, it got better. At first, I experienced it several times a week. Now it happens at the most once a month during my period. It can sometimes happen at that time of the month because of the hormonal changes.

Along with the night sweats (or even sweating more during the day), you may also notice a general increase in your body temperature. Your hands and feet may feel a lot warmer than they were before. You may especially notice it after a meal. This is, of course, a good sign.

Insomnia

I suffered from insomnia while I had an eating disorder and even in my recovery when my body was still a work in progress. At the time, I didn't think it was related to my eating disorder, but the more I read about the symptoms and the effects of dieting, restriction, purging, overexercising, damaged hormones, and metabolism, the clearer it became that the insomnia was related to my eating disorder, and recovery could heal it. And it did!

If you have metabolic and hormonal damage, it can be the reason why you wake up at two or four every morning and find it difficult to fall back to sleep. Or why it can take you such a long time to fall asleep in the first place. For me, it was very often like this. I couldn't fall asleep easily, and I would wake up during the night with thoughts rushing through my head. I often just got out of bed and stayed up.

My insomnia went away about eight to twelve months into my recovery. It took some time, but it happened. Now I very rarely wake up at night, and if I do, I usually just fall asleep again very soon afterward.

Another thing related to your slow metabolism that can be a contributor to insomnia is that you need to pee frequently – sometimes several times at night, even when you don't drink much before you go to bed. What helps with this is to recover, obviously, by eating enough food with concentrated sources of calories, adding salt to your foods, drinking only when thirsty (not drowning yourself with water), and resting your body from exercise and reducing overall stress.

Amenorrhea (Loss of Period)

Calorie restriction, overeating, binge eating, purging, overexercising, being underweight, low weight, low body fat, deficiency of vitamins or minerals and macronutrients such as fats, too much stress, fast weight loss, unhealthy weight loss, hormonal imbalance (dieting is a recipe for hormonal imbalance), and having an eating disorder in general are some of the main causes of losing your period.

If the body is constantly running on a deficit and is under stress (restriction and overexercising is very stressful to our body!), then it will stop producing enough reproductive hormones and focus instead on keeping you alive. It figures that the environment is not safe for pregnancy. Your body is not strong or healthy enough to carry a child.

Many girls who have lost their period may think that having no period is preferable and life is much easier because they don't have to worry about cramps, bleeding, or PMS. Many who have written to me don't see the big deal about losing their period, and some don't care if they have it or not.

However, losing your period is a clear sign that something is very wrong and your health is in decline. Not having menstruation means you can't get pregnant, but it also means that if not treated ASAP, you can develop osteopenia, and if that progresses, you will have osteoporosis. Osteopenia and osteoporosis both mean low bone density. The first one is curable, but if it develops into osteoporosis, then it's not.

Osteoporosis is a disease which breaks your bones down over time. As your bones lose mass, they become very thin and brittle and are easily broken or fractured. Something as simple as sneezing can result in a broken rib, and a little stumble may lead to a fractured spine. In a nutshell – you become fragile as glass. While any bone in your body can be affected, the most common areas for fracture in people with osteoporosis include the hips, spine, wrist, and ribs.

Now, before you panic, it's always best to first go to see your doctor for professional advice and get a bone density scan. The best is the DEXA scan.

How to Get Your Period Back

1. **Eat enough calories, and eat them regularly.** Make sure you eat your MinnieMaud calorie guideline amounts plus pay attention to any additional hunger or extreme hunger. And do not skip meals. Eat frequently, every two to three hours.

2. **Eat enough carbs and enough fats and concentrated sources of calories.** Do not get your calories only from watery fruits and veggies, but eat more calorie-packed foods such as bread, pastry, pasta, rice, potatoes, cookies, chocolate, oils, nut butter, nuts and seeds, avocado, coconut milk, etc.

3. **Skip all exercise. Rest as much as possible, and sleep as much as possible.** Only light walking or everyday tasks are okay. Walk to the fridge to get more food and then back to the couch – you get the point.

4. **Lower your stress.** The biggest stressors in an eating disorder are, of course, not eating enough calories, restricting, overexercising, purging, etc., so if you avoid those things in recovery, it's a good step forward. But also, limit any other stress as much as you can – school or work stress, stressors within relationships, and so on. If you have a lot of stress in your everyday life, then maybe find some things that will help you relax or de-stress such as meditation, listening to soothing music, taking a hot bubble bath, reading a novel, or anything

else you can think of. This is not the right time to start running an hour a day to "relieve stress." Remember point 3!

5. **Give it time.** Do all the above things, continue doing it, and just give it time. Some women may get their period back in the first weeks and some in a few months – it really depends. The information here is quite general, and every case is different. When you get at least three consecutive periods (the more, the better, of course), you'll know that things are working properly again.

I have received numerous messages from girls who have done those exact things and got their period back. One girl did not have a period for five years and got it back! So there is definitely hope, and your body is not broken.

I Feel So Full and Bloated! I Can't Eat So Much Food!

It can be very hard to start eating enough food when you come from a past of restriction or low-calorie dieting. Often times it makes us experience digestive issues and feel fat, bloated, and generally very uncomfortable.

We became so used to restricting. We're used to that feeling of "emptiness" in our stomach when we come from anorexia or that feeling that we have to purge when we feel too full if we come from bulimia. A full belly signals panic in our minds!

And restriction would be our automatic response to feeling full.

But you have to understand that if you want to achieve full recovery, then restriction or purging isn't an option anymore. This uncomfortable feeling will pass, and it will get so much better in time – the first weeks and months can be the toughest.

You need enough calories and food to come out of a place of restriction and restore your body. You might feel like bingeing, and you might have extreme hunger. You might get indigestion and feel constipated, bloated, and gassy all the freaking time! I get it! I had it! But it will get better...I promise!

If you keep going back to restriction and eating small amounts of foods or purging after you feel too full, you only delay your recovery!

The worst thing you can do when you feel too full is to restrict or purge. Remember, every time you purge, recovery cannot happen! When you purge, your body thinks you're still in a famine and there's not enough food coming in – and staying in. It will keep sending you signals of extreme hunger. It will keep urging you to overeat and binge. Only when you stop all restrictive behaviors will things get better.

> *Sit with yourself until the urges subside. Remind yourself that they are temporary and that they will pass. The first time you do this will probably be the hardest... It can feel impossible that the urge will ever end unless you act on it...*

> *But that's not true. Every single thing on this planet comes and goes – this urge will be no different.* –Shaye, 5 Stepping Stones to Bulimia Recovery

If you find it very hard to eat enough calories because it makes you so bloated and fills you up too quickly, then focus on eating more calorie dense foods – more fats, more processed foods, and definitely more carbs! Don't fill your belly with low-calorie veggie salad and watermelon!

Bad Hair, Skin, and Nails

If you have an eating disorder, your skin is pale and dry, your nails are brittle, and you may even experience hair loss. When you start recovery, these things do not get better immediately, and they might even get worse for a time. But yes, it's normal!

When your body starts to recover from restriction, its first priority is to restore the primary organs and functions. In terms of health, your hair, skin, and nails are the least important, and they can wait.

But as you recover more, and your body – your organs, bones, digestion, metabolism, and hormones – starts to function optimally…then you will eventually restore your beauty, too! Your nails will grow stronger, your hair will become thicker, your skin will glow, and your eyes will sparkle.

We all have different health backgrounds, and I am not saying that everything will be absolutely perfect after recovery because everyone is different. I can only share with you my own experience.

My hair used to fall out like crazy, and it became very thin, but now it's back to its normal condition. I learned that hair falling out can be a sign of stress that may have occurred even six months prior. Lots of stress (like dieting or an eating disorder) literally makes our hair fall out. Even my eyebrows became thinner for a while, but now I've noticed they have become thicker again. I used to have many small pimples on my skin, but at the end of my recovery, this also got a lot better. Also, my teeth got whiter!

Many people experience acne in recovery. This, again, is normal. Your hormones go through a lot of changes and have to rebalance. It has nothing to do with the food. Yes, if you have restricted many foods (or food groups), it may seem that every new food you eat will aggravate acne (remember the "raw curse!"), but it is most likely hormonal. When I started recovery, it felt like every new thing and every "junk food" I ate caused my acne to get worse, but now that I am fully recovered, I can see that I can eat gluten, occasionally some junk food, oils and fats, and sugars, and they have no effect on my skin. I might get a few pimples around the time of the month I get my period, but this again is hormonal.

I think that, in terms of beauty, starting your recovery as soon as possible and not relapsing back to restriction is the most important thing. Also, make sure you sleep and rest enough and get some sunlight and reduce stress so your body can put the most energy toward recovery.

Relapse

Relapses are hard. They're scary, and they're difficult, and you may feel recovery isn't working. Relapses can make you lose all hope of ever getting better. I had many relapses in recovery, but it was all a part of the learning process! Just remember that nothing is broken! You have to get up and keep going!

Everybody has experienced some sort of relapse in recovery. You're not alone, and you're not a failure. You're a human being just like the rest of us!

The most important thing is to learn from your relapse. What were the warning signs? What triggered you? How can you avoid it next time? If you learn from it, you can brush off the dust and continue along your road to recovery.

Here are some of the triggers for relapse so you know what to avoid:

1. **Restriction of any kind**

Sometimes people relapse after a short period in recovery – they still do not comprehend fully that restriction will *never* lead to recovery. They may start to have "innocent" ideas of how to "speed up" the recovery process by shutting down their extreme hunger and following "intuitive eating" when they are not ready for that just yet. They'll start an "intuitive-eating diet" where they only allow themselves to eat until full and do not respond to their extreme hunger because that would be "bingeing" and "wrong" and will only result in "unnecessary" weight gain.

I have to stress that intuitive eating comes after recovery, and you do not have to force it to happen. If you do, it might just be another form of restriction because the recovery symptoms like extreme hunger, bloating, water retention, and digestive issues are just freaking you out.

Another example is that you may feel "ready" – way too soon in your recovery – to start exercising again. You convince yourself that from now on you're just being "healthy" or you "looove to run" or it's your "me time." In some cases, it might be true, but if you find yourself being more and more religious about it, and you feel guilty if you miss a day (or a month or a year) of exercise, it is very likely (and probable) that you're not doing it for pure fun and enjoyment but because you think you "have to." In your head, the weight gain in recovery is "unnecessary."

Or you may start to exercise again despite still having many symptoms of starvation: no menstruation, still feeling cold all the time, gaining weight easily when you eat until fullness, bloating, retaining water, constipation. These are clear signs that you should continue to avoid all exercise and eat, rest, repeat.

There are so many of these kinds of examples of how people fall back into restriction. It might also include an "I'm gonna get healthy" kind of mindset (the restrictive-obsessive healthy, not the full recovery healthy). Maybe you're not calorie restricting, but you're becoming more and more obsessed about clean eating. You start to read labels, worry about what you can eat if you're going out with friends, or leave out foods because they're "toxic." And not allowing yourself to eat some particular foods is how you slowly develop food restriction. It's when you're drooling over the thought of having pizza, but you choose to be "healthy" and order steamed veggies with "dressing on the side." You get the point.

2. **You start to collect "thinspiration" pictures on your Pinterest account**

This one is just as an example, but I hope you know what I mean in general. If in any way you start to engage in (or you never actually stopped) looking for images, videos of perfect bodies, or health gurus who are skinny, you're engaging in the eating disordered brainwash. Remember when we talked about being brainwashed in a previous chapter? Yup, that's what's happening. You are still doing the things that keep your eating disorder alive. You follow fitness accounts on Instagram or other social media platforms, you look for diet advice to be "lean and healthy," – blah blah blah. Stop it!

3. **Focusing on weight loss**

I know that water retention and bloating are both very uncomfortable. Gaining ten pounds in a day is a bitch, and you want to make it pass, but you have to let it go and just wait it out! It will even out as long as you do not relapse.

With weight gain – bloating, water retention, indigestion, or real weight gain – most people hope they will be the exception. *Maybe I'll be different! Maybe I am the unicorn, and I won't gain weight. Or if I do, it's not because of healing but because something is very wrong – and I have to eat less!*

But I'm 101% sure you are not different, and weight gain of some sort (yes, even when already weight restored or even overweight) will happen to you in recovery. Why am I so sure? Because it happens simply because you finally stopped all restrictive behaviors. You start eating enough, and your metabolism is still slow, so you will have bloating, water retention, more food in your system, and slower digestion – and all of these factors contribute to weight gain in recovery. But for the most part, it's not "real" weight gain. Yes, you will gain some real weight like fat, muscle, and bone mass if your body needs it – and if it's needed, it's essential, and you can't do anything about it! But if you choose to go through full recovery – eat enough and stop exercising, purging, and participating in any other restrictive behaviors – your metabolism will go back to normal, and you'll restore your body's normal functions. It's the best thing you can do for your weight!

4. **Too much worry about healthy eating**

Eating healthy overall is great, and everybody should learn about nutrition basics like eating more whole foods. Concern about our health is normal, and we should definitely pay attention to it, but I'm talking about the extremes here – the type of healthy eating that makes you miserable and unhealthy instead of making you happy and healthy. The kind of eating that puts you in a very tight restrictive box and gives you an eating disorder. So many of the people who write to me also come from a past of clean eating and orthorexia-like tendencies.

If they feel their health is not "optimal," they automatically start to blame their "unhealthy" diet and beat themselves up about the pizza they had a few days ago because that *must* be the cause of all their crappy symptoms, not the fact that they are recovering from an eating disorder. So this triggers them to "eat clean" from that point on. They might slowly exclude some things from their diet, and little by little, they fall back into the obsession. They see other "health conscious" people posting triggering food photos on Instagram #glutenfreeforlife and automatically feel guilty about what they're eating.

Intuitive eating is quickly forgotten, and instead, it's hello rules, food fears, and obsessions!

The way I got myself out of this behavior in recovery was to always remind myself that I wanted to keep eating all the foods I genuinely like, and I wanted to continue being an intuitive eater because it was important for my mental health, not just my physical body. Our mind and body are interconnected. They work together.

I knew that restricting the "unhealthy" foods actually made me crave them even more in the long run. Restriction made me binge-prone and obsessed. It's only when I allow all kinds of foods in my diet, with no restriction, that I don't crave them so often or in as large amounts. I saw that for my physical health, it was wiser to eat them every now and again and moderately than to restrict them completely and then have binge episodes, cravings, food related stress, and obsession.

5. Former triggering eating disorder behaviors

Any diet behavior will trigger you to relapse and can be a sign that you are already relapsing. Weighing and measuring yourself, body-checking, Paleo/low-fat/gluten-free diet recipe searching or following –all of these previous eating disorder behaviors are signs of relapse or impending relapse. Communicating with other eating disordered people who are not recovering can be a trigger for you as can calorie counting to make sure you do not eat "too much" or eating from blue dishes with chopsticks.

6. Trying to be perfect in recovery

It's important to realize that recovery is not another diet where you fail. Even though I listed here all possible triggers for your eating disorder, I want to tell you that it's not possible to be one hundred percent perfect in recovery. Erasing all your triggers and going to full recovery with absolutely no setbacks? Maybe it happens in recovery fairyland, but that's not real life. Recovery is a journey, and all mistakes are learning experiences.

Nobody expects you to be perfect. Be realistic instead! Expecting to be perfect is another sure way to trigger relapse because if something goes wrong (and it will!), you might just give up altogether because you'll automatically think it isn't working. If you climb a mountain and fall a few steps back because there were some loose rocks you didn't expect, it doesn't mean you have to go all the way back down and start again from ground zero. Taking a few steps back does not mean you have to start from the beginning. Instead, celebrate the road you have traveled thus far in your recovery, and just continue going!

Eating Healthy

People get very upset when I recommend that they eat their fear foods, the foods they have been restricting, or processed foods or (do I dare say it?) junk food in recovery. They think my message is that the only way to be eating disorder free is by eating McDonald's and KFC. But that's not true, and it's not what I'm saying. At all.

Our body needs nutrition, no doubt about it. Eating whole foods, fruits, veggies, whole grains, and nuts and seeds is important for our overall health and well-being. But letting go of the "good" and "bad" foods mindset is important. I don't eat McDonald's and KFC because I simply do not crave those foods. But eating my fear food in recovery actually made me *want* to eat healthier in the long run. There was no restriction anymore, and no food was off-limits. Therefore, I could really listen to my body and my intuition, rather than to my fears and guilt. Letting myself eat these "unhealthy" foods made me naturally want healthier foods. Isn't that great!? Isn't that what we want? To naturally crave more whole foods, more nutritious foods? And to crave them naturally rather than forcing it? Eating some junk food without stress and guilt is *much* better and healthier than having an eating disorder. There is no health in an eating disorder.

The major point I want to get across is that if you let yourself eat absolutely everything and anything you want, and you get rid of the mental restriction and fear of foods, your body can make the right choices based on your love and kindness toward it and not your rules, fears, restriction, and guilt.

Another point for recovery is to eat the foods you actually crave. If you don't crave a food, don't eat it. If you don't care about potato chips, there's no need to eat them! For example, I have never craved meat. I don't like the taste or the thought of it, and it makes me sick to my stomach just thinking about it, so I don't eat it. I don't even eat soy-based fake meat products because the texture is just too similar to meat.

But I did crave butter. I didn't crave it for nutritional needs but because I had a big fear of eating it during my eating disorder – it was all mental! So to recover, I had to eat butter and make peace with it. And I did. But I rarely eat it anymore. There is no craving because there's no guilt about eating it. I had to overcome my mental fear of the "unhealthy" foods to be eating disorder free.

Interestingly, one girl wrote to me that during her eating disorder, she was actually restricting healthy foods. So for her, it was time to start eating healthy foods and make peace with them. As you can see, the point is not to only eat junk foods and skip healthy foods. The point is not about the food, but the *mentality* – the fear, guilt, shame, and restriction. We have to restore the normal relationship with foods, not particularly for nutrition, but for mental reasons first and foremost.

Being Vegan/Vegetarian

Most eating disorder experts do not recommend being vegan in recovery and I can understand why: in today's world veganism is rather confused with restrictive diets, juice-cleanses, detoxes, having orthorexia-like obsessions over foods and losing weight.

If you are vegan for restrictive reasons – to be skinny, to eat "clean," to limit "unhealthy" foods, to be in your food comfort zone, to diet, to feed your eating disorder – then I do not recommend being vegan. Veganism revolves around more than food, it's about animals. It's a moral stand. That's it. It is not a diet.

I am vegan for ethical reasons. I believe you can be vegan in recovery if you were vegan before you had an eating disorder or any restrictive habits or if it is one hundred percent for ethical reasons. If one is against cruelty to other beings and does not want to consume products that support cruelty, then it is not an eating disorder. If someone is eating vegan foods or plant-based foods for health and well-being, and it does not harm their mental health or develop into obsessions and eating disorders, then of course there is no problem. But if it triggers an abnormal relationship with foods, and you are not doing it because of animals but specifically for dieting reasons, weight loss, and so on, then stop it.

You can read more about my personal story about being vegan and what it was like for me in recovery here: http://followtheintuition.com/being-vegan-in-recovery/

In the next chapter, we will finally discuss intuitive eating (a normal, healthy way of eating), and this is where you want to be after recovery. This is the place where you will finally find true freedom and get back your normal eating habits. I will share my best tips on how to eat after hunger and fullness signals and how I transitioned to intuitive eating.

CHAPTER 5
Intuitive Eating

Intuitive eating is a natural way of eating. It encourages people to respect their bodies, honor their appetite, reject dieting, and pursue healthy behaviors regardless of weight. Intuitive eating is a built-in mechanism of our body just like breathing or the need for sleep.

Nobody counts how many breaths they take each day. Or thinks that if they accidentally take too many breaths, they need to restrict their breaths so as to not have too much breath in their lungs. If they did restrict breaths, however, it would lead either to hyperventilating or, if the body's needs are not met, death. Okay, this comparison may seem ridiculous, but I think it can show how crazy food restriction is. In the first chapter, I explained how our bodies do not work that way.

We can forget how to eat intuitively if we experience food and eating problems like those discussed in this book. Our eating gets out of balance, and our hunger signals stop functioning normally. But even so, intuitive eating is still a part of us, and our bodies are very capable of restoring it.

Intuitive eating is about listening to your body. It's about eating what you want, when you want, and how much you want. It's about following your body and your inner guide but also, as a human being, using your knowledge, wisdom, and common sense about foods. It is not about eating junk food only for taste without paying attention to your body's signals. Or eating only salad and fruit all day and not letting yourself enjoy some pizza, pasta, or bread if you crave it. Your body will tell you which foods are good to eat at any given moment, and it can vary from day to day. You should use your knowledge about nutrition to make the best choice while at the same time considering your body's signals, cravings, and feelings.

Intuitive eating does not completely eliminate some types of foods or label food as either good or bad. Rather, the message is to eat all kinds of foods without restriction but pay attention to your inner guidance, your body signals, your cravings, your knowledge of nutrition, and your feelings. We eat for our body's nutrition but also to feed our soul and to feel happy and in balance. That is the main reason why intuitive eaters do not restrict "unhealthy" foods but rather see them as food for the soul and something to help them feel in balance – these are often referred to as "play foods."

Knowledge about nutrition is not enough to achieve healthy balanced eating and to be free from eating problems. If you already have an eating disorder, you know it's true. Besides, there is so much conflicting information about nutrition and food these days that you don't even know what's right. Often times nutritional knowledge dominates our intuitive knowledge. We use our brain but don't listen to our body – or vice versa. We need to do both in balance, not solely one or the other.

Following your inner guidance is a more effective way to maintain a healthy weight and body than adhering to restrictive diets. It helps you create a healthy relationship with foods and a complete freedom and trust in yourself. Diets only give you the illusion that you're in control when in reality you are out of control! The diet starts to control you!

A normal eater never diets, always eats what she wants, and never counts calories or macronutrient grams. She listens to her cravings but also uses some common sense and nutritional knowledge about foods. She never develops the urge to binge and never thinks about food obsessively. She does not diet, and therefore, her mind is not preoccupied with it.

But a person who diets and counts calories, reads food labels, counts fat grams, weighs herself, and has lots of food anxieties around foods is controlled by fear. This person has a weekly binge on their "cheat day," followed by a day at the gym with a religious exercise regimen. She is constantly preoccupied with food and body-related thoughts. So who is more in control here, and who is controlled by a diet and eating disorder?

In today's world, we eat when we're not hungry and deny ourselves food when we're starving. We eat because we don't want to "waste food," even when stuffed. We starve because it's already past 6 pm and we "can't" eat. We choose a low-calorie salad instead of a creamy pasta because "you have to eat your greens!" We eat a very low-fat diet because "the fat you eat is the fat you wear." Or we avoid sugar at all costs because "sugar is like cocaine." We stop eating when we're half full because "eating until full is greedy." And so on and on! We listen to what society or someone else tells us we should do, and we do not listen to our own bodies. We have forgotten how to trust our hunger cues. No wonder why so many have eating problems.

What is intuitive eating for me?

People forget what it's like to eat intuitively after coming from restrictive diets and eating disorders. I think the more you try to follow some plan or rules, the more you can lose your inner guidance for intuitive eating.

If you had a restrictive past with food, becoming an intuitive eater will not happen overnight. You have to relearn it. The reason I say re-learn is because I think that just as we were born to breathe intuitively, everybody was born as an intuitive eater. It's when we start to mess with this natural instinct, however, that we start to develop problems.

If you're starting your recovery from an eating disorder or a history of restrictive eating, your body signals are skewed, and you will need a period of recovery. The length of recovery is very different for everybody. For some, it might take just a few months, and for others, it may take few years. I started to feel better immediately as I let go of all the rules and restrictions I had. But it took a lot longer to really learn well all the new and normal ways of eating, to let go of the guilt and fear around food, and to learn to trust my body again. This happened much more gradually, and it took me at least half a year to start to feel more normal again and one year to recover completely.

Now I can say that if I continue to do the things that helped me recover, my eating disorder will never come back. I am an intuitive eater again, and I wanted to write down what intuitive eating is for me so maybe you will get some inspiration for your recovery.

Next is my personal interpretation of what intuitive eating is for me. I was inspired to define it following Ellyn Satter's (an internationally known authority on this topic) version of "What is Normal Eating?"

> *Intuitive eating is something that just happens, without you having to think about it. Intuitive eating is eating when you are hungry and stopping when you are satisfied. It is eating the foods you like and eating until you've had enough. Not stopping when you think you should, but when you feel truly satisfied. Intuitive eating is also eating sometimes when you are sad, bored, or just because it feels good, without having negative feelings about it – there are no rules of when you*

can and cannot eat! Intuitive eating is eating without guilt or control. It is eating the foods you like and what feels good in your body at any particular time. Food selection can vary from day to day depending on what satisfies your hunger the best at any given moment. Intuitive eating is having nutritious foods but also allowing any other foods because you simply enjoy them. It's not only about food, but it's also about how you feel. It can be eating three times a day, or five, or six, or munching along the way. It's about leaving some delicious food on the plate because you are full and satisfied and you know that you can always have this food again later on. Intuitive eating is sometimes eating "too much" but truly enjoying yourself and doing it without guilt. Intuitive eating is also not eating enough sometimes because you are in a hurry, you are not as hungry, or whatever life situation happens. Intuitive eating is not about control or mistakes. Intuitive eating takes some time in your life, but you know that it is only one important area of your life. Intuitive eating is flexible and not restrictive. It can vary from day to day depending on your hunger cues and feelings.

You have to figure out what intuitive eating is for YOU. What do you like to eat? How much? How does it make you feel? Do you truly enjoy what you eat? Are you satisfied after you eat? Do you feel any restriction? Do you feel guilty about what you eat? Do you worry about eating certain foods? Do you eat until you feel sick? Do you count calories to make sure you don't overeat?

I told you what intuitive eating is for me, and now I also want to tell you what intuitive eating is not in my personal opinion.

Intuitive eating is not about restriction or any kind of deprivation. It is not about counting calories for weight loss. It is not about stuffing yourself until you can't think. It is not about masking your true cravings behind massive amounts of "clean food." It is not about what you THINK you should eat and allowing only what is "healthy." It is not about feeling guilty every time you eat something "bad" or "unhealthy." It is not about allowing a "cheat day" because you should eat what you want every single day. It is not about eating certain foods, at a certain time, in certain amounts. It is NOT about rules and an unnatural control of food and what to eat.

Extreme Hunger Conflicts With Intuitive Eating

Learning about intuitive eating was a big part of my recovery and why I finally let go of restriction. I read a book by Nina V, *Recover from Eating Disorders,* and it really made me see that if I wanted to get rid of my bulimia and food obsessions and return back to intuitive eating, I had to start listening to my body and what it craves and never restrict again.

I started my recovery with intuitive eating. I started to let go of the "good" and "bad" food mindset. I promised to never restrict again as I understood that it simply does not work. I ate everything I wanted and tried to let go of the guilt around food and eating.

But in intuitive eating they tell you to not "overeat" since eating too much is not "intuitive." Intuitive eating is all about getting back to your normal hunger cues and eating like somebody who is a normal eater. That's all good, and eating normally is what we want to achieve in the end, *but* if we come from an eating disordered past where we restricted calories and maybe even purged or became underweight, our body will need a period of recovery with an adequate amount of calories. So for recovery from eating disorders, trying to eat "intuitively" might not be enough. In recovery, sometimes you will "binge" – meaning you'll have periods of extreme hunger – and this is a normal part of recovery.

Somebody who comes from dieting may think that 1500 calories a day is plenty to restore the body and stop bingeing. They may think if they have water retention and bloating in recovery and feel uncomfortable, it means they should eat less to be more "intuitive." But this may only feed the problem. We will go through some uncomfortable and even scary phases in recovery which are actually *very normal* (extreme hunger, bloating, indigestion, etc.), but they don't talk about these things in intuitive eating.

When you have a restrictive past, you will find it very hard to eat according to your hunger cues. Maybe you haven't had normal hunger cues for years! You will get there for sure, but it will take time. To get there, you have to eat without restriction and respond to your extreme hunger when it strikes.

In intuitive eating, extreme hunger is considered "overeating." Extreme hunger will freak out somebody who follows intuitive eating since, in their understanding, it's not normal. They see extreme hunger as an enemy. Something to suppress and get rid of ASAP rather than embrace. This sends the wrong message to someone with an eating disorder, and they may even fall back to restriction because they think that recovery simply does not work for them.

When I started my recovery with intuitive eating, I also experienced extreme hunger, and I was so scared and confused. I thought I was "bingeing." I didn't know it was normal and would pass as long as I always ate as much as I wanted and didn't restrict after. Extreme hunger will make you feel like you're bingeing, but it's just your bodies response to the previous starvation – no matter how short or long a period you dieted or restricted. It doesn't matter if you're underweight, normal weight, or overweight, extreme hunger can still happen, and it's normal in recovery.

After I read about the MinnieMaud recovery guidelines and learned that we actually need to eat 2500-3000 calories minimum in recovery, respond to our extreme hunger, and stop exercising, I finally recovered. This was the missing link for me in intuitive eating that kept me "trying to not eat too much" in a semi-recovered state. When I finally ate the recommended amounts without guilt and responded to my extreme hunger, the overwhelming hunger started to fade away, and my hunger cues normalized. My body finally got what it wanted and needed so much – enough food without me compensating or stressing about "eating too much." And science proves that bingeing aka extreme hunger is very *normal* after restriction – just reread the Minnesota Starvation Experiment.

Don't get me wrong – intuitive eating was still a major part of my recovery, but I always say that I combined intuitive eating with MinnieMaud guidelines. I needed them both to recover. However, after recovery, you follow only your hunger cues and intuitive eating.

What's wrong with the "eat when hungry and stop when full" recommendation in recovery?

In intuitive eating, it's considered normal to "eat when hungry and stop when full." But if you come from a place of serious restriction, your hunger cues may lead to only 1200 calories before you feel totally full! You cannot recover on this amount, and you need to train your body to be able to eat and digest more food to restore your health. Your stomach is simply not used to normal volumes of foods. In recovery, you need many more calories to recover your organs and body functions. You don't need energy just for everyday tasks, you need plenty of energy to recover all the damage that dieting or an eating disorder has done to your body.

For someone who has been eating very low amounts of foods, normal hunger signals can actually be switched off as a protective mechanism, something that may have been an evolutionary protective mechanism in the past to help us through periods of famine. So if someone comes from serious calorie restriction, they may need to eat more than they are hungry for at first to actually restore their normal hunger signals and stomach capability, allowing them to fit in and digest the proper amounts of foods again. That's why someone coming from anorexia might not be able to recover by simply following the "eat when hungry stop when full" recommendation.

Mental Hunger

Before we continue discussing why intuitive eating is actually good for you during your recovery and after recovery, I want to talk about the last reason why intuitive eating in recovery may not be all you need.

On many intuitive eating websites and in many books, it says to eat only when truly physically hungry and not to eat for emotional reasons. But in my experience, this advice may not work and could give the wrong impression to someone who is recovering. This kind of thinking can lead the recovering person to think it's wrong to eat when their stomach isn't yet rumbling or if they crave something even if not physically hungry.

In the third chapter, I talked about why emotional eating is not always "emotional" (especially in recovery) but true hunger. When we have an eating disorder, our hunger and fullness signals are messed up. The stomach's signals and the brain's signals for hunger and fullness are no longer synchronized. That's why someone with an eating disorder may not feel physically hungry yet will still want to eat. The person may not eat, thinking it's only mental hunger or emotional hunger, but in my experience, it is actual true hunger, and you need to respond.

I also thought I had an emotional eating problem, but now that I'm fully recovered, I never eat for emotional reasons. If you come from a past of dieting, you may think you only eat for emotional reasons, but it's actually your restrictive past sending you the signals to eat, not some "emotional void." To get your hunger/fullness signals working normally again, you have to follow your hunger no matter what – even if you feel it's just "mental" or "emotional."

When I tried to be rational about my hunger and not eat when I thought it was just "mental hunger," I continued to be obsessed. I wasn't listening to my body, and I still felt restricted. But once I started to eat whenever my body sent me a signal – mental or physical – I recovered. And now I truly do not eat for mental or emotional reasons. My hunger and brain signals are synchronized.

> *When a person is energy balanced, then hunger, fullness, and satiation are all synchronized. But after just a few weeks*

(let alone months or years) of catabolizing your own body, now things are asynchronous when you begin to reverse the damage....

Your enteric nervous system is receiving information that the physical aspects of energy absorption are at peak levels, yet the central nervous system continues to receive information that more anabolism (building up of tissue) is required to return to an energy-balanced state.

Try not to get too caught up in what descriptions your conscious mind comes up with as you move through these phases of recovery. Eating is your job. The anxieties about whether it is "normal," "emotional," "the stomach has adapted to more food" are just that: anxieties. And I'm sure no one would be keen on betting against the probability that these are eating-disorder-generated anxieties either!

If you feel the need to eat more, then it doesn't matter what description gets placed on it after the fact, the drive to eat is fundamentally sound and all about energy restoration, or anabolism.

And when you reach your energy balanced state yet again, then all your hormones and neurotransmitters will be providing the same message at the same time so hunger, fullness and satiation will not be creating any more strange cross-talk in your mind.[123]

Intuitive Eating Is Awesome!

Now when I have explained, in every possible way, why following only intuitive eating in recovery might not be the sole answer you need, I want to tell you why intuitive eating is actually very good for recovery and after recovery.

Intuitive eating is not another diet with rules or a program to follow. In this book, I use the term "intuitive eating" to describe a normal way of eating, one that happens naturally. I do not describe it as something I learned from a book but rather as something gained from my own personal experience with being fully recovered.

Intuitive eating and what feels right for each individual can vary. You need to find your own inner wisdom about foods and eating, and the end result should be that you never have to think about eating or feel you have to somehow force it or control it. What I describe here is for general guidance on what is normal eating so you know what to expect after recovery.

You will get back to intuitive eating in your recovery. Your hunger cues will normalize gradually. In time, you will feel more in tune with your body and what it truly needs.

Science Behind Intuitive Eating

1. **Intuitive eating helps with weight management and lessens behaviors associated with eating disorders.**

    - Department of Pediatrics in University of Minnesota conducted a study where they *"explored intuitive eating among young adults according to socio-demographic characteristics and body mass index (BMI), and examined associations between intuitive and disordered eating behaviors."* What they found was that *"Intuitive eating (i.e., reliance on physiologic hunger and satiety cues to guide eating) has been proposed as a healthier, more effective, and more innate alternative to current strategies of weight management.... Males and females who reported trusting their body to tell them how much to eat had lower odds of utilizing disordered eating behaviors compared to those that did not have this trust. Females who reported that they stop eating when they are full had lower odds of chronic dieting and binge eating than those who do not stop eating when full. Overall, this study found that intuitive eating practices are inversely associated with a number of harmful outcomes. Clinicians should discuss the concept of intuitive eating with their young adult patients to promote healthier weight-related outcomes."*[124]

- *"Researchers at the University of Missouri have found that "Eat for Life", a new wellness approach that focuses on mindfulness and intuitive eating as a lifestyle, is more effective than traditional weight-loss programs in improving individuals' views of their bodies and deceasing problematic eating behaviors."*[125]

- Department of Human Nutrition from University of Otago report that *"Women with high Intuitive*

Eating Scale (IES) scores had significantly lower body mass index, which suggests that people who eat in response to hunger and satiety cues have unconditional permission to eat and cope with feelings without food and are less likely to engage in eating behaviors that lead to weight gain."[126]

- American Psychological Association reports that The Intuitive Eating Scale (IES) *"was developed in a sample of college women to measure adaptive forms of eating, such as eating based on physiological rather than emotional cues.... [A]nalysis identified 4 factors: Unconditional Permission to Eat, Eating for Physical Rather Than Emotional Reasons, Trust in Internal Hunger/Satiety Cues, and Awareness of Internal Hunger/Satiety Cues.... IES scores were related inversely to body mass index, body dissatisfaction, negative affect, pressure for thinness, and internalization of the thin ideal, and positively to satisfaction with life and positive affect."*[127]

- Iowa state University conducted *"the first experimental study to test the effectiveness of an intuitive eating intervention designed to increase adaptive eating practices and reduce eating disorder risk factors.... As hypothesized, after the intervention, the experimental group demonstrated significantly greater adherence to intuitive eating practices and significantly less dieting attitudes and practices relative to the control group.... Overall these results present empirical evidence that the intuitive eating model can be a promising approach to disordered eating prevention in a variety of service delivery modalities."*[128]

2. **Intuitive eating promotes healthy eating and reduces overeating without feelings of restriction.**

   - Journal of the Academy of Nutrition and Dietetics observed negative effects of restrained eating on eating behaviors and concluded that a more positive approach to healthy eating is needed. Their main goal was to determine whether sensory-based intervention influenced eating-related attitudes and behaviors among restrained women, as well as reliance on physical signals for hunger and satiety. A sensory-based intervention taught women about hunger and fullness cues, eating sensations based on the senses (taste, touch, hearing, smell, and sight), and pleasurable associations with eating. Women in the intervention group scored higher on the Intuitive Eating Scale. They concluded that *"sensory-based intervention can be a promising approach to improve eating-related attitudes and behaviors among restrained women, without exacerbating other behaviors such as restrained eating."*[129]

   - The journal of BMC Complementary and Alternative Medicine conducted a study Imagine HEALTH to promote healthy lifestyle behaviors and to prevent the early onset of type 2 diabetes and cardiovascular disease risk in obese Latino adolescents. *"...[Our] findings suggest that intuitive eating can be safely used in obese adolescents without fear of sustained consumption of unhealthy foods. In other words, no sustained increases in calories, sugars or fats were seen despite the curriculum suggesting all foods are allowable, dieting is counterproductive, and portion size should be addressed using awareness of internal satiety and hunger signals rather than external rules."*[130]

3. **Dieting may disrupt intuitive eating. Intuitive eating helps to reduce dieting mentality.**

    - Department of Psychology, University of North Texas, found that *"dieting to lose weight, with its focus on restriction of caloric intake, may disrupt intuitive eating processes. In a sample of 669 middle school boys and 708 girls, regardless of sex or exercising, dieting was related to feeling less free to eat what was wanted and to eating more to soothe emotions than to satisfy actual physical hunger. These findings suggest that different weight loss approaches - dieting vs. exercising - have unique relationships to young adolescents' intuitive eating and these associations tend to be stable across sex. Longitudinal studies now are needed to examine how dieting that begins in childhood or early adolescence might have long-term effects on the progression of intuitive eating."*[131]

- A study, conducted by American Journal of Health Behavior, aim was *"to evaluate the effectiveness of the "My Body Knows When" intuitive eating program tailored to assist Fort Drum military spouses in rejecting the dieting mentality.... The intuitive-eating program was able to significantly transition participants away from a dieting mentality....towards intuitive-eating lifestyle behaviors.... IE [intuitive eating] is a holist approach to long-term healthy behavior change and would benefit from an extended support system to improve effectiveness."*[132]

4. **Intuitive eaters have better body image and self-esteem, and less eating disorder symptoms.**

    - Journal of Counseling Psychology *"measured individuals' tendency to follow their physical hunger and satiety cues when determining when, what, and how much to eat."* The results of this study were positively related to body appreciation, self-esteem, and satisfaction with life. There were less eating disorder symptoms, body shame and internalization of media appearance ideals. *"...scores also garnered incremental validity by predicting psychological well-being above and beyond eating disorder symptomatology."*[133]

    - The University of North Carolina at Charlotte, Department of Psychology, studied the link between self-compassion and intuitive eating. They found that *"self-compassion has been linked to*

> *higher levels of psychological well-being... The present findings also suggest the need for additional research as it relates to the development and fostering of self-compassion as well as the potential clinical implications of using acceptance-based interventions for college-aged women currently engaging in or who are at risk for disordered eating patterns."*[134]

For you to understand intuitive eating better and relearn it, it's helpful to know about hunger cues and how to get back in tune with them. Next is all the information I have acquired in my journey to recovering intuitive eating and normal hunger signals.

Hunger

There are different kinds of hunger sensations. You might feel the emptiness of your stomach, a craving for some specific food, or even just the feeling of, *Hmm...I want something...*

If you are in recovery, you've very likely forgotten what hunger even feels like – when to eat, when to stop eating, and how much to eat. In my experience, this will all come naturally in time as your body recovers and goes through different stages of recovery, but here I want to explain some things I have learned about hunger.

First and foremost, I want you to understand that you are a human being and you need to eat. You need to eat enough for your body to be healthy and function normally. If you eat less than you need, your body will suffer.

Eating can be a physical necessity, but it can also be emotional. Eating is essential for both physical and mental health. I do not believe that we should eat only for physical need, ignoring the pure enjoyment of eating or not eating when we need it for comfort or pleasure.

Just as human beings need art and music for pleasure and not just for a physical need, we may also need food for pleasure and for aesthetic needs. The food we eat will nourish our body, but the pleasure, enjoyment, and satisfaction we get from food will also nourish our soul. If we feel guilty about food and deny ourselves food for pleasure, we will not get true satisfaction from eating, and the foods may not even fulfill our appetite. Eating should fill our multidimensional needs. One is not better than the other – they are all important.

Michelle, from fatnutritionist.com, describes three different kinds of hunger sensations[135]:

1. Mechanical Hunger

2. Aesthetic Hunger

3. Chemical Hunger

Mechanical hunger is the most common and most understood type of hunger. It's basically the feeling of hollowness, an empty stomach, and a growling stomach. You know you're ready to eat when that happens. However, if you've been dieting or restricting, even this kind of hunger may be unrecognizable at first. But don't worry – you'll get there as you recover.

This hunger normally happens several hours after eating, depending on how much you ate for your last meal and what kinds of activities you've done since then. This type of hunger normally takes some time to develop and doesn't occur shortly after a proper meal.

However, if you are in recovery, it's very normal to either not feel this kind of hunger at all or to feel it shortly after a meal. In recovery, you can feel hungry even when you aren't physically hungry.

Aesthetic hunger is a desire for a particular food. Having a craving. Some people also refer to it as a "mouth hunger" or just appetite. Eating for aesthetic reasons is similar to listening to your favorite music for pleasure. I believe we need food to nourish our body physically, but we also need to satisfy our emotional appetites with delicious food. To feel nourished and satisfied at every level, we need to eat food for pleasure and enjoyment.

Even when you eat something when you're not particularly hungry – let's say someone offers you ice cream, and you eat it for pleasure – there's actually no problem! You have to trust your body to make its own corrections. If I eat something between meals, then normally my appetite will decrease a little bit for the next meal or perhaps the next day. The body will balance things out!

You deserve to eat delicious food, you deserve to eat free of guilt, you deserve to eat for pleasure and to feel your cravings are truly satisfied both physically and emotionally.

Bottom line – aesthetic hunger is a legitimate need since emotional health is a hugely important part of overall health. Because as Ellyn Satter, internationally recognized authority on eating and feeding, says, *"when the joy goes out of eating, nutrition suffers."*

Chemical hunger is the feeling that "something is still missing." You may feel you ate enough, but you may still be craving more food – something did not quite hit the spot. Some people experience this type of hunger when they haven't eaten enough fruits and veggies in several meals. Your body needs nutrition and whole foods to be in balance and will let you know when it needs more. Sometimes you may feel a particular craving because you've been trying to eat what you think you should, but you're not eating what you actually want. Your cravings haven't been satisfied.

Chemical hunger can also come from low blood sugar – that shaky, weak, lightheaded feeling you get when you've entirely forgotten to eat or something delayed your eating like work responsibilities or being stuck in traffic. These feelings don't come directly from the stomach. They come from your blood, your glycogen stores, and sometimes even depleted vitamin and mineral stores. You need to eat regularly.

This is a very short version of the different types of hunger, how they make you feel, and why you need to satisfy all of them. If you make sure to address each of these three types of hunger, you will feel satisfied with your foods every time. Conversely, if you don't feel satisfied or feel like something is out of place, refer back to these different types of hunger signals to see what might be missing or out of balance.

Fullness

This is not where I tell you how to stop eating when you "reach number 6 on the hunger scale" or to stop eating when you are "full but not overly full." Rather, I want to explain that when your body recovers, you recover from your eating disorder both physically and mentally. When that happens, you will naturally go back to your normal hunger cues and lose the ability to eat beyond fullness.

If your nutritional, caloric, and aesthetic needs for food are satisfied, you will stop eating after you are full. The reasons for your previous overeating will no longer be there – you will not be restricting calories, the fear of next restriction will be over, your body will be recovered, you will eat what feeds your nutritional needs and also what satisfies your cravings. Also, you will have recovered your mental health as well, so you will no longer have a restrictive mindset or an unhealthy relationship with foods and your body. The mental aspect is a huge part of your eating disorder and why you're triggered to overeat.

Basically, what this means is that you have to recover from your eating disorder in order to be able to eat when hungry and stop when full and do it naturally. It's impossible to do it while you still have an eating disorder. If your body is messed up, you won't get normal hunger and fullness signals. But once your body recovers physically and mentally, you will also recover your normal hunger cues and be able to stop eating when you are full.

I lost my ability to overeat when I recovered from my eating disorder. I had bulimia, and believe me, I thought I would never be able to eat normally again. I also thought that my stomach was stretched out, and I would therefore always eat too much. But the thing is that I was genuinely hungry for that much food in my recovery. I had abused my body for so long – throwing up my food, overexercising, and restricting many foods I craved. But despite all that, I now eat when hungry and stop when full.

How to Recover Normal Hunger Cues

I think recovering your normal hunger cues is definitely one of the big goals in eating disorder recovery as this will mean you can finally listen to and trust your body and rely on your body's signals. Having normal hunger cues is also a key to intuitive eating, and this is where we want to be in the end.

How to know when you're ready to eat after hunger cues:

1. Your weight appears stable (weighing yourself is not necessary to determine that).

2. You lost your period during your restriction and have achieved minimum of three consecutive periods in a row.

3. You're eating enough calories, eating regularly, and responding to your hunger wherever it leads you, and it is comfortable to do so.

4. Most recovery symptoms are gone – no bloating or water retention, no more feeling cold or tired all the time, etc.

5. You don't worry about food as much anymore and generally feel freer around foods.

You may still worry about eating to hunger cues a little bit, but this is can be a sign that shows your commitment to recovery. If you are too confident about eating to hunger cues it might mean you are still far away from being ready.

And now I'm going to give you a little recap of everything we've already talked about because all of these are essential to restore normal hunger signals!

#1 Physical Essentials

You cannot recover your normal hunger cues without a strong physical foundation. If your body is still undernourished, and you continue to compensate for calories, it will surely keep your hunger cues messed up. Your body is still running on a deficit, and the bodily functions are not normal.

I've already talked about all of these physical aspects, but please make sure these things are taken care of:

1. Eat enough calories! Make sure there is no restriction. For me, it helped to make sure I ate at least 2500+ calories every day. Please refer back to Chapter 2. Eat enough and respond to extreme hunger, but use some common sense and do not hurt yourself either. Just gradually train your body to be able to eat normal amounts.

2. Skip exercising. As long as you exercise, you're still running on a deficit, and your body will not go to full recovery. Please see Chapter 2 again about this subject.

3. Stop all food restriction – no "clean" eating or eliminating foods you crave. Food restriction only keeps you in eating disorder status and far away from restoring your normal hunger cues and trusting your body to tell you what it needs.

4. Stop all compensation – no purging, exercising, skipping meals, laxatives, diuretics, etc.

5. Eat regularly! If you had an eating disorder or did extreme dieting, your eating may have been chaotic or out of control in many ways, so it's crucial to eat regularly so your body sees there is a constant flow of energy coming in and no sign of food deprivation. If the baseline of regular eating is made, and you feel you can trust your hunger signals, you will continue to eat intuitively.

#2 Mental Essentials

1. Refrain from all triggers! There are many different things that trigger people to relapse or go into restrictive thought patterns. Here are some examples – weighing and measuring, body-checking, watching triggering stuff on media, comparing your body to others, interacting with disordered people, wearing tight clothes that don't fit, and so on.

2. Separate yourself from ED thoughts. Train your brain to replace all ED thoughts with positive and realistic ones, those that will help you recover.

3. Be aware of mental restriction! Even when you eat enough calories and eat what you want, please pay attention to your thought patterns. Do you still verbally punish yourself when you eat until full or feel uncomfortable after eating? Do you tell yourself you're fat or you shouldn't eat so much? This can increase your stress signals and confuse your body in terms of

food – what and how much is okay to eat. Be sure you do not engage in this negative mental talk.

4. Love your body as it is. Feed your body with positive and loving thoughts. Work on your body image. Unbrainwash yourself from all the dieting and "perfect" body nonsense.

5. Have the right mindset in recovery. Believe that recovery is possible!

#3 Food Is Always Available and There Is No Restriction Coming!

When I felt ready in my recovery to start to follow my hunger cues, I started to notice that sometimes I would eat more even when I wasn't hungry or when I actually didn't even want to eat. I was eating either from my old habits (I had strong neurological connections to bingeing as we talked about in Chapter 3) or from a fear that food would be restricted again (the same thing what the Minnesota men reported after being recovered).

In my eating disorder, it was normal for me to do something restrictive after a big meal – either exercising more, starting with a "clean" diet the next day, or purging. So I realized that my mind and body were just so used to the binge-restriction cycle that every time I ate enough, I ate like it was the last time I would be allowed to eat. I ate like somebody who was still dieting. My brain was still somewhat connected to all of the old habits. Not so much physically, but mentally. At least that's how it felt.

If you are familiar with dieting and have experienced binges after diets, then you know that when you binge, you feel very guilty. In your mind, you may think, *Okay, I messed up my diet, so I might as well eat all the food – and as much as I can. And then starting tomorrow, I will be good again.* It's a very typical way to think if you are a constant dieter or have an eating disorder. It's the fear of an upcoming restriction that makes you want to eat, eat, eat. It's the fear that the next diet is right around the corner. Bingeing can come from the fear that food is going to be restricted again – your brain still remembers your old behavior patterns.

So in recovery, you can start telling yourself, your body, and your mind: *Food is always going to be available for me. There is no restriction coming ever again.* This will help you rewire your brain to know that there is no restriction coming, hence the urge to binge is not needed anymore.

Say those things and affirm them to yourself every time you feel out of touch with your body and your hunger. Still eat enough, but tell yourself that you are not going to diet anymore or restrict in any way so your body can start to believe that it doesn't have to eat more out of fear of future restriction. Our mind needs to catch up to our physical recovery to find balance.

Recently, I have received many messages regarding this exact observation. People who have been in recovery for quite some time and are eating enough, responding to extreme hunger, and not compensating in any way are still ending up overeating and feeling terrible. So here, it might be the same thing I experienced. You have to rewire your brain to believe that the trauma of the eating disorder is completely over and there's no need to hold on to the survival response of bingeing. It's important to affirm to your brain every time you eat that there is no need to eat past comfortable fullness because the restriction is over, and the food will always be there to eat again when you are hungry.

Don't suppress your hunger, but continue to tell your body and your brain that there is no restriction coming. In this way, you can start to change the old mental pattern of the binge-restrict cycle. However, remember that the physical essentials, such as eating enough and not compensating, have to be taken care of first so this change can happen.

#4 Notice How Your Body Feels

Start paying attention to your body's signals. At first, this can be very tricky and confusing. You may not even know what signals indicate hunger or fullness. It was that way for me – I had no idea! But as I started to pay attention to my body and how I felt before, after, and while I was eating, I began to have a clue, and it just got better and better the more I recovered. So don't give up!

Notice your hunger. At what point are you actually getting slightly hungry but not yet hungry enough to have a full meal? At what point do you know you're hungry and ready to eat? At what point do you feel like having only a snack?

If you feel overly hungry in just an hour after your meal, ask yourself some questions. Did you eat enough at your last meal, or did you maybe eat too little? Did you have a more active day today (or even yesterday) and need more fuel?

Notice your fullness. When do you feel slightly full? When do you feel comfortably full and content? When do you feel overly full?

If you feel overly full even three to four hours after a meal, maybe you ate past your physical fullness signals. Or if you feel you have extreme hunger and are still a long way from full recovery, you may want to take a few breaths, wait until your stomach feels better, and then continue eating if you're still hungry.

Did you like the food you ate? Did you choose what you craved at that moment? Did it taste good? Did it satisfy you? If not, then why? What do you want to eat – something salty or something sweet? Do you want to eat a full meal or maybe just a snack?

At first, you may not know the answers to any of these questions, but you will as time goes by. And asking yourself these questions really helps you become more in tune with your body.

For me, it was kind of difficult at the beginning. I would rush my eating and forget to feel my body and taste the food – my body and mind was still in an eating disorder, and I felt like I had to binge because the next restriction was coming. But soon I learned that I didn't have to be afraid of restriction anymore and could listen to my body and really start to eat what I truly wanted and enjoy it. I could eat what I wanted to eat, satisfy my hunger and cravings when needed, and eat as much as I had to in order to feel good and satisfied until my next meal or snack.

Start to ask yourself these kinds of questions to become more in tune with your body and notice its signals and hunger cues – it will take time, but starting to notice these things helped me a lot, and it will help you, too.

5# Eat What You Crave

The longer I tried to suppress my cravings and eat only "healthy" foods, even when I craved something else, the further I drifted from my body's signals and normal hunger cues.

To change that and get better, I started to ask myself, *Elisa, what do you want to eat for your next meal? You can have whatever you want!* I asked this question in a very caring, positive voice, out of love for myself. I began to feel very happy every time I went to the store – I could choose whatever foods I wanted! It was a feeling of pure freedom not to restrict anything anymore and allow myself to eat what I craved. It didn't matter if I wanted chocolate, fruit, pasta, or salad – it was all good. Additionally, if I didn't want a particular food, I didn't have to eat it.

Very early on in recovery, I learned that if I always ate what I craved and what I wanted to eat without restricting anything, then my hunger cues stayed normal. But as soon as I tried to control my food or eating, I would mess it up.

Now I never restrict, and I eat all kinds of foods. I normally just eat my everyday foods and home-cooked meals because I know what I like and do not like. But sometimes I like to experiment with new things and buy some foods for pure interest and enjoyment – I don't care if the food is "healthy" or "unhealthy." I've also noticed that, regarding my freedom with foods, I generally eat in a quite healthy and balanced way, and I do think it's so easy to do that because I don't have any rules or restrictions. By allowing myself to eat "unhealthy" foods, I actually crave them less often. I never binge on them anymore simply because I feel I can have them again whenever I want. If no foods are restricted, there are no cravings! It may sound impossible for a militant dieter, but it's true. And it's very liberating!

All these things I mentioned helped me to recover my normal hunger cues. Remember that once you have all the physical and mental essentials of recovery as a base, your normal hunger cues can return.

It's Not Black and White!

Your head is probably spinning around from all the information in this book – what to do, what not to do, this is okay, that's not okay, do this, but don't do that! Some information may even seem unnecessary, weird, wrong, contradicting…stupid?

So don't take everything I say too literally. I want you to trust yourself and listen to *your* intuition. I gathered all this information from different sources, and I put together what essentially worked for ME. This is my experience. I adjusted things a little bit here and there when I felt the need. I didn't follow anybody's advice one hundred percent but used the information and adjusted my recovery according to my needs.

I don't want you to take this recovery book as black and white. You may have even noticed that I am not giving out only one and only option to every recovery issue. For example, with counting calories and following the MinnieMaud guidelines, I have showed you every possible way to go and that recovery is achievable with or without counting, it really depends on every individual. And so is it with other recovery stuff – it is not always black and white.

If you feel something is completely not resonating with you, then do what you need to do to make it suitable for YOU. Try different things to see what works. You will definitely go through some trial and error, so don't get upset if something doesn't work for you as it did for me. Be open to trying out the things I mention, but be smart enough to find your own way.

I am not here to say *do this, this, and this, and then you will get one hundred percent the same results I did.* Every person requires a little bit of a different approach. We are complex biological creatures, not mathematically identical robots. This one little book can't possibly be the sole answer to millions of people who suffer from eating disorders.

I used all this information very instinctively. Some days, I felt the need to make sure I was eating enough, so I followed the MinnieMaud calorie guidelines. Other days, I felt the need to listen to my body and intuition, so I did. Sometimes I felt the need to eat more frequently, and on some days, I ate only a few big meals. If I saw something was not working, I asked myself, *What isn't working, and what should I change?* The answers came to me through different sources, and I tried whatever fit my situation. If something felt good and helped my recovery, I continued doing it. If something felt unnecessary and kept me stuck, I stopped doing it.

I read a lot about recovery and saturated my brain with information. I didn't stop with one book but read a lot of books. I read about the experiences of people who were in recovery and those of people who have recovered successfully. From every information source, I took what felt right and left out what did not. So you, too, can also take what you want from this book and continue learning and searching for more ideas on your own.

Ultimately, it does not matter how exactly you manage to recover, but that you do recover and do it healthfully and for LIFE!

FREE Bonus E-Book!

Thank you so much for reading my book! I spent over three years learning all the information it took to fully recover and then spent a year and a half writing this book. I put my heart and soul into it, and I hope it can help someone with problems similar to those I had when I was in the middle of my eating disorder, not knowing what to do or how to start recovery. If this book helped you to gain some knowledge, insight, or encouragement to start your recovery, then I request you to kindly write your review on my Amazon book page. Your feedback is very important as it will help the book reach out to people who might need it!

To say thank you, I want to give you a free bonus e-book: "**50 Common Eating Disorder Recovery Questions Answered!**" You can access it here: eepurl.com/bThF9L

HOW TO RECOVER
Recap of Everything We Have Learned

1. **Stop following diets and rules** – Stop following diets or eating programs, stop following someone else's rules, stop counting calories or macronutrients, stop listening to "health gurus" and following what works for other people. You have to design your own lifestyle and do what works for YOU! Never restrict, deprive, diet, fast, do intermittent fasting or crazy cleanses, overexercise, or any of that – this will only mess up your body's natural signals and hunger cues. Dieting is one of the biggest causes of eating disorders, bingeing, and all kinds of food-related issues, so do not do it! Intuitive eating comes from *your* body's signals, not someone else's! (Refer back to Chapter 1).

2. **Recover your body** – Before you can eat intuitively without trouble, you may need to go through a recovery period to undo the damage your eating disorder (or

dieting) has done to your body. This may require a period of making sure you eat enough, a period of extreme hunger, skipping exercise, letting go of the "good and bad foods" mindset, and so on. This is all part of the road to intuitive eating, and you should not feel discouraged by it! (Refer back to Chapter 2).

3. **Restore your normal relationship with food** – Instead of only eating what you think you "should" eat or what you think is "healthy," ask yourself this question: *If any food is available to me, what food do I want to eat?* If you don't want something, don't eat it. But if you want something, eat it until satisfied. If you crave something, eat the exact food you crave. Focus on developing a healthy relationship with food. Healthy eating should come from listening to your body, not from restriction. And remember, eating "unhealthy" foods is much better than having an eating disorder or constant food-related stress. This can actually make you unhealthy and give you more cravings than you realize. You should feel in balance with eating. Good nutrition feeds the body on all levels – body, mind, and soul. (Refer back to Chapters 2 and 5).

4. **Separate yourself from the ED thoughts** – ED thoughts are just "neurological junk" created by years of restriction and ED behavior. This is not the real you! To recover, you have to change those negative thoughts to positive ones, the ones that will help you recover.

RECAP OF EVERYTHING WE HAVE LEARNED

You have to un-brainwash yourself from the ED and your damaging beliefs. (Refer back to Chapter 3).

5. **Start loving your body and yourself as you are right now!** – When you always have this "ideal body" at the back of your mind, you will always remain fearful of foods, calories, eating enough, and eating what you crave. You have to work on your body image and self-love and self-worth. Full recovery cannot come when you still hate your body or the way it looks. This mental picture in your head of your "perfect body" will only hold you back from following your body's intuitive signals. It's essential to work on your body image and your image of yourself to recover mentally. (Refer back to Chapter 3).

6. **Get away from triggers** - Stop all triggering behaviors such as following triggering accounts on social media, looking for "thinspiration" pictures, or searching for diet recipes. Stop weighing and measuring yourself. Surround yourself with people who are normal eaters, those who do not diet or engage in negative body talk. Find new hobbies and new interests. Do things that have nothing to do with food or eating. Take a new positive direction in your life. (Refer back to Chapter 3).

7. **Let recovery symptoms pass by giving them the right conditions** – Numerous recovery symptoms will surface. Some will be uncomfortable, and some may even be scary. However, this is how our body recovers,

and this period will pass as long as you give your body the right conditions and just wait it out. In any case, consult your doctor! (Refer back to Chapter 4).

8. **Eat when hungry, and stop when full** – Before full recovery, it is very normal to have mixed up hunger and fullness signals. You will get there in time. As you recover, start listening to your body and its hunger signals. Never try to eat less than you are hungry for. Start to notice your hunger before, after, and even during meals. Also, affirm to your brain that the trauma of the eating disorder is completely over and there's no restriction coming ever again, hence no more overeating is needed! Practice eating intuitively. Don't worry – at first, you may find it hard, but it will get better as you recover! (Refer back to Chapter 5).

Endnotes

1. Kathryn Hansen, *Brain Over Binge: Why I Was Bulimic, Why Conventional Therapy Didn't Work, and How I Recovered for Good* (2011), Kindle edition, accessed February 5, 2016.

2. Nina V, *Recover from Eating Disorders: Complete Eating Disorder Recovery* (2011), e-book, accessed February 5, 2016, http://www.helpforeatingdisorder.com.

3. Richard Kerr and Ali Kerr, *Bulimia Help Method: A Revolutionary New Approach That Works* (2014), Kindle version, accessed February 5, 2016.

4. "Dangers of Dieting," Eating Disorders Victoria, accessed February 5, 2016, http://www.eatingdisorders.org.au/eating-disorders/disordered-eating-a-dieting/dangers-of-dieting.

5. G. C. Patton, J. B. Carlin, et al. "Adolescent Dieting: Healthy Weight Control or Borderline Eating Disorder?" *Journal of Child Psychology and Psychiatry and Allied Disciplines* (1997), accessed February 5, 2016, http://www.ncbi.nlm.nih.gov/pubmed/9232476.

6   Jennifer A. O'Dea, "Studies of Obesity, Body Image and Related Health Issues Among Australian Adolescents" (2010). Journal of Student Wellbeing, Vol. 4(2),10, accessed March 19, 2016, http://ojs.unisa.edu.au/index.php/JSW/article/download/721/545.

7   A. E. Field, S. B. Austin, et al. "Relation Between Dieting and Weight Change Among Preadolescents and Adolescents (2003)," Pediatrics, accessed February 5, 2016, http://www.ncbi.nlm.nih.gov/pubmed/14523184.

8   J. Kenardy, W. J. Brown, et al. *Dieting and Health in Young Australian Women, European Eating Disorders Review* (2001), accessed 5 February 2016, http://onlinelibrary.wiley.com/doi/10.1002/erv.388/abstract.

9   Todd Tucker, *The Great Starvation Experiment: The Heroic Men Who Starved so That Millions Could Live* (2008), Kindle version, accessed 5 February 2016.

10 *Clinical Guidelines on the Identification, Evaluation and Treatment of Overweight and Obesity in Adults* (1998), Obesity Education Initiative, National Institutes of Health, National Heart, Lung, and Blood Institute, online book, accessed February 5, 2016, http://www.nhlbi.nih.gov/files/docs/guidelines/ob_gdlns.pdf.

11 *The Great Starvation Experiment, 1944-1945* (2011), Mad Science Museum, accessed February 5, 2016, http://www.madsciencemuseum.com/msm/pl/great_starvation_experiment.

12   *The Great Starvation Experiment.*

13   Spinardi, Josie, *How to Have Your Cake and Your Skinny Jeans Too: Stop Binge Eating, Overeating and Dieting for Good, Get the Naturally Thin Body You Crave from the Inside Out* (2013), Kindle version, accessed February 5, 2016.

14   "The Effects of Starvation on Behavior," Cure Zone, accessed February 5, 2016, http://www.curezone.org/forums/am.asp?i=1430817.

15   *The Great Starvation Experiment.*

16   J. E. Dellava, P. Policastro, D. J. Hoffman, "Energy Metabolism and Body Composition in Long-term Recovery from Anorexia Nervosa" (2009), PubMed, accessed February 5, 2016, http://www.ncbi.nlm.nih.gov/pubmed/19107831.

17   Bailor, Jonathan. *A Calorie Myth: How to Eat More and Exercise Less with the Smarter Science of Slim* (2014), Kindle version, accessed February 5, 2016.

18   G. L. Blackburn, G, T. Wilson, B. S. Kanders, L. J. Stein, P.T. Lavin, J. Adler, and K. D. Brownell, "Weight Cycling: The Experience of Human Dieters" (1989), *American Journal of Clinical Nutrition,* PubMed as cited in Bailor, Jonathan, A Calorie Myth.

19   *Spinardi, How to Have Your Cake.*

20   *Spinardi, How to Have Your Cake.*

21 Priya Sumithran, MB, BS, Luke A. Prendergast, PhD, et al, "Long-Term Persistence of Hormonal Adaptations to Weight Loss" (2011), *The New England Journal of Medicine,* accessed February 5, 2016, http://www.nejm.org/doi/full/10.1056/NEJMoa1105816?viewType=Print.

22 Katherine Liberty, "The Alarming Link Between Diets and Bulimia" (2011), Bulimia Help, accessed February 5, 2016, http://www.bulimiahelp.org/articles/alarming-link-between-diets-and-bulimia.

23 Reflections on Body Image," All Party Parliamentary Group on Body Image and Central YMCA, online magazine, accessed February 5, 2016, http://issuu.com/bodyimage/docs/reflections_on_body_image/69.

24 Kathy A. Benedetto, SPE, LPC, LMFT, Stephen Todd Callahan, MD, MPH, Rhonda Rose, RN, BSN, and Edwin S. Rogers, PhD, ABPP, "Eating Disorders in Children and Adolescents," online document, accessed February 5, 2016, https://www.tn.gov/assets/entities/behavioral-health/attachments/Pages_from_CY_BPGs_195-207.pdf.

25 Irene Alton, "Eating Disorders," online document, University of Minnesota, accessed February 5, 2016, http://www.epi.umn.edu/let/pubs/img/adol_ch12.pdf.

26 H. Walter Kaye, *Puzzling Symptoms: Eating Disorders and the Brain* (2014), A F.E.A.S.T Family Guide to the Neurobiology of Eating Disorders, 7, online document, accessed February 5, 2016, https://c.ymcdn.com/sites/www.feast-ed.org/resource/collection/DBF23DC3-CF99-488E-9FC6-A51632E8012E/Puzzling_Symptoms_LTR_11.20.2014.pdf.

27   "Global Market for Weight Loss Worth US $586.3 Billion by 2014," Markets and Markets, accessed February 5, 2016, http://www.marketsandmarkets.com/PressReleases/global-market-for-weight-loss-worth-$726-billion-by-2014.asp.

28   Harriet Brown, *Body of Truth: How Science, History, and Culture Drive Our Obsession with Weight and What We Can Do about It* (2015), Kindle version, accessed February 5, 2016.

29   "Weight Watchers Works. For Two Out of a Thousand. (And They Probably Weren't Fat to Begin With.)" (2008), Fat Fu accessed February 5, 2016, https://fatfu.wordpress.com/2008/01/24/weight-watchers/.

30   Traci Mann, A. Janet Tomiyama, Erika Westling, Ann-Marie Lew, Barbra Samuels, and Jason Chatman. "Medicare's Search for Effective Obesity Treatments, Diets Are Not the Answer" (2007), University of California, online document, accessed February 5, 2016, http://janetto.bol.ucla.edu/index_files/Mannetal2007AP.pdf.

31   Randy E. McCabe, Traci L. McFarlane, Marion P. Olmsted, *Overcoming Bulimia Workbook: Your Comprehensive Step-by-Step Guide to Recovery* (2003), e-book, accessed February 5, 2016, https://books.google.com.au/books?id=S-dq5hXfIZ4C&pg=PA48&lpg=PA48&dq#v=onepage&q&f=false.

32   Stephan Guyenet, "The Body Fat Set Point" (2009), Whole Health Source, Nutrition, and Health Science, accessed February 5, 2016, http://wholehealthsource.blogspot.com.au/2009/12/body-fat-setpoint.html.

33   Stephan Guyenet, "The Body Fat Set Point" (2009), Whole Health Source, Nutrition, and Health Science, accessed February 5, 2016, http://wholehealthsource.blogspot.com.au/2009/12/body-fat-setpoint.html.

34   Brown, *Body of Truth*, accessed February 6, 2016.

35   Gwyneth Olwyn, "Bingeing is Not Bingeing" (2012), Youreatopia, accessed February 6, 2016, http://www.youreatopia.com/blog/2012/10/31/bingeing-is-not-bingeing.html.

36   K. H. Pietiläinen, "Does Dieting Make You Fat? A Twin Study" (2011), *International Journal of Obesity* 36: 456-464 as cited in Brown, *Body of Truth*, accessed February 6, 2016.

37   Leigh Anderson, "Can Prescription Drugs Cause Weight Gain?" (2014), Drugs.com, accessed February 6, 2016, http://www.drugs.com/article/weight-gain.html.

38   A. Tschoner, J. Engl, M. Laimer, S. Kaser, M. Rettenbacher, et al. "Metabolic Side-Effects of Antipsychotic Medication" (2007), PubMed, accessed February 6, 2016, http://www.ncbi.nlm.nih.gov/pubmed/17627711.

39   M. Victor Montori, Managing the Metabolic Adverse Effects of *Antipsychotic Drugs in Patients with Psychosis* (2011), Australian Prescriber, online document, accessed February 6, 2016, http://www.australianprescriber.com/magazine/34/4/issue/159.pdf.

40   Brown, *Body of Truth*.

41 "User Reviews for Ortho Tri-Cyclen" (p. 2), accessed February 6, 2016, http://www.drugs.com/comments/ethinyl-estradiol-norgestimate/ortho-tri-cyclen-for-contraception.html.

42 Stuart Wolpert, "Simply Being called 'Fat' Makes Young Girls More Likely to Become Obese" (2014), UCLA Newsroom, accessed February 6, 2016, http://newsroom.ucla.edu/releases/simply-being-called-fat-makes-young-girls-more-likely-to-become-obese.

43 Sandy Calhoun Rice, "Nutrition & Metabolism Disorder Overview" (2013), Healthline, accessed February 6, 2016, http://www.healthline.com/health/nutrition-metabolism-disorders.

44 Matt McMillen, *Is Depression Wrecking Your Weight?* WebMD, accessed February 6, 2016, http://www.webmd.com/depression/features/depression-and-weight-connection.

45 Portia de Rossi, *Portia de Rossi on Oprah (4 of 4),* YouTube video, accessed February 6, 2016, https://www.youtube.com/watch?v=ZmcJ6r4GfXk.

46 J. Kiyah Duffey, M. Barry Popkin, "Energy Density, Portion Size, and Eating Occasions: Contributions to Increased Energy Intake in the United States, 1977–2006" (2011), PLOS Medicine, accessed February 6, 2016, http://www.plosmedicine.org/article/info%3Adoi%2F10.1371%2Fjournal.pmed.1001050.

47 Bailor, *A Calorie Myth,* accessed February 6, 2016.

48 M. L. McCullough, D. Feskanich, M. J. Stampfer, B. A. Rosner, F. B. Hu, D. J. Hunter, J. N. Variyam, G. A. Colditz, and W. C. Willett. "Adherence to the Dietary Guidelines for Americans and Risk of Major Chronic Disease in Women" (2000), *American Journal of Clinical Nutrition*, PubMed as cited in Bailor, Jonathan, *A Calorie Myth*.

49 Bailor, *A Calorie Myth*.

50 Bailor, *A Calorie Myth*.

51 Matt Stone, *Diet Recovery: Restoring Hormonal Health, Metabolism, Mood, and Your Relationship with Food* (2013), Kindle version, accessed February 6, 2016.

52 Scott Abel, *Understanding Metabolism: The Truth About Counting Calories, Sustainable Weight Loss, and Metabolic Damage* (2015), Kindle version, accessed February 6, 2016.

53 Abel, *Understanding Metabolism*.

54 Bailor, *A Calorie Myth*.

55 D. M. Lyon and D. M. Dunlop. "The Treatment of Obesity: A Comparison of the Effects of Diet and of Thyroid Extract," Oxford University Press, online document, accessed February 6, 2016, http://qjmed.oxfordjournals.org/content/1/2/331.

56 Bailor, *A Calorie Myth*.

57 Barbara Brehm, *Psychology of Health and Fitness, Applications for Behavior Change* (2016), Google books, accessed January 6, 2016, https://play.google.com/

store/books/details?id=wMCrAwAAQBAJ&rdid=book-wMCrAwAAQBAJ&rdot=1&source=gbs_vpt_read&pcampaignid=books_booksearch_viewport.

58   M. Rosenbaum and R. L. Leibel, "Adaptive Thermogenesis in Humans" (2010), PubMed, accessed February 6, 2016, http://www.ncbi.nlm.nih.gov/pubmed/20935667.

59   G. L. Thorpe, "Treating Overweight Patients," *Journal of the American Medical Association*, PubMed, as cited in Bailor, *A Calorie Myth*.

60   Bailor, *A Calorie Myth*.

61   Taeko Kajioka, Shigeki Tsuzuku, et al, "Effects of Intentional Weight Cycling on Non-Obese Young Women" (2002), ScienceDirect, accessed February 6, 2016, http://www.sciencedirect.com/science/article/pii/S0026049502868822.

62   R. L. Leibel and J. Hirsch, "Diminished Energy Requirements in Reduced-Obese Patients," PubMed, as cited in Bailor, *A Calorie Myth*.

63   Ruth, August 15, 2014, comment on *"In Defense of Eating Junk Food in Eating Disorder Treatment,"* Science of Eating Disorders, accessed February 6, 2016, http://www.scienceofeds.org/2014/08/15/in-defense-of-eating-junk-food-in-eating-disorder-treatment/.

64   Ruth, August 15, 2014, comment on *"In Defense of Eating Junk Food in Eating Disorder Treatment,"* Science of Eating Disorders, accessed February 6, 2016, http://www.scienceofeds.org/2014/08/15/in-defense-of-eating-junk-food-in-eating-

disorder-treatment/.http://www.youreatopia.com/blog/2013/3/31/minniemaud-guidelines-for-recovery-from-a-restrictive-eating.html.

65 Karen Kersting, "An Evolutionary Explanation for Anorexia?" (2004), American Psychological Association, accessed February 6, 2016, http://www.apa.org/monitor/apr04/anorexia.aspx.

66 Gwyneth Olwyn. "I Need How Many Calories?!!" (2011), Your Eatopia, accessed February 6, 2016, http://www.youreatopia.com/blog/2011/9/14/i-need-how-many-calories.html.

67 *Dietary Energy Intakes for Energy.* IOM. (Washington, DC: National Academies Press, 2005), 164-222, as cited in Marion Nestle and C. Malden Nesheim, *Why Calories Count:* From *Science to Politics* (2012), Kindle version, accessed February 5, 2016.

68 M. Mary Boggiano, C. Paula Chandle, et al, "Combined dieting and Stress Evoke Exaggerated Responses to Opioids in Binge-eating Rats" (2005), University of Alabama at Birmingham, online document, accessed February 5, 2016, http://www.chc.ucsf.edu/coast/pdfs/2010%20Symposium%20Presentations/boggiono_rats.pdf.

69 M. M. Hagan and D. E. Moss, "An Animal Model of Bulimia Nervosa: Opioid Sensitivity to Fasting Episodes" (2012), PubMed, accessed January 6, 2016, http://www.ncbi.nlm.nih.gov/pubmed/22465439.

70   C. T. Fry and David Klein, Your Natural Diet: Alive Raw Foods (2004), accessed February 6, 2016 from amazon.com.

71   *The Great Starvation Experiment.*

72   *The Great Starvation Experiment.*

73   Monica Rodriguez, "The Health Benefits of Junk Food" (2014), Monica Rodriguez, accessed February 6, 2016, http://www.monicarodriguez.com/2014/07/07/the-health-benefits-of-junk-food/.

74   Matt Stone, "Rest and Refeeding" (2015), 180 Degree Health newsletter, accessed February 6, 2016.

75   Maddy Moon, "I Stopped Doing Cardio and This Happened" (2015), Maddy Moon, accessed February 6, 2016, http://maddymoon.com/i-stopped-doing-cardio/.

76   Abel, *Understanding Metabolism.*

77   S. Timothy Church, K. Corby Martin, et al, "Changes in Weight, Waist Circumference and Compensatory Responses with Different Doses of Exercise among Sedentary, Overweight Postmenopausal Women" (2009), The National Center for Biotechnology, accessed February 6, 2016, http://www.ncbi.nlm.nih.gov/pmc/articles/PMC2639700/.

78   Alan C. Utter et al. "Influence of Diet and/or Exercise on Body composition and Cardiorespiratory Fitness in Obese Women" (1998), *International Journal of Sport Nutrition,* accessed February 6, 2016, http://www.ncbi.nlm.nih.gov/pubmed/9738131.

79   T. G. Nazem and K. E. Ackerman, "The Female Athlete Triad" (2012), The National Center for Biotechnology, accessed February 6, 2016, http://www.ncbi.nlm.nih.gov/pmc/articles/PMC3435916/.

80   Caroline Haagen, "Your Brain on Restriction" (2015), The Fuck It Diet, accessed February 7, 2016, http://thefuckitdiet.com/2015/12/22/your-brain-on-restriction/.

81   *"Recovery - True Inspirational Stories,"* National Association of Anorexia Nervosa and Associated Disorders, accessed February 7, 2016, http://www.anad.org/my-recovery-story/.

82   *"Recovery - True Inspirational Stories,"* National Association of Anorexia Nervosa and Associated Disorders.

83   *"Recovery - True Inspirational Stories,"* National Association of Anorexia Nervosa and Associated Disorders.

84   *"Eating Disorders and Peer Pressure"* (2013), Secure Teen, accessed February 7, 2016, http://www.secureteen.com/peer-pressure/eating-disorders-and-peer-pressure/.

85   Evelyn Tribole and Elyse Resch, *Intuitive Eating: A Revolutionary Program That Works* (2012), Kindle version, accessed February 7, 2016.

86   Diane Neumark-Sztainer, "Dieting and Disordered Eating Behaviors from Adolescence to Young Adulthood: Findings from a 10-year Longitudinal Study" (2011), *Journal of the American Dietetic Association*, PubMed, accessed February 7, 2016, http://www.ncbi.nlm.nih.gov/pubmed/21703378.

87   E. Enriguez, G. E. Duncan, et al, "Age at Dieting Onset, Body Mass Index, and Dieting Practices, A Twin Study" (2013), PubMed, accessed February 7, 2016, http://www.ncbi.nlm.nih.gov/pubmed/24025547.

88   Diane Neumark-Sztainer et al, "Obesity, Disordered Eating, and Eating Disorders in a Longitudinal Study of Adolescents: How Do Dieters Fare 5 Years Later?" (2006), PubMed, accessed February 7, 2016, http://www.ncbi.nlm.nih.gov/pubmed/16567152.

89   Barbara Brody, "The Link Between Trauma and Binge Eating" (2015), WebMD, accessed February 7, 2016, http://www.webmd.com/mental-health/eating-disorders/binge-eating-disorder/features/ptsd-binge-eating.

90   "Stories," Orthorexia, accessed February 7, 2016, http://www.orthorexia.com/stories-from-readers/.

91   "Depression/Unhappiness and Poor Body Image/Body Dissatisfaction," Researchomatic, accessed February 7, 2016, http://www.researchomatic.com/Depression-Unhappiness-And-Poor-Body-Image-Body-Dissatisfaction-122632.html.

92   *"Depression/Unhappiness and Poor Body Image/Body Dissatisfaction,"* Researchomatic.

93   Julie K. L. Dam, *How Do I Look?* (2000), *People* online, accessed February 7, 2016, http://www.people.com/people/archive/article/0,,20132200,00.html.

94   G. Pope, M.D. Harrison, A. Phillips, M.D. Katherine, et al. *The Adonis Complex: The Secret Crisis of Male Body Obsession* (2000), Google books, accessed February 7, 2016, https://books.google.com.au/books?id=Jo-LHyyIy_kC&pg=PA30&lpg=PA30&dq#v=onepage&q&f=false.

95   Dennis Hummel et al, *Visual Adaptation to Thin and Fat Bodies Transfers Across Identity* (2012), PubMed, accessed February 7, 2016, http://www.ncbi.nlm.nih.gov/pubmed/22905232.

96   E. Anne Becker, A. Rebecca Burwell, et al, Eating Behaviors and Attitudes Following Prolonged Exposure to Television Among Ethnic Fijian Adolescent Girls, (2002), *The British Journal of Psychiatry*, accessed February 7, 2016, http://bjp.rcpsych.org/content/180/6/509.

97   "Body Image," BWell Health Promotion, Brown University, accessed February 7, 2016, http://www.brown.edu/campus-life/health/services/promotion/nutrition-eating-concerns-eating-concerns-and-body-image/body-image.

98   M. Kendyl Klein, "Why Don't I Look Like Her? The Impact of Social Media on Female Body Image" (2013), Claremont McKenna College, online document, accessed February 7, 2016, http://scholarship.claremont.edu/cgi/viewcontent.cgi?article=1749&context=cmc_theses.

99   L. G. Boothroyd et al, "Visual Diet Versus Associative Learning as Mechanisms of Change in Body Size Preferences" (2012), PubMed, accessed February 7, 2016, http://www.ncbi.nlm.nih.gov/pubmed/23144929.

100 Harriet Brown, *Body of Truth: How Science, History, and Culture Drive Our Obsession with Weight and What We Can Do about It* (2015), Kindle version, accessed February 5, 2016.

101 Linda Bacon, PhD. S. Judith Stern, ScD, et al, "Size Acceptance and Intuitive Eating Improve Health for Obese, Female Chronic Dieters" (2005), Weight Management Psychology, online document, accessed February 7, 2016, http://www.weightmanagementpsychology.com.au/wp-content/uploads/2014/05/JADA-HAES-study-2005_105.pdf.

102 Erik Fisher et al, "Social Comparison Body Image: An Investigation of Body Comparison Processes Using Multidimensional Scaling" (2002), *Journal of Social and Clinical Psychology*, online document, accessed February 7, 2016, http://jkthompson.myweb.usf.edu/articles/Social%20Comparison%20and%20Body%20Image.pdf.

103 Portia de Rossi, *Unbearable Lightness: A Story of Loss and Gain* (2011), Kindle version, accessed February 7, 2016.

104 *Programming Your Subconscious Mind* (2012), Calm Down Mind, accessed February 7, 2016, http://www.calmdownmind.com/programming-your-subconscious-mind/.

105 Julia Layton, "How Brainwashing Works" (2006), How Stuff Works, accessed February 7, 2016, http://science.howstuffworks.com/life/inside-the-mind/human-brain/brainwashing.htm.

106 Alun Palmer, "I Was So Brainwashed in North Korea Death Camp I Betrayed My Family: Survivor's Shocking Story" (2013), *Mirror*, accessed February 7, 2016, http://www.mirror.co.uk/news/world-news/north-korea-death-camp-survivor-1814554.

107 Gwyneth, Olwyn. (2013). *Relapse: An Inevitability?* Your Eatopia, accessed 7 February 2016 from http://www.youreatopia.com/blog/2013/4/13/relapse-an-inevitability.html

108 "Definition of Emotional Eating" (2012), MedicineNet, accessed February 7, 2016, http://www.medicinenet.com/script/main/art.asp?articlekey=46450.

109 Janet Tomiyama et al, "Low Calorie Dieting Increases Cortisol" (2010), American Psychosomatic Society, online document, accessed February 7, 2016, http://www.chc.ucsf.edu/coast/pdfs/news/article_Tomiyama_psychosomaticmed.pdf.

110 Hansen, *Brain Over Binge.*

111 Nina V, *Recover from Eating Disorders.*

112 Richard Kerr, "What if Everything the Media told You About Bulimia Nervosa Was Wrong?" (2014), Amalie Lee, accessed February 7, 2016 http://amalielee.com/2014/12/10/what-if-everything-the-media-told-you-about-bulimia-nervosa-was-wrong/.

ENDNOTES

113 de Rossi, *Unbearable Lightness*, accessed February 8, 2016.

114 Frederic Patenaude, "12 Reasons Why I Don't Eat 100% Raw" (2012), accessed February 8, 2016 from http://www.fredericpatenaude.com/blog/?p=2686.

115 Gwyneth Olwyn, "Tummy Troubles" (2014), Your Eatopia, accessed February 9, 2016, http://www.youreatopia.com/blog/2014/2/9/tummy-troubles.html.

116 Gwyneth Olwyn, "Is it Normal to Gain This Much?" (2015), Your Eatopia, accessed February 8, 2016, http://www.youreatopia.com/usual-questions/2015/6/4/is-it-normal-to-gain-this-much.

117 Becca, "Matt Stone Interview – Diets and Your Metabolism" (2014), Eat More 2 Weigh Less, accessed February 8, 2016, http://eatmore2weighless.com/matt-stone-diets-metabolism/.

118 Olwyn, *Bingeing is Not Bingeing*, accessed February 8, 2016.

119 Julia. "Weight Redistribution After Gaining Weight" (2015), Lord Still Loves Me, accessed February 8, 2016, http://www.lord-still-loves-me.com/weight-redistribution/.

120 Gwyneth Olwyn, "Phases of Recovery From A Restrictive Eating Disorder" (2012), Your Eatopia, accessed February 8, 2016, http://www.youreatopia.com/blog/2012/11/23/phases-of-recovery-from-a-restrictive-eating-disorder.html.

121 Shaye Boddington, *5 Stepping Stones to Bulimia Recovery*, e-book, accessed February 8, 2016.

122   Ellyn Satter, "What is Normal Eating?", Ellyn Satter Institute, accessed February 8, 2016, http://ellynsatterinstitute.org/hte/whatisnormaleating.php.

123   Gwyneth Olwyn. "Extreme Hunger II: Profoundly Disturbing" (2013), Your Eatopia, accessed February 9, 2016, http://www.youreatopia.com/blog/2(). 013/4/9/extreme-hunger-profoundly-disturbing.html.

124   K. N. Denny, K. Loth, et al, "Intuitive Eating in Young Adults. Who is Doing it, and How is it Related to Disordered Eating Behaviors?" (2013), Pub Med, accessed February 9, 2016, http://www.ncbi.nlm.nih.gov/pubmed/23063606.

125   H. Bush, L. Rossy, et al, "Eat for Life: A Worksite Feasibility Study of a Novel Mindfulness-Based Intuitive Eating Intervention" (2014), University of Missouri-Columbia, Science Daily, accessed February 9, 2016, https://www.sciencedaily.com/releases/2014/07/140707134331.htm.

126   C. E. Madden, S. L. Leong, et al, "Eating in Response to Hunger and Satiety Signals is Related to BMI in a Nationwide Sample of 1601 Mid-age New Zealand Women" (2012) [Epub ahead of print], as cited in https://www.intuitiveeating.com/content/studies, accessed February 9, 2016.

127   S. A. Dockendorff, T. A. Petrie, et al, "Intuitive Eating Scale for Adolescents" (2012), American Psychological Association, accessed February 9, 2016, http://psycnet.apa.org/psycinfo/2012-23495-001/.

128   S. Young. "Promoting Healthy Eating Among College Women: Effectiveness of an Intuitive Eating Intervention"

(2010), Iowa State University, Gradworks, online document, accessed February 9, 2016, http://gradworks.umi.com/34/18/3418683.html.

129 S. Young. "Promoting Healthy Eating Among College Women: Effectiveness of an Intuitive Eating Intervention" (2010), Iowa State University, Gradworks, online document, accessed February 9, 2016, http://gradworks.umi.com/34/18/3418683.html.

130 M. J. Weigenberg et al, "Imagine HEALTH: Results from a Randomized Pilot Lifestyle Intervention for Obese Latino Adolescents Using Interactive Guided Imagery" (2014), BMC Complementary & Alternative Medicine, accessed February 9, 2016, http://bmccomplementalternmed.biomedcentral.com/articles/10.1186/1472-6882-14-28.

131 J. Moy and T. A. Petrie. "Dieting, Exercise, and Intuitive Eating Among Early Adolescents" (2013), PubMed, accessed February 9, 2016, http://www.ncbi.nlm.nih.gov/pubmed/24183151.

132 R. E. Cole and T. Horacek "Effectiveness of the 'My Body Knows When' Intuitive-eating Pilot Program" (2010), PubMed, accessed February 9, 2016, http://www.ncbi.nlm.nih.gov/pubmed/20001186.

133 T. L. Tylka. (2013). The Intuitive Eating Scale-2: Item Refinement and Psychometric Evaluation with College Women and Men, PubMed, accessed 9 February 2016 from http://www.ncbi.nlm.nih.gov/pubmed/23356469

134 S. J. Schoenefeld and J. B. Webb. (2013). Self-compassion and Intuitive Eating in College Women: Examining the Contributions of Distress Tolerance and Body Image Acceptance and Action, PubMed, accessed 9 February 2016 from http://www.ncbi.nlm.nih.gov/pubmed/24183143

135 Allison, Michelle, "How Does Hunger Feel?" (2011), The Fat Nutritionist, accessed February 10, 2016, http://www.fatnutritionist.com/index.php/lesson-three-how-does-hunger-feel/.

Printed in Great Britain
by Amazon